WILD
SPAIN

A TRAVELLER'S GUIDE

FREDERIC V. GRUNFELD

WITH TERESA FARINO

INTERLINK BOOKS
An imprint of Interlink Publishing Group, Inc.
NEW YORK

First American edition published 2000 by
INTERLINK BOOKS
An imprint of Interlink Publishing Group Inc.
99 Seventh Avenue • Brooklyn, New York 11215 and
46 Crosby Street • Northampton, Massachusetts 01060

Library of Congress Cataloging-in-Publication Data
Grunfeld, Frederic V.
    Wild Spain : a traveller's guide / by Frederic V. Grun-
feld.
        224p. 21.0 x 14.9cm.—(Wild guides)
    Includes bibliographical references and index.
    ISBN 1-56656-322-4 (pbk.)
    1. Natural history—Spain—Guidebooks. 2. Natural
areas—Spain—Guidebooks. 3. Spain—Guidebooks. I.
Title. II Series: Wild guides (Interlink Books)
QH171.G785   2000
508.46—dc21   99-17868
                                                    CIP

Printed in Hong Kong

EDITOR: SIMON RIGGE

Art Direction and Book Design: Ivor Claydon and Bob
Hook
Assistant Editors: Sarah Bevan, Lisa Cussans, Nicholas
Lim
Researcher: Dolores Udina
Picture Researcher: Kate Duffy
Senior Editorial Assistant: Laura Smith-Spark
Editorial Assistants: Linda Aitken, Ruth Bourne, Fenel-
la Dick, Charlotte Lawrence, Joan Lee, Lieta Marziali,
Sophia Ollard, Gail Reitano, Rebecca Skipwith, Sam
Thorne, Henrietta Valder, Sally Weatherill
Production Assistants: Zoë Hall, Marie-Anne Poncet
Artwork: Maggie Raynor
Maps: Oxford Cartographers
Captions: David Black, Ferdie McDonald

Front cover caption: The rugged landscape of the Sierra
de Albarracín rises above the city of Teruel.

THE GENERAL EDITOR

DOUGLAS BOTTING has travelled to Brazil,
South Yemen, the Sahara, Arctic Siberia and to
many European wild places. His books include
One Chilly Siberian Morning, *Wilderness Europe*
and *Rio de Janeiro*. He has recently written a biography of the author and conservationist, Gerald Durrell.

THE AUTHOR

FREDERIC GRUNFELD is a writer and cultural historian who lived in Mallorca from 1961
until his death, shortly after completing this
book. He travelled throughout Spain and wrote
extensively for Time-Life Books on countries in
Europe and beyond. His biography of Auguste
Rodin won him a Pulitzer Prize nomination.

CONTRIBUTORS

TERESA FARINO is a freelance environmental
journalist and consultant with a special interest
in Spain and Portugal. She wrote the chapter on
Northern Spain as well as the exploration zones

for Monfragüe and Aiguamolls de l'Empordà,
and contributed greatly to the ecological and geological material in the text.

NORMAN RENOUF, who contributed to the
fact-packs, is a freelance travel writer and pho-
tographer. He has written extensively about
many countries in western Europe as well as the
mid-Atlantic region of the USA, where he now
lives.

PHILIPPA FRASER, who researched and wrote
sections on the Canary Islands' national parks, is
a freelance journalist fluent in five languages, including Spanish and Chinese.

DOLORES UDINA, who made extensive contri-
butions to this book, is a translator and freelance
Catalan writer.

CONSULTANTS

DAVID BLACK is a writer and editor who has
contributed to many nature books including Gerald and Lee Durrells' *Practical Guide For The
Amateur Naturalist*.

CONTENTS

ABOUT THE SERIES

What would the world be, once bereft
Of wet and of wildness? Let them be
left,
O let them be left, wildness and wet;
Long live the weeds and the wilderness
yet.

Gerard Manley Hopkins: Inversnaid

These books are about those embattled refuges of wildness and wet: the wild places of Europe. But where, in this most densely populated sub-continent, do we find a truly wild place?

Ever since our Cro-Magnon ancestors began their forays into the virgin forests of Europe 40,000 years ago, the land and its creatures have been in retreat before *Homo sapiens*. Forests have been cleared, marshes drained and rivers straightened: even some of those landscapes that appear primordial are in fact the result of human activity. Heather-covered moorland in North Yorkshire and parched Andalusian desert have this in common: both were once covered by great forests which ancient settlers knocked flat.

What then remains that can be called wild? There are still a few areas in Europe that are untouched by man — places generally so unwelcoming either in terrain or in climate that man has not wanted to touch them at all. These are indisputably wild.

For some people, wildness suggests conflict with nature: a wild place is a part of the planet so savage and desolate that you risk your life whenever you venture into it. This is in part true but would limit the eligible places to the most impenetrable bog or highest mountain tops in the worst winter weather — a rather restricted view. Another much broader definition considers a wild place to be a part of the planet where living things can find a natural refuge from the influence of modern industrial society. By this definition a wild place is for wild life as well as that portmanteau figure referred to in these pages as the wild traveller: the hill walker, backpacker, bird-watcher, nature lover, explorer, nomad, loner, mystic, masochist, *aficionado* of the great outdoors, or permutations of all these things.

This is the definition we have observed in selecting the wild places described in these books. Choosing them has not been easy. Even so, we hope the criterion has proved rigid enough to exclude purely pretty (though popular) countryside, and flexible enough to include the greener, gentler wild places, of great natural historical interest perhaps, as well as the starker, more savage ones where the wild explorers come into their own.

These are not guide-books in the conventional sense, for to describe every neck of the woods and twist of the trail throughout Europe would require a library of volumes. Nor are these books addressed to the technical specialist — the caver, diver, rock climber or cross-country skier, the orchidhunter, lepidopterist or beetlemaniac — for such experts will have data of their own. They are books intended for the general outdoor traveller — including the expert outside his field of expertise (the orchidhunter in a cave, the diver on a mountain top) — who wishes to scrutinize the range of wild places on offer in Europe, to learn a little more about them and to set about exploring them off the beaten track.

One of the great consolations in the preparation of these books has been to find that after 40,000 years of hunting, clearing, draining and ploughing, Cro-Magnon and their descendants have left so much of Europe that can still be defined as wild.

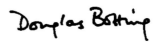

WILD SPAIN: AN INTRODUCTION

'Among European countries Spain stands unique in the range of her natural and physical features. In no other land can there be found, within a similar area, such extremes of scene and climate as characterize the 400 by 400 miles of the Iberian peninsula. Switzerland has alpine regions loftier and more imposing, Russia vaster steppes and Norway more arctic scenery; but nowhere else in Europe do arctic and tropic so nearly meet as in Spain. Contrast, for example, the stern grandeur of the Sierra Nevada, wrapped in eternal snow, with the almost tropical luxuriance of the Mediterranean shores which lie at its feet.'

These words are as true today as when they were first published more than a century ago in the opening paragraph of a pioneering book about hunting, natural history and exploration in Spain. Its authors were Abel Chapman and Walter J. Buck; its title: *Wild Spain*, alias *España Agreste*.

In many respects I have followed in their footsteps when writing my own report on wild Spain. It is still the 'wildest' country in Europe; not far from any of the big cities you can always find areas that are light years removed from modernity. Half an hour from Madrid begins the Sierra de Guadarrama, with its towering cliffs and bizarre rock formations, its ancient footpaths winding through forests of beeches, poplar and pine. Behind Barcelona looms the massif of Montserrat; behind Girona the extinct volcanoes of Olot; behind Oviedo the mountains of the Cantabrian range; behind Málaga the Serranía de Ronda. Take a bus to the outskirts of almost any city and you can walk from the last stop to a wild place in as little as an hour or two.

The *Wild Spain* of today is for people who want to walk quietly through some of the world's most splendid countryside, breathing some of the last unpolluted air of Western Europe. It is designed to help hikers and explorers who want to get away from it all. I have tried to think of their needs both in choosing the areas to be covered and in selecting the factual information to be annexed to each entry. I myself have been a hiker-wanderer in Spain for many years, and in writing this book have renewed acquaintance with many areas of the country that I first got to know 15 or 20 years ago.

Some of *Wild Spain's* exploration zones require strenuous activity: climbing, pitching a tent, backpacking and so on. But I should like to stress that we have confined our entries mainly to those areas that have been officially reserved for such purposes: national and regional parks, and the like. Indeed, I have had to make a selection of what I regard as the finest of these, for there are far more forest reserves and state lands than you could cover even in fragmentary fashion, and thus the line had to be drawn somewhere to keep the guide from having as many entries as the telephone directory. The exhaustive *Inventario Nacional de Paisajes Sobresalientes,* published by DGCN (the Directorate General for Nature Conservation), comprises two 500-page volumes, and yet each of the 'outstanding landscapes' of Spain receives only one picture and a few lines of description.

Spain is indescribably rich in rugged landscapes, and I could easily fill a second volume with other wild places. No matter where you might happen to be you will have no difficulty finding remote areas of your own to explore. 'Our Spain begins where byways end,' declared Chapman and Buck. 'We write of her pathless solitudes, of desolate steppe and prairie, of marsh and mountain-land — of her majestic sierras, some well-nigh inaccessible, and, in many an instance, untrodden by British foot save our own. Lonely scenes these, yet glorified by primeval beauty and wealth of wildlife. As naturalists — that is, merely as born lovers of all that is wild, and big, and pristine — we thank the guiding destiny that early directed our steps towards a land that is probably the wildest and certainly the least known of all in Europe — a land worthy of better cicerones than ourselves.'

These are precisely the feelings with which

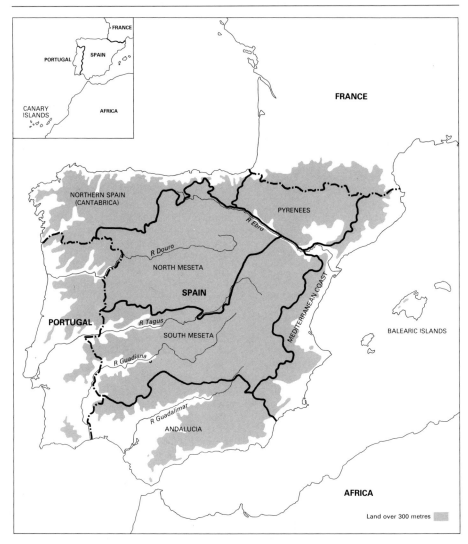

I approached the writing of this book. Yet like my predecessors I did not mean to disparage the other, cultured Spain. Indeed wild Spain usually co-exists in close proximity with the Spain of the castles, ancient villages and medieval churches. At the end of a walk through the Pyrenees you will come to a village of thousand-year-old fieldstone houses, clustered around a church containing a masterpiece of Romanesque mural painting or a crucifix that might otherwise adorn the Cloisters of the

Metropolitan Museum. If you wander through Las Hurdes of Extremadura (an area where Luis Buñuel shot a famous documentary) you will come upon churches that have a human skull placed in a niche on an outside wall, to remind church-goers of the souls of their departed ancestors. Nature and people have here worked hand-in-glove for two thousand years or more, and as a result the ruins augment the effect of the landscape: 'to come on San Pere de Roda looming shattered on its Catalonian mountain,' writes Rose Macaulay in *Fabled Shore*, 'San Miguel de Cullera, the Cartujas near Jerez and at Porta Coeli, so lovely in their desolation, as much utterly one with their background as ancient mouldering trees, has a breath-taking excitement that the carefully ordered trimness of our own Tintern or Fountains or Glastonbury can-not give.' If you travel along these worn paths you will find, as she did — and as do so many other visitors — that there is nothing more fascinating than wandering through Spain: 'it seems still, to each fresh and eager tourist, to have a wild virgin quality, as if oneself were its first ravisher for centuries.'

THE KEY TO SPAIN'S WILD PLACES

THE SHAPE OF THE WILD

One reason why there are so many more wild places in Spain than in the rest of Europe is that Spain has the highest mean altitude of any country in Europe, barring Switzerland. Spain is basically a highland plateau, 'a huge table-mountain', as Chapman and Buck call it, framed and intersected by ranges of still loftier mountains, but with hardly any lowlands except along some of the major rivers, such as the Ebro Valley, and in thin alluvial strips along the coasts.

About 40 per cent of peninsular Spain is taken up by the wind-blown, largely treeless Meseta, with its torrid summers and freezing winters. Much of the rest consists of mountains: the Pyrenees, the Picos de Europa, the Sierra de Gredos, the Sierra Morena, the Sierra Nevada and so on, which serve to hem in this great inland plateau. Few natural routes traverse these ranges, and the alluvial plains of the coast are sharply cut off from the interior. As a result, Spain incorporates as many different kinds of landscape as it does ethnic groups. The rest of the world usually thinks of Spain in terms of white-washed Andalusian patios and lace mantillas, but there is so much more to it than that. Along the Bay of Biscay Chapman and Buck found a region 'absolutely Scandinavian in type', with its abrupt peaks and deep valleys and rivers abounding in salmon.

On the Mediterranean shore lies Almería, with Europe's only true desert. At the other extreme are the inundated rice-fields of the Ebro delta and L'Albufera de València: when you see the local farmers working ankle-deep in their rice paddies you could easily imagine yourself to be in South-East Asia. And then there are the Spanish island groups; by virtue of their climate and geography the Balearics and the Canaries have both become favourite seaside playgrounds, to which endless flights of aeroplanes bring millions of tourists every year. Yet they have managed to hold their own: Mallorca, with its most Mediterranean of mountain landscapes to offset the overcrowding of its sandy beaches, and the Canaries, which counterbalance their tourist invasions by setting aside their most dramatic landscapes as national parks.

WILD HABITATS

The huge range of habitats in Spain — the result of ancient geological processes and the effects of climate — makes it difficult to divide them neatly into a handful of categories. Here I have attempted to describe them briefly under the four greatest landscape divisions present, between which some overlap is inevitable.

Mountains: more than 35 per cent of Spain exceeds 800 metres (2,600 feet) in height; peripheral areas lifted above the central plateau are rucked into a series of mountain ranges. The north has two great east-west ridges, the *Pyrenees* and *Cordillera Cantábrica*. The flora ranges from Mediterranean to Atlantic, from pines to beech woods, with high numbers of endemic species: fritillaries, gentians, narcissi and pasque-flowers, especially in traditional haymeadows, and in the alpine zone (2,500-3,000 metres/8,200-9,850 feet). The fauna is exceptional: large mammals include wolves, bears, wild boar, chamois; smaller beasts of note are salamanders and asps, and these mountains are the last stronghold of the Pyrenean desman. Raptors occur in large numbers, especially vultures, owls and eagles, with two outstanding birds of the region being the capercaillie and wallcreeper; butterflies boast many endemic races, some confined to a single valley in the Pyrenees. The extreme south of Spain is dominated by the *Sierra Nevada*, running parallel to the coast and containing the southernmost glacier in Europe. The slope vegetation is highly Mediterranean, with a typical 'hedgehog' zone of spiny, drought-resistant shrubs; but the peaks have snow-tolerant flora unrivalled in Western Europe for the number of endemic species: glacier toadflax, Nevada saxifrage, daffodils, buttercups and crocuses. The Nevada blue butterfly is found only in these mountains. Further north is the *Sierra de Cazorla*, with endemic species of violet, butterwort and columbine, but it is more famous as the headquarters of the Spanish ibex. The central Spanish mountains — *Sierras de Gredos, Francia & Guadarrama* — are less imposing, oak- and pine-clad in the lower reaches, with brooms, cistuses and heathers above, and few alpine zones; hawks, eagles and kites abound, with warblers, wheatears and shrikes in the valleys, and ibex in the Gredos peaks.

Plains: make up much of the central plateau and are the least 'wild' of Spain's habitats in that man has almost inevitably had some influence. Many outstanding landscapes and wildlife features are associated with the *subterranean water supply*, e.g. Tablas de Daimiel, now drying out; Laguna de Gallocanta, famed for the European crane and red-crested pochard; Laguna de Fuente de Piedra, with more than 3,000 breeding pairs of flamingo; Laguna de Zóñar, with the white-headed duck and purple gallinule. The arid, half-cultivated *steppe* habitat is also very interesting, especially for its birds: great and little bustard, pin-tailed sandgrouse, red-necked nightjar, Andalusian hemipode, stone curlew, quail, white storks and many lark species and harriers, as well as for a group of plants rapidly diminishing in Europe: arable weeds. A feature of the south-western plains is the *dehesa*, evergreen oak 'parklands' over rich pastures which are the supreme Spanish habitat for small birds: golden oriole, woodchat shrike, roller, azure-winged magpie and bee-eater. The *dehesa* is also famed as the breeding ground of the threatened Spanish imperial eagle, black vulture and black-winged kite; Monfragüe, in Extremadura, also has black storks on its barren cliffs.

Coastal features: *dunes* have a rich flora that varies with their position on the Cantabrian-Atlantic, Mediterranean or southern Atlantic coasts and includes many rare and endemic plants (*Corema album, Romulea clusiana, Linaria arenaria*), as well as sea daffodils, sea holly and the stablizing marram grass; the dunes are threatened by the popularity of Spain's beaches as holiday resorts. *Coastal marshes* have halophytic vegetation including glassworts, sea lavenders and sea plantains, but birds are of greater importance here, including migrating egrets, herons, bitterns and breeding black-

winged stilts at Aiguamolls de l'Empordà, and lesser grey shrikes inland; the superlative aquatic avifauna in Doñana National Park includes marbled teal, crested coot, ruddy shelduck, ferruginous duck and glossy ibis. *Cliffs* are important for specialist flora and for birds; on the northern Atlantic coast, shags and guillemots breed; on Gibraltar, peregrine, blue rock thrush and the famed Barbary partridge.

Islands: may combine elements of the other three categories. *Canaries* (seven islands) are partly volcanic and highly influenced by both oceanic and Saharan climates; the highest mountain in Spain - El Teide - is on Tenerife. There are almost 600 endemic plant taxa, including Canary laurels, Canary pine, Teide violet, many species of tree-spurge and viper's bugloss; milkweed butterflies are also to be found. On the *Balearics* (four main islands) the flora is less rich than on the Canaries, but equally unique with Balearic peony and Balearic cyclamen; the fauna is more diverse, including cliff-nesting Cory's shearwater and Eleonora's falcon; Hermann's tortoise, Mallorcan midwife toad and Lilford's wall lizard are all highly localized and endangered species.

PROTECTED WILD PLACES

Spain has a long history of protecting its wildest and most beautiful countryside by law; some of the foremost national parks in Europe were established in the mountains of Northern Spain as early as 1918: Ordesa in the Pyrenees and Covadonga (now part of the Picos de Europa park) in the Cordillera Cantábrica. Today there are twelve national parks, covering more than 300,000 hectares (740,000 acres). Four of these are in the Canary Islands; the most recent, in the Sierra Nevada, was created in 1998.

During the reafforestation effort begun after the Civil War, many *reservas nacionales de caza* (national hunting reserves) were established. These covered a vast area of more than 1.5 million hectares (3.7 million acres), mostly in mountainous zones. Following the promulgation of the 1978 constitution, when the 17 Spanish autonomies were established, the newly formed regional governments inherited the management and protection of these hunting reserves. Today, many of them have been transformed into natural parks and nature reserves.

The old state institution for nature conservation, ICONA, has been superseded by the Directorate General for Nature Conservation

less at right angles to the east-west thrust of the principal chain. As a result there is no easy way to get from the Catalan Pyrenees to the Basque Pyrenees unless you descend to the lowlands of the Ebro valley. East-west travel in the mountains involves a complicated series of twisting, narrow roads that lead from one cross-compartment to another.

I am always grateful for these impediments to travel, since they have served to protect vast areas from exploitation and development. Tucked away in inaccessible valleys are innumerable quiet corners that are surprisingly untouched by the fell hand of the late 20th century. For alpinists and expert skiers there are the high mountains; for hikers and back-packers, lush meadows and magnificent forests; for families with small children, village inns on the banks of shallow mountain streams where toddlers can splash and float toy boats. Sadly, many Pyrenean mountain villages have been abandoned by their inhabitants and now stand in ruins. But where the villages are still inhabited, the conjunction of peasant architecture and mountain scenery is often nonpareil.

Here are fieldstone houses and Romanesque churches that seem to grow out of their hilltop sites like so many stone mushrooms. Except for telephone and electric lines you could easily imagine yourself back in the Middle Ages. Virtually the entire region makes good rambling country, and, indeed, some of the most enjoyable areas for walks and explorations are not among the loftiest peaks but further down, in gentler valleys like that of the Río Isábena, which is flanked by peaks in the 1,500-2,000-metre (4,900-6,500-foot) range. Here there is even a whole cathedral in miniature, one of the most astonishing Romanesque buildings in existence, which looks out across fields and meadows. I had never heard of the cathedral of Roda de Isábena until someone described to me this amazing edifice in the middle of nowhere. It was built a thousand years ago when a local count attained a certain regional autonomy, and his brother became the first bishop of this newly independent countship, notwithstanding that the entire see could not have numbered more than two or three thousand inhabitants. Atop the count's tiny hill-side 'capital' they built a perfect little 10th-century cathedral, complete in every way, although it takes up only about as much space as the average parish church. When I first came across it some years ago, I found that this architectural jewel was being looked after very well by an aristocratic priest who spent most of his time in overalls, restoring medieval stonework and repairing the ancient carvings: it was clear that here, in this forgotten valley, he had found his life's vocation looking after this sleeping beauty of an abandoned cathedral.

Throughout the Pyrenees you're apt to make discoveries of this kind: crystal-clear mountain lakes and glacier-fed waterfalls; remnants of ancient castles and monasteries; alpine meadows smothered in wild flowers and populated with chamois; monumental remains of Bronze Age inhabitants about whom nothing is known except that somehow they managed to survive in this inhospitable terrain. On the whole, wildlife is abundant and well cared for in the major national parks of the Pyrenees — Ordesa and Aigüestortes — which harbour sizeable populations of such fauna as roe deer and wild boar, eagles, vultures and falcons, as well as fox and ermine. In addition to these nationally protected areas are a whole range of regionally declared and managed parks and reserves, among the best of which are the *parques naturales* of Posets-Maladeta (Benasque; Aragón) and Cadí-Moixeró and La Garrotxa (Cataluña).

Topographically, the Pyrenees are usually divided into three regions — the Navarran, Aragonese and Catalan regions. The mountains of Navarra are gentler and less rugged than the rest of the Pyrenees, and the villages look correspondingly more prosperous: it is a lot easier to farm the lush, gradual slopes at the western end of the range. At the head-waters of the valleys of Ansó and Hecho loom the highest peaks in the region, the Pic d'Anie (2,507 m/8,225 ft), the Pic de Laraille (2,147 m/7,044 ft) and Mesa de los Tres Reyes (2,348 m/7,703 ft), the point where the kingdom of Navarra adjoined its neighbouring kingdoms of Aragón and Bearn.

The Aragonese Pyrenees, at the centre of the chain, extend eastward from this meeting place and include the highest summits of the range: Aneto in the Maladeta ridge, which at 3,408 metres (11,181 feet) is the second highest peak in peninsular Spain, Posets (3,371 m/11,060 ft) and Monte Perdido (3,355 m/11,007 ft). This central nucleus also contains the wildest scenery, with deep gorges, immense rock walls, and natural amphitheatres such as that of Piedrafita. Yet nestled among the loftiest mountains is the famous spa of Panticosa, a sort of high-altitude Baden-Baden, with a small casino and a little park for summer visitors who come to take the waters in the world's most improbable hydrotherapy centre. Benasque, still farther east, is the steepest-walled valley

of the central Pyrenees and the jumping-off point for excursions to both Aneto and Posets.

On the eastern slope of the towering peak of Aneto begins the Vall d'Aran, and with it the Catalan Pyrenees. Here the frontier with France curves northward before dipping south again to make way for the independent principality of Andorra, one of the world's most interesting mountain states. Andorra was once the Bhutan of Europe, but in recent years the prosperity of its tax-free shops and a flourishing tourist industry have ended its erstwhile isolation. Yet its form of government has hardly changed in 500 years. In the Middle Ages it was jointly ruled by the bishops of Urgel and the counts of Foix; now its co-princes are the bishop of Urgel and the president of France, on whom have devolved the feudal rights formerly exercised by the counts of Foix.

East of Andorra, just north of the border town of Puigcerdà, lies another feudal anomaly, the small Spanish township of Llívia, which is entirely surrounded by French territory. But mountains are no respecters of boundary lines. They continue to present a barrier to north-south traffic almost to the Mediterranean shore, maintaining their elevation with remarkable uniformity, through the provinces of Lleida (Lérida) and Girona (Gerona), until at last a sudden dip occurs in that part of the range called the Montes Alberes, which allows the Perpignan-Girona motorway to cross the mountains without difficulty. The last outrunners of the Pyrenees form a small peninsula in the Mediterranean that culminates in the Cabo de Creus, just north of the teeming bird habitats of the Golfo de Roses.

The Catalan Pyrenees contain some

of the finest nature reserves in the whole of Spain. The national park of Aigüestortes in the province of Lleida is certainly the best known, but all the surrounding region — especially the valleys drained by the Río Noguera Ribagorçane — is ideally suited to long hikes and to rambling nature-cum-Romanesque-village explorations. Another important valley, that of the Río Segre, is dominated by the ancient citadel of the bishops of Urgel — the town of La Seu d'Urgell (Seo de Urgel) which provides a convenient base from which to explore the eastern Pyrenees. (My favourite European work of art is the great book of the *Apocalypse Commentary* of Beato de Liébana, in the episcopal museum of La Seu d'Urgell.)

The Valle de Aran, enclosed to the north and south by parallel ridges of the Pyrenees, shelters meadows filled with orchids

Although the Catalan Pyrenees become more densely populated as you move eastwards, Girona province offers some splendid mountain terrain in the Ripoll, Garrotxa and Alt Empordà regions. La Garrotxa is something very special — a region of steep cliffs and small hidden valleys, punctuated by the craters of scores of extinct volcanoes, an extraordinary intrusion in this part of Spain.

A word about the terminology of these mountains: the peaks are called *puigs* in Catalunya (Cataluña), *pueyos* or *puertos* in Aragón, *poyos* in Navarra, and *puys* in France — all are thought to derive from *podium*, the Latin for an elevation. Depressions at the heads of valleys or the necks of ridges are called *colls* in Catalan and *collados* in Castilian Spanish; the passes that lead over them are known as *puertos* — gates, doorways — or *portil-*

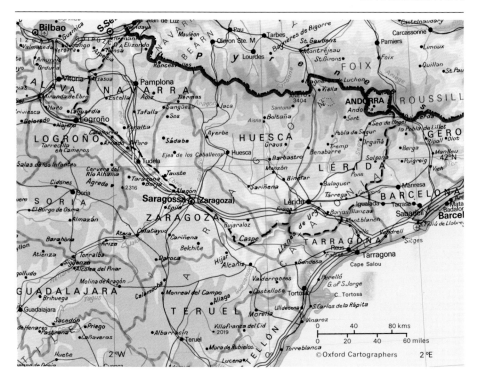

los (or in other words, small doors). There are about 70 or 80 passes in all, and the great majority are still negotiable only on foot, impassable during the snowed-in months and dangerous in the summer.

Indeed, the most significant change that the 20th century has wrought is that people are now coming to the Pyrenees for pleasure rather than just as smugglers, hunters or shepherds.

Thus what Richard Ford wrote about these mountains in the middle of last century, is still demonstrably true — that Nature 'here wantons in her loneliest, wildest forms. The scenery, sporting, geology and botany, are Alpine, and will repay those who can "rough it" considerably, [those] who love Nature with their heart, strength and soul, who worship her alike in her shyest retreats, in her wildest forms.'

BEFORE YOU GO
Maps: Michelin 1:400,000 Nos. 443 and 442.

GETTING THERE
By air: the principal airport for international arrivals is Barcelona. Many international charter flights arrive at Girona. Bilbao, Pamplona, San Sebastián, and Zaragoza are served by internal flights from both Barcelona and Madrid.

When not closed by bad weather, the airport at La Seu d'Urgell (Seo de Urgel) offers a very convenient means of getting to the heart of the Pyrenees.
By sea: Barcelona is the nearest major port for access to the eastern Pyrenees, Bilbao and Santander the nearest for the western end.
By car: from France, you can approach the Pyrenees from

either the east or west, on the main roads running along the coast, or via one of the mountain pass roads.

The roads connecting the different regions of the Pyrenees are mainly secondary and tertiary grades.
By rail: from Madrid there are frequent trains to Barcelona, Bilbao, Lleida, San Sebastián, Vitoria and Zaragoza; and less frequent services to Canfranc,

15

Girona, Huesca, Jaca and Pamplona.
From Barcelona there are frequent trains to Madrid, Lleida and Girona; and less frequent services to Bilbao, Irún, Logroño, San Sebastián and Vitoria. For information, call RENFE in Madrid, T: (91) 328 90 20, or check the schedules on RENFE's web-site, www.renfe.es.
By bus: to travel to Barcelona or San Sebastián by bus from major European cities is a feasible though time-consuming means of reaching the Pyrenees. There are good regional bus services between all major towns and most mountain villages. As these are operated by many different companies, and timetables are subject to change, check with the local tourist office for more information.

WHERE TO STAY
The best towns and villages in which to find accommodation are listed in the entries for individual exploration zones.

ACTIVITIES
Walking/climbing: in summer, walking in the Pyrenees is generally fairly easy; it is only in the most mountainous parts, such as Huesca, that the going gets tough. In winter you will need crampons and some experience.
Mountaineering clubs:
Federación Aragonesa de Montañismo, Albareda, 7, 50004 Zaragoza, T: (976) 22 79 71; Federación Catalana de Montañismo, Rambla, 41, 1°, 08002 Barcelona, T: (93) 412 07 77; and Federación Navarra de Deportes de Montaña y Escalada, Paulino Caballero, 13, 31002 Pamplona, T: (948) 42 78 48, F: 42 78 35, e-mail: f.n.montaña.jet.
Guided walks/adventure holidays: Federació d'Entitas
16

Excursionistes de Catalunya, Rambla, 41, 1°, 08002 Barcelona, T: (93) 412 07 77, F: 412 63 53, and www.feec.es.
Fishing: there is good trout fishing all through the Pyrenees, notably in the head-waters of such rivers as Segre, Garona, Cinca, Aragón and Gállego. Salmon fishing is confined to the western Pyrenees, notably in La Bidasoa, Navarra. Check with the local tourist office for seasons and permits.
Fishing clubs: Federación Aragonesa de Pesca, C/ Padre Marcellán, 15, 50015 Zaragoza, T: (976) 73 08 27; Federación Catalana de Pesca, Avda. Madrid, 118, entrlo 1°, 08018 Barcelona, T: (93) 330 48 18.
Skiing: the major ski resorts of the Spanish Pyrenees are:
Girona (972): Masella, 89 81 06; La Molina, 89 20 31; Vallter 2000, 74 03 53; Valle de Núria, 73 07 13.
Lleida (973): Baqueira-Beret, 64 50 25; Tuca Malh Blanc, 64 10 50; Llessui, 62 01 96; Port Ainé, 62 03 25; Super Espot, 63 50 13; Port del Comte, 48 09 50; Aránser, 51 50 09; Lies, 35 15 11; Tavascan, 62 63 00; Bonabè, 62 62 69; Sant Joan de l'Erm, 35 21 62; Tuixén-La Vansa, 37 00 34; Boí-Taüll, (93) 414 66 60.
Huesca (974): Cerler, 55 11 11; Panticosa, 48 72 48; Formigal, 49 00 49; Candanchú, 37 31 92; Valle de Astún, 37 30 34.
Navarra: Auritz-Burguete and Ibañeta.

FURTHER INFORMATION
Barcelona (93): tourist office, Gran Vía Corts Catálanes, 658, T: 301 74 43, F: 412 25 70. Red Cross, T: 205 14 14, F: 205 62 15.
Girona (972): tourist office, Rambla de la Libertad, 1, 17004, T: 22 65 75, F: 22 66 12. Red Cross, T: 23 01 31, F: 20 88 83.
Huesca (974): tourist office, C/

Coso Alto, 23, 22003, T: 22 57 58. Red Cross, T: 22 11 86, F: 24 29 54.
Lleida (973): tourist office, Avda. de Madrid, 36, T: 27 09 97, F: 27 09 49. Red Cross, T: 26 00 90, F: 26 48 96.
Pamplona (948): tourist office, C/ del Duque de Ahuma, 3, 31002, T: 22 07 41, F: 21 14 62. Red Cross, T: 22 64 03, F: 22 27 66.
San Sebastián (943): tourist office, Fueros, 1, 20003, T: 42 62 82, F: 43 17 46. Red Cross, T: 27 68 11, F: 29 39 17.
Zaragoza (976): tourist office, Torreón de la Zuda, Glorieta Pío XII, 50003, T: 39 35 37. Red Cross, T: 22 48 80, F: 21 92 61.

FURTHER READING
Jacquie Crozier, *Birdwatching Guide to the Pyrenees* (Arlequin Press, 1998);
Bob Gibbons & Paul Davies, *The Pyrenees* (B. T. Batsford Ltd, 1990);
Paul Jenner & Christine Smith, *Landscapes of the Pyrenees* (Sunflower, 1990);
Henry Myhill, *The Spanish Pyrenees* (London, 1966);
Kev Reynolds, *Walks and Climbs in the Pyrenees* (Cicerone, 1994);
A. W. Taylor, *Wild Flowers of the Pyrenees* (London).

La Garrotxa

A parque natural with an ancient volcanic landscape contrasted with trees, shrubs and farmland 11,908 ha (29,425 acres)

La Garrotxa, with its astonishing parade of volcanic cones amid neatly terraced fields, is a fascinating aberration. Volcanic action is virtually unknown in the Iberian peninsula, and in many ways the topography of La Garrotxa (literally, 'torn earth') resembles that of some beached South Sea island, forming a 'fantastic and inaccessible natural fortress', as the Catalan writer José Pla describes it.

As if in response to this challenge, the people of La Garrotxa have, over the centuries, endowed the valley with a series of equally fascinating and dramatic structures, so that the balance between the natural and the manufactured is beautifully maintained. Here is the town Castellfollit de la Roca ('the Mad Castle of the Rock'), poised on the edge of a basalt abyss overlooking the Río Fluvià; the town of Besalú, with its Roman bridge and medieval towers at the confluence of the Fluvià and the Río Capellades; and villages such as Santa Pau, in the centre of the volcanic plain, with massive fieldstone houses and arcaded streets. This last village must be one of the oldest inhabited places in Catalunya for there is a megalithic menhir on the Pla de Reixac. Out of the same volcanic soil

grows the famous beech forest known as La Fageda d'En Jordà.

The volcanic eruptions that shook this region took place no less than 17,000 years ago — long enough to have covered the basalt with a heavy layer of topsoil that has produced splendid meadows and rich farmland. Time has lined the craters with a carpet of trees and shrubs, but their outlines are still visible; the crater of Santa Margarida, for example, is nearly 350 m (1,150 ft) in diameter, and there are a dozen other notable extinct volcanoes, such as Montolivet, Treiter, Garrinada and Croscat.

Before you go *Maps:* IGN 1:25,000 and 1:50,000 No. 257; IGN 1:200,000 Mapa Provincial of Girona. *Guide-books:* Carlos de Hita, *Pirineo Catalan* (Anaya, 1998). **Getting there** *By car:* from Girona, take the C150 to the volcanic region just west of Banyoles (Bañolas). The southern road between Banyoles and Olot is the shortest distance between these 2 points. The northern route is more picturesque; it follows the Río Fluvià and touches on both

Besalú and Castellfollit de la Roca, 2 of the most interesting towns in La Garrotxa.

By bus: there is a regular service from Girona to Olot. 'Barcelona Bus', T: (93) 232 04 59, operates buses from the Estació del Nord in Barcelona to Girona, T: (972) 50 50 29.

Where to stay: La Garrotxa is only 54 km (30 miles) from Girona, which has a range of good accommodation. Olot has several hotels, including the 4-star Riu Olot, T: (972) 26 94 44, F: 26 67 03, the 1-star La Perla, T: (972) 26 23 26, F: 27 07 74, and Albergue Torre Malagrida, T: (972) 26 42 00, F: 27 18 96. Besalú has the 1-star Siqués, T: (972) 59 01 10, F: 59 12 43.

Interesting *casas rurales* include: Mas Salvanera, T: (972) 59 09 75, in Beuda; La Miana, T: (972) 22 30 59, in Sant Ferriol and Can Jou, T: (972) 19 02 63, in Sant Jaume de Llierca.

Outdoor living: the camp-site near Olot, Les Tries, T: (972) 26 24 05, is open 1 Apr-30 Oct. South of Olot, in San Felio de Pallerols, La Vall d'Hostoles, T: (972) 44 41 04, is open 15 June-30 Sept with space for 126.

Activities *Walking:* from Olot to the Volcà de Santa Margarida, the largest crater, via the beech forest, La Fageda d'En Jordà; or follow the Río Fluvià down the Vall d'En Bas, which will take you through a series of pretty villages.

Viewpoints: there are a number of good views across the volcanoes — notably, overlooking the Sierra de Finestres, near the *château* at Santa María de Finestres; by Puigsacalm; and north at Santa Bárbara de Prüneres.

Further information *Tourist offices:* Mulleres, Pl. del Mercat, 17800 Olot, T: (972) 26 01 41; Pl. de la Libertat, 1, 17850 Besalú, T: (972) 59 02 25; and Girona, p16.

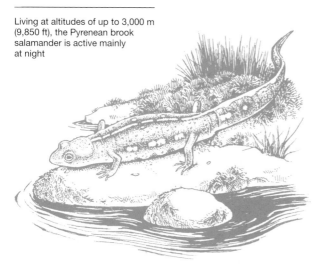

Living at altitudes of up to 3,000 m (9,850 ft), the Pyrenean brook salamander is active mainly at night

Cadí-Moixeró

A parque natural near Puigcerdà in the eastern Pyrenees
41,342 ha (102,156 acres)

The astonishingly varied and beautiful Pyrenean countryside of Cadí-Moixeró provides a wonderful setting for lone rambles and quiet strolls. It comprises mountain ranges and several other massifs, together with all their valleys, meadows and forests. More than two dozen villages and hamlets are set against a superb backdrop of mountains that are snow-capped for half the year.

These mountains are lower, gentler and on the whole more user-friendly than, for example, the high peaks of the Montes Malditos, near Maladeta. The chains of Cadí and of Moixeró, which are the park's dominant physical features, together extend for about 30 kilometres (20 miles) from east to west and are linked by the Pas de Tancalaporta (the 'close-the-door' pass). There is more than enough scope for serious mountain-climbing here. You will find the 2,647-metre (8,685-foot) Puig de la Canal Baridana (also called Puig Vulturó), the highest peak in the Cadí range, and the Pedraforca, at 2,497 metres (8,192 feet), rising from the 900-metre (2,950-foot) valley floors. The most common starting-points for assaults on the Pedraforca are the villages of Gósol and Gisclareny. Both can also be enjoyed as bases for walks through adjoining valleys.

As you explore the area, it will become apparent that the ecosystems are alpine rather than Mediterranean: dense forests and fertile meadows contrasting with the rugged contours of limestone massifs. Low temperatures and high humidity support species not usually associated with Spain. Above 2,000 metres (7,000 feet) there are typically alpine meadows full of gentian and other high-mountain flowers; on the lower slopes, forests of mountain pine with juniper and rhododendron. There are large stands of silver fir and beech trees on wet, shady ground on the southern slopes; oaks, maple and aspen occur in sizeable numbers, as well as Scots pine and box wood (*Buxus sempervivens*), which gives off its strongest fragrance when the leaves are heated by the summer sun.

The highest mountain pass in this region is the 1,800-metre (5,905-foot) Collada de Toses, which has the richest alpine flora in the whole of the eastern Pyrenees. The screes abound with parnassus-leaved buttercup (*Ranunculus parnassifolius*), a thickset perennial with shining green leaves and pink-tinged flowers, growing with the attractive yellow crucifer, decumbent treacle-mustard (*Erysimum decumbens*); both are limestone-loving plants. Another handsome species is the diminutive Rhaetian poppy (*Papaver rhaeticum*). The beautiful *Ramonda myconi* is found in these mountains too.

The park's animals are also alpine in character. The Pyrenean chamois lives on the highest peaks during the summer; in winter the herds move downhill to the southern slopes. Red and roe deer are common and golden eagles, buzzards and capercaillies may be seen too.

BEFORE YOU GO
Maps: IGN 1:25,000 and 1:50,000 Nos. 215, 216, 217, 253, 254 and 255; IGN 1:200,000 Mapas Provinciales of Barcelona, Girona and Lleida.
Guide-books: Agustí Jolis & M. Antònia Simó, *Cerdanya* (Editorial Montblanc-Martin, 1986) and *Pedraforca* (Editorial Montblanc-Martin, 1969).

GETTING THERE
By air: small airport at La Seu d'Urgell has flights to Cadí-Moixeró. Sometimes closed in bad weather.
By car: there are 4 main routes to the park. The N152 from Barcelona to Puigcerdà via Vic and Ripoll brings you to the Collada de Toses at the eastern end of the park. The C1411, branching off from the N-11 from

Barcelona towards Berga and Bellver de Cerdanya, follows the Río Llobregat, then crosses the Cadí tunnel; the same road, branching off towards the west before Guardiola de Berguedà, runs through the southern part of the park. The C1313 from Puigcerdà to La Seu d'Urgell skirts the park's northern limits.
By rail: a regular service runs from Barcelona to Puigcerdà by

way of La Molina and Alp. **By bus:** Alsina Graells, Estació del Nord in Barcelona, T: (93) 265 68 66, operates services from Barcelona to La Seu d'Urgell, and from La Seu to Puigcerdà.

WHERE TO STAY
Try 2-star Pensión Triuet in Gósol, T: (973) 37 00 72, and 2-star Hotel Bellavista, T: (973) 51 00 00, F: 51 04 18, in Bellver de Cerdanya.
Outdoor living: Solana del Segre in Bellver de Cerdanya, T: (973) 51 03 10.
Refuges: inside the park, there are a number of well-tended shelters, most open during the summer months only. The Refugi Cèsar A. Torras, 2,037 m (6,683 ft), can be reached by a 1.5-km (1-mile) forest path

from Martinet via Montellè. The Refugi de l'Ingla, 1,510 m (4,954 ft), and Refugi del Pla de les Esposes, 1,500 m (4,921 ft), are both near Bellver de Cerdanya; in winter, the keys are available from the Agent Forestal del Medi Natural in Bellver de Cerdanya. The Refugi Cortgal d'en Vidal, 1,650 m (5,413 ft), 8 km (5 miles) from Urús, is often blocked by snow during the winter. The Refugi de Rebost, 1,670 m (5,479 ft), stands within the boundaries of Bagà; keys are available from the Unió Excursionista de Catalunya in Bagà. The Refugi d'Erols de Baix, 1,450 m (4,085 ft), is on the road from La Pobla de Lillet. The Refugi de Sant Jordi, near Bagà, is accessible only on foot.

ACTIVITIES
Walking: well- marked trails throughout the park. About 9 hrs are required for the north-south excursion from Martinet to Gósol through the Coll de l'Homme Mort and the Pas dels Gosolans.
Guides: for the Servei de Guies de Natura (wildlife-guide service) consult the town halls of Bellver de Cerdanya and La Seu d'Urgell. For long mountain walks, contact the experienced guide Joan Cassola, Escoles d'Olià, Bellver de Cerdanya, T: (973) 51 01 90.
Further information *Tourist offices:* Pl. de S. Roc, s/n, 25720 Bellver de Cerdanya, T: (973) 51 02 29, and Lleida, p16. *Mountaineering club:* Federación Catalana de Montañismo, p16.

Aigüestortes & Estany de Sant Maurici

A magnificent national park of mountains, lakes and meadows, just west of Andorra
ZEPA
10,230 ha (25,280 acres)

**\\\ \\\ **

This is, without question, the jewel of the Catalan Pyrenees, and except for Ordesa to the west, there is not a more pristine and breathtaking area in the entire Pyrenean region. Indeed, it has some of the finest mountain scenery in the whole of Europe, a magnificent conjunction of meadows, peaks, lakes, streams and forests. Aigüestortes means 'twisted waters' in Catalan, in the sense of 'rough' or 'uneven'; now that the park falls under the jurisdiction of the Generalitat de Catalunya, its entire name is officially designated in Catalan even within the Generalitat's Spanish-language publications. (Privately published books in Castilian still refer to it as the Parque Nacional de

The deep, unruffled waters of the Estany Negre de Peguera lie trapped in one of the glacial depressions of Aigüestortes

19

Aigües Tortes y Lago San Mauricio.) The park covers an area of 10,230 hectares (25,280 acres) and is divided into two nearly equal halves: the Aigüestortes zone in the west, near the Boí valley, and the Lake Sant Maurici zone in the east. A crest of high mountains, including the Pala Alta de Serrader (2,982 metres/9,783 feet), the Pic de Contraig (2,966 metres/9,730 feet) and the Gran Tuc de Colomers (2,932 metres/9,619 feet), marks the park's boundary on the north and underlines its inaccessibility. Until the end of the last century this was one of the most isolated regions in the whole of Europe, and no one except shepherds and big game hunters ever came this way. There were no roads leading into the area, and no bridges spanning the dizzying precipices that have to be crossed. But with the age of hydro-electric power, the utility companies moved in, building roads, bridges, dams and generating stations. These signs of a now rather antiquated modernity are kept largely out of sight, however, and do little to detract from the mountain splendours of what has justly been called a 'Pyrenean paradise'. The only thing that might diminish enjoyment of this paradise is the weather: it rains a great deal, and snows even more. In Sant Maurici,

during the average year there are 50 days of rain and 100 of snowfall.

The rounded valleys and rough-cut mountain tops — imposing masses of granite and slate — were formed during the Primary era some 200 million years ago; were up-thrust and folded by plate-collision pressures during the Tertiary; and finally were carved, ground and polished by glacial action during the early phases of the Quaternary era, which gave the mountains their present distinctive shape and scooped out the hollows for 140 or so lakes. Some of these lakes are nearly 50 metres (165 feet) in depth, thanks to the implacable abrasive energy of the Pyrenean glaciers. These lakes are the special glory of Aigüestortes: most are of a spectacular clarity and brilliance, and some are fed by waterfalls.

The vegetation follows much the same pattern as that of Ordesa, with fir, beech and silver birch forests in areas up to 2,000 metres (6,600 feet); only the twisted black pine can hold its own above that limit. The Pyrenean chamois flourishes in the high meadows, and golden eagles build their nests in caves on sheltered butresses. There are otters in the lakes and grouse and capercaillie in generous numbers inhabit the woods.

BEFORE YOU GO
Maps: IGN 1:25,000 and 1:50,000 Nos. 181 and 182; IGN 1:200,000 Mapa Provincial of Lleida.
Guide-books: Enric Balasch & Yolanda Ruiz, *El Parque Nacional de Aigüestortes i*

Estany de Sant Maurici (Planeta, 1998).

GETTING THERE
By car: there are two main access routes to the park. For the western entrance – the Aigüestortes sector – take the

N230 from Lleida to Vielha via Alfarràs and Benabarre. Just past Pont de Suert, turn east on L500 towards Caldes de Boí (Caldas de Bohí). Or from Lleida take the C1313 to Balaguer, the C147 to La Pobla de Segur and then the C144 to Pont de Suert.

Access to the eastern side and Estany de Sant Maurici (Lago San Mauricio) is provided by the C147 from Balaguer to Esterri d'Aneu via La Pobla de Segur; 6 km (4 miles) before Esterri d'Aneu turn west on LV5004 toward Espot.
By rail: there is a limited *Regional* service from Lleida to La Pobla de Segur.
By bus: Alsina Graells, T: (973) 27 14 70, operates one bus a day Mon-Fri, in the afternoon, between Lleida and La Pobla

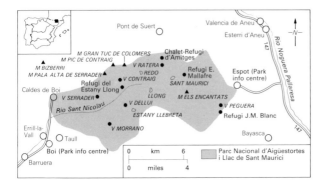

de Segur; and one bus each morning between La Pobla de Segur and Pont de Suert, and from Pont de Suert to Caldes de Boí. Also daily buses run from Barcelona and Lleida to Esterri d'Aneu and Vielha, which stop at the crossroads leading to Espot (7 km/4½ miles from the village).

WHERE TO STAY
Three villages near the western sector of the park – Caldes de Boí, Boí and Erill la Vall – and the town of Espot on the east offer accommodation. Try, in Caldes de Boí, the 4-star Hotel Manantial, T: (973) 69 62 10, F: 69 60 58, or the Casa Rural Les Cabanasses, T: (973) 29 70 33; in Erill la Vall, the 2-star Pensión L'Aut, T: (973) 69 60 48, F: 69 61 26, and the charming La Plaça, T: (973) 69 60 26, F: 69 61 28; in Espot, the 2-star Hotel Saurat, T: (973) 62 41 62, F: 62 40 37; in Vilamur, the Casa Rural Casa Blasi, T: (973) 62 17 80, is worth a visit. To the east, in La Seu d'Urgell, try the 4-star Hotel El Castell, T: (973) 35 07 04, F: 35 15 74.
Outdoor living: 2 sites in Espot are open during the summer:

La Mola, T: (973) 62 40 24, and Sol i Neu, T: (973) 62 40 01.
Refuges: Refugi E. Mallafré, T: (973) 62 40 09, at the foot of Els Encantats near Lake Sant Maurici, open 1 June-30 Sept; Refugi del Estany Llong, T: (973) 69 62 84, in Sant Nicolau Valley, open 17 June-10 Oct; and Refugi J. M. Blanc, beside the Estany Tort de Peguera in the Peguera valley, and the Refugi d'Amitges, near the Estany d'Amitges in the Ratera valley, open 1 June-30 Sept. The rest of the year call T: (93) 315 23 11.

ACTIVITIES
Walking: approaching from the west, the normal route is to follow the course of the Río Sant Nicolau, along whose banks runs a road that can barely be negotiated by Land Rovers; it leads uphill past the lake known as the Estany Llebreta ('of the small hare') to the plain of Aigüestortes. Here are the trail-heads for most of the footpaths leading into the surrounding mountains.
Climbing: many of the ascents are simple climbs even for beginners; few are more than 1-

Pyrenean snake's head (*Fritillaria pyrenaica*) has large, nodding bell-shaped flowers of a brownish-purple colour with green markings

day excursions. For detailed information, contact the Federación Catalana de Montañismo, p16.

FURTHER INFORMATION
Tourist offices: Prat del Guarda, 2, 25597 Espot, T/F: (973) 62 40 36, and Lleida, p16.
Park office: Camp de Mart, 35, Lleida, T: (973) 24 66 50.

Vall d'Aran

A botanical treasure-house in an isolated corner of the high Pyrenees, on the border with France

In Spanish eyes the Vall d'Aran is the valley of all valleys (the word *aran* means 'valley'). It is a green and fertile oasis of forests and meadows, enclosed by jagged mountain summits. In spring, the valley comes alive with meadows of horned pansy (*Viola cornuta*), alpine pasque-flower (*Pulsatilla alpina*) and four species of daffodil — the pale Lent lily (*Narcissus pallidiflorus*) and

The ptarmigan, a mainly arctic and alpine bird, has its southerly outpost in the Pyrenees, where it inhabits scree and stony plateaux

the pheasant's-eye narcissus (*N. poeticus*) as well as *N. abscissus* and *N. bicolor* — all in great swathes of purple, white and yellow. Autumn heralds the arrival of merendera (*Merendera montana*) and a purple-flowered crocus (*Crocus nudiflorus*), which sprout from the cut meadows.

The crystalline rocks in the tributary valley of the Río Iñola support three of the more spectacular geranium species: bloody cranesbill (*Geranium sanguineum*) with its crimson flowers grows alongside dusky cranesbill (*G. phaeum*), its blackish-purple petals turned back like fragile cyclamen, while the shadier sites beneath overhanging rocks are home to the Pyrenean cranesbill (*G. pyrenaicum*). In late May, it is easy to overlook the graceful arches formed by the purple-and-green chequered bells of the Pyrenean fritillary (*Fritillaria pyrenaica*) hidden among the heathers and brooms on these acid slopes. And the woods and meadows are full of herbs and wild flowers useful to witches or practitioners of alternative medicine, such as arnica, liquorice and several varieties of what the Aranese call 'mountain tea'.

The Vall d'Aran used to be cut off from the rest of Spain as soon as the first snows blocked the mountain passes leading to the south and east. There was only one pass that remained open all year — and it led northward, to Argut-Dessous, in France. Thus the kings of Spain were never able to visit their Aran domains during the winter unless they travelled by way of France. Not until 1948, and the completion of the tunnel to Vielha (Viella), was the area accessible from Spain all year round. Even then there were days when, in the words of the old joke, you couldn't get there from here. Now snow-proof approaches have been built at both ends of the tunnel, the Vall d'Aran need never be cut off from the mother country.

The abundance of snow here in the high Pyrenees has proved to be a great boon to the economy of this once-pastoral district. The ski resorts of Baqueira-Beret and La Tuca are among the finest in the country, in terms of both the terrain and snow conditions. But the valley's ski boom has also brought with it the usual aesthetic disfigurements of ski-resort architecture. Vielha, once a beautiful half-medieval town, now resembles a French *station de ski*, and some of the ancient villages further up the valley have acquired a sudden modernism that has practically extinguished their original field-stone and slate-roof architecture.

Still, the Vall d'Aran has the potential makings of a great national park, although it hasn't yet been turned into one. There are marvellous walks through the forests and the valleys of the Río Garona, numerous cross-country ski trails and plenty of scope for climbing: among the surrounding peaks is Maubermé (2,880 metres/9,450 feet), on the French border.

The profusion of wild flowers in the meadows of the Valle de Benasque provides a summer paradise for butterflies and moths

BEFORE YOU GO
Maps: IGN 1:25,000 and 1:50,000 Nos. 148, 149 and 181; IGN 1:200,000 Mapa Provincial of Lleida.
Guide-book: Ramon de Semir i de Arguer, *La Vall d'Aran turistica y documental* (Editorial Alpina, 1984).

GETTING THERE
By car: the C230 from Lleida leads to Vielha through the Túnel de Vielha. The C142

runs from Esterri d'Aneu to Port (Puerto) de la Bonaigua, the south-eastern pass into the Vall d'Aran. From France, the N125 joins the N230 in Pont de Rei; or, from the north-west, D618 joins the Spanish C141 at the Portillo de Bossòst.

By bus: there is a regular service operated by Alsina Graells from Barcelona and Lleida to Vielha and Baqueira-Beret. For further information, T: (93) 265 68 66 in Barcelona, or T: (973) 27 14 70 in Lleida.

WHERE TO STAY
Accommodation is plentiful in the Vall d'Aran, with Vielha,

At 1,000-2,000 m the woods of the Vall d'Aran are made up of beech and birch interspersed with conifers such as black pine and fir

BUTTERFLIES IN THE VALL D'ARAN

Aran is such a special valley botanically that it is hardly surprising that it holds a number of rather scarce butterflies as well. These include the alpine grizzled skipper (*Pyrgus andromedae*) and the chequered skipper (*Carterocephalus palaemon*). The clouded apollo (*Parnassius mnemosyne*), a beautiful creamy-white butterfly with charcoal and yellow circular markings and a wingspan of some 7.5cm (3in), is not a rare species internationally, but it has an endemic sub-species here — *republicanus* — which occurs in only a few localities in Spain. The larvae feed off various plants of the poppy family, such as fumitories, and also from stonecrops. As expected, it is a mountain species, flying between 1,200-2,000m (3,900-6,500ft) during June and July, often in damp meadow areas.

Also localized around the Aran area is the silvery argus (*Pseudaricia nicias*), a species found only where there is an abundance of meadow and wood cranesbills (*Geranium pratense* and *G. sylvaticum*) between 1,200-1,700m (3,940-5,580ft). This butterfly is found only in the Pyrenees, the south-west Alps, Finland and Russia; the Aran population is described as a separate race (*judithi*).

Salardú and Bossòst offering a wide choice. Try the 3-star Parador de Viella, T: (973) 64 01 00, F: 64 11 00, or the 2-star Hotel Arán, T: (973) 64 00 50, F: 64 00 53, in Vielha; or the 3-star Hotel Tuc Blanc, T: (973) 64 43 50, F: 64 60 08, in Salardú.
Outdoor living: of the campsites try the Era Yerla d'Arties at Arties, T: (973) 64 16 02, or the Artigane at Arròs, T: (973) 64 01 89 — but you can camp in any of the mountain areas *de utilidad pública*; contact the tourist office for details.

ACTIVITIES
Walking: there are numerous

scenic routes, for example, the simple walk to the Circo de Saboredo, at the south-eastern end of the valley; the trail begins at the end of a forest road that starts at Salardú and hugs the western bank of the Río Garona de Ruda as far as the Font de Campo ('spring of the meadow'), from where a 1-hr ascent brings you to the Estany Major of Circo de Saboredo, a superb high-mountain region with 35 lakes and tarns of all sizes, which is ideal for camping.
Climbing: the Pic de Maubermé offers several strenuous but not too difficult climbs as well as rock climbing. For detailed

information, see *Pyrenees Andorra and Cerdagne* by Arthur Battagel (Reading, 1980), or consult the mountaineering club, Federación Catalana de Montañismo, p16.
Fishing: there are some 200 lakes, or *estanys*, full of trout, and many of these are truly spectacular. Enquire at the tourist office in Vielha for seasons and permits. Fishing club, Federación Catalana de Pesca, p16.

FURTHER INFORMATION
Tourist offices: Sarriulera, 6, 25530 Vielha, T: 64 01 10, F: 64 05 37; Lleida, p16.

Valle de Benasque

The highest mountains of the Pyrenees, which are rich in wildlife and provide plenty of scope for climbers; contained mostly within the Parque Natural de Posets-Maladeta
33,267 ha (82,203 acres)

The Valle de Benasque runs like a green-and-blue ribbon between the two glacier-capped massifs of the Posets and the Macizo de la Maladeta. At 3,408 metres (11,181 feet) the Maladeta's Aneto is the highest mountain in the Pyrenees; Posets is second, at 3,371 metres (11,060 feet).

In the more sheltered southern half of the valley are the villages of Sahún, Eriste, Anciles, Cerler and Benasque. Going higher and farther north means getting into really harsh weather, with scarcely a ray of sunshine during the winter months. Even in summer the weather is tricky, as elsewhere in the Pyrenees. The streams and rivers are at their fullest then. June and August, incidentally, are the stormiest months, and the storms here in the past have sometimes proved fatal to climbers and hikers.

Quaternary glacial action was the sculp-

tor of the Pyrenees. It gradually reduced the upthrust mountains, cracking them and sanding them down. Igneous rock acquired needle-sharp profiles, peaks and crests. Limestone and slate were split into small pieces and took on rounded forms, producing underlays for the gently curving meadows, that grazing livestock like so much.

The higher reaches of the valley are so rich in wildlife, the area really should be turned into a national park. The Picos de Eriste and Vallibierna (Valhiverna) are inhabited by hundreds of Pyrenean chamois. There are weasels, hares and marmots; the last-named are said to make the trip from France, in groups, to the high meadows of the Esera, there to hibernate in deep burrows during the winter. The capercaillie lives here in the most inaccessible parts of the forest: it is such a remarkable bird that a simple word like 'grouse' will not do — the Spanish call it *urogallo*. It flies very swiftly for such a heavy bird, and has splendid black-blue plumage, a small beard and red circles around the eyes.

In summer the whole of the Valle de Benasque becomes one irresistible field of wild flowers, rampant with orchids and gentians, irises and forget-me-nots.

The rocky outcrops of the Macizo de la Maladeta support a jumble of matted globularia (*Globularia coridifolia* ssp. *nana*), clinging to the bedrock like moss, together with the irregular pink flowers of fairy foxglove (*Erinus alpinus*) and the yellow Pyrenean toadflax (*Linaria supina*) which grows outwards from a central point, the flowerstems radiating like the spokes of a bicycle.

In the Puerto de Benasque alpine mouseear (*Cerastium alpinum*) and the tiny pink-and-green cushions of moss campion (*Silene acaulis*) hug the stony ground, while the screes are held together by the trailing stems of Pyrenean vetch (*Vicia pyrenaica*).

There are dozens of lakes and tarns — here called *ibons* — in the Posets massif. Most of them lie above 2,500 metres (8,200 feet), and some lie higher than the Coma de la Paul glacier, at 2,570 metres (8,430 feet).

Following the Río Esera toward the north-east, the slopes become steeper and the landscape still more rugged. At the Plan del Hospital begins the twisting trail to the pass known as the Portillón de Benasque (2,445 metres/8,020 feet); this is the old path to France, carved out by smugglers, soldiers and pilgrims during the Middle Ages.

Curiously enough, the name Montes Malditos rests on a misunderstanding. La Maladeta, in Aragonese, simply means 'the highest mountain'. But the French travellers assumed the word meant *maudit*, 'accursed', and the highly descriptive Maladeta was thus transformed into the pejorative and sinister Montes Malditos, 'the accursed mountains'. They are nothing of the kind, and the great glacier that runs along the ridge is one of the seven wonders of Spain.

BEFORE YOU GO
Maps: IGN 1:25,000 and 1:50,000 Nos. 148, 149, 180 and 181; IGN 1:200,000 Mapa Provincial of Huesca.

GETTING THERE
By car: whether you start from Lleida, Huesca or Zaragoza, the gateway to Benasque is the village of Graus, on N230 from Lleida, N240 from Huesca. From Graus, the A139 leads north to Benasque and all the villages of the valley.
By bus: two buses daily, operated by Alto Aragonesa, T: (974) 21 07 00, in both directions, connecting Lleida, Huesca, Graus and Benasque.

WHERE TO STAY
Benasque has several hotels, including the 3-star Ciria, T: (974) 55 16 12, F: 55 16 86, and the 1-star Hostal El Puente, T: (974) 55 12 79. Nearby, in Eriste, try the charming La Caseta del Sastre, T: (974) 55 13 09, and in Sahún, the rustic Casa Falisia, T: (974) 55 13 40.
Outdoor living: for official sites, Aneto, in Benasque, is open all year round with space for 450 people, T: (974) 55 11 41; and

Ixeia, T: (974) 55 21 29, north of Benasque, also open all year round with capacity for 250 people. The Plan d'Están, at the end of the Pista de Vallibierna, and Llanos del Hospital in the Erera valley, are good areas for pitching a tent.
Refuges: Angel Orús, T: (974)

An alpine marmot adopts an alert posture, ready to issue a short sharp whistle if danger threatens

34 40 44, in the Valle de Eriste, and Refugio de Estós, T: (974) 55 14 83, in the Valle de Estós, both open all year.

ACTIVITIES
Walking/climbing: the ruined Cabañas de Sallent near the turbulent stream known as the Aigüeta de Eriste at 2,080 m (6,825 ft), marks the starting point for the standard excursion to the Pico de Posets, which takes 4 hrs of steady climbing through the gorges of the Llardaneta.

There are half a dozen standard ways of climbing to the Maladeta and the Pico de Aneto, which affords a breathtaking view of the entire range. The shortest begins at La Renclusa, the *refugio* maintained by the Centre Excursionista de Catalunya. Cross-country skiers find this a magnificent area in the winter; in summer the climb to Aneto is one of the great Pyrenean experiences.
Mountaineering club:
Federación Aragonesa de Montañismo, p16.

FURTHER INFORMATION
Tourist office: Huesca, p16.

25

Ordesa

The isolated Ordesa canyon and the great Monte Perdido dominate this dramatic national park on the Franco-Hispanic border
Biosphere Reserve, ZEPA, European Diploma , World Heritage Site
15,608 ha (38,568 acres)

Ordesa is full of geological curiosities like these natural limestone buttresses

Ordesa is magnificent enough when the sun is shining but absolutely awe-inspiring during a thunderstorm. I've been caught in several of them, for even during the summer months there's always a good chance of rain in the high Pyrenees. I remember one particularly violent downpour when it seemed that we were being treated to a replay of Noah's flood: it was early July, but the skies opened up, water descended in sheets and hailstones ricocheted from my hat. All of this was pleasant enough at the end of a hot day, but then a mist began moving up the valley and as the rain continued to fall, great cascades of dirty yellow water came pouring off the rock walls, dislodging a shower of small stones that bounced and splashed their way into the valley. It made me think of the medieval Aragonese mountain-dwellers, fighting off invading armies of lowlanders by pelting them with rocks.

The next day was clear and beautiful. We proceeded up the valley past caves and waterfalls, following the path of the Río Arazas. When we finally caught sight of our destination, the superb Circo Soasa, a young Catalan woman turned to me. 'I've never been to Canada,' she said, 'but this is what I imagine it to be like — this sense of space, a crystal stream, majestic mountains, this uncluttered landscape.'

The Valle de Ordesa has always been considered something quite special and extraordinary by people with eyes to see. Of course, the local shepherds had always known about this isolated canyon but Louis Ramond de Charbonnières, a French alpinist, is regarded as its modern 'discoverer'. One day at the turn of the century, while looking down from the summit of Monte Perdido, he decided to go down and investigate the great sickle-shaped depression, which had been scooped out of the calcareous bedrock by Quaternary glaciation. He published a description of what he found in his *Voyages au Mont-Perdu* (1901).

26

Three of the national park's constituent valleys — Ordesa, Añisclo and Pineta — form the legs of a kind of tripod supporting the great massif of Monte Perdido ('lost mountain'), whose 3,355-metre (11,000-foot) summit lies just south of the Franco-Hispanic frontier, and whose northern slope includes the famous French gorge known as the Cirque de Gavarnie. The fourth valley, Las Gargantas de Escuaín, carries its moun-tain waters down towards the south-east and the village of Tella: it is the least known of the park's valleys but far from the least in-teresting, with its great flanking walls of rock, some of them reaching a height of 300 metres (984 feet), and the mysterious dol-men that stands in a meadow above Tella.

Monte Perdido is the highest of the three high mountains known as Las Tres Sorores ('the three sisters') that dominate the park;

27

the other two are El Cilindro de Marbore (3,328 metres/l0,920 feet) and El Sum de Ramond (3,262 metres/10,700 feet). The mountain chain was formed by cataclysmic pressure at the beginning of the Tertiary period. Then the glaciers began their slow work: in the Quaternary a frozen sea covered Las Tres Sorores and there were rivers of ice in the canyons that have become the Ordesa, Añisclo and Pineta valleys. What makes Ordesa geologically unusual is that it runs parallel to the main spine of the Pyrenees, unlike most of the other valleys, which are perpendicular to it.

The Ordesa valley is a tongue of green vegetation running for 15 kilometres (9½ miles) between two imposing walls of bleached, calcareous rock. Looming above the beech trees, the pines and dark green firs are the dramatic rock cornices known as *fajas* — balconies of stone formed by erosion — which afford magnificent views of the canyon and its many waterfalls.

Pyrenean chamois, currently multiplying at a furious rate, are fond of the vertiginous terraces of the valley. Ordesa has one of Europe's largest populations of chamois, but

In Spain the lammergeier (or bearded vulture), is confined to the Pyrenees, with a population of 60 pairs

the Spanish ibex, or *cabra montés*, which the park was intended to protect, has not done nearly as well: there are said to be no more than 15 ibex in the park these days.

The lammergeier has one of its major European strongholds in these mountains and indeed is found only in the Pyrenees in Spain today. Formerly, it was easy to see at Ordesa, but sightings have been more irregular in recent years and you would be well advised to search somewhere else: the area of Santa Cruz, west of Jaca, has this grand bird, as do the towering pinnacles above the monastery of Riglos to the south. With a wingspan of 2.5 metres (eight feet) and a long, wedge-shaped tail, they are easily recognized, especially the adults which have golden-hued underparts and a habit of dropping bones to break them prior to extracting the marrow. The sheer cliff faces of Ordesa are also home to the elusive wallcreeper, a grey moth-like rock-climber that continually flicks its wings to show bright scarlet feathers. Higher up are snow finches on the bare screes and, lower, citril finches are found where the trees and bare ground meet.

Apart from these endangered species, Ordesa constitutes a favourable habitat for 171 species of birds, 32 mammals, eight species of reptiles and five amphibians. Wild boar are a fairly common sight, and there are otters and foxes in the valleys. There is one species of poisonous snake, the asp (*Vipera aspi*s). The Ordesa valley is also home to a specific race of the Spanish argus butterfly (*Aricia morronensis ordesiae*), found nowhere else in the world.

In the valleys the predominant trees are firs and beeches that grow strong and tall up to altitudes of about 1,700 metres (5,575 feet); above 2,300 metres (7,550 feet) the only tree hardy enough to survive is the dwarf mountain pine whose short, contorted trunk reflects its struggle against the elements. The park's botanists take particular pride in its wild flowers, which include the edelweiss — in Spanish, *el pie de león* ('lion's foot') or *flor de nieve* ('snow flower') — gentians, orchids and anemones. The alpenrose (*Rhododendron ferrugineum*) grows in the shade of the pine, while violets and belladonna prefer the shelter of the fir forests.

BEFORE YOU GO
Maps: IGN 1:25,000 and 1:50,000 Nos. 146 and 178; IGN 1:200,000 Mapa Provincial of Huesca.
Guide-books: Enric Balasch & Yolanda Ruiz, *El Parque Nacional de Ordesa y Monte Perdido* (Planeta, 1998); Oscar Díez Sanchez & Luis Lorente Villanueva, *El Parque Nacional de Ordesa y Monte Perdido* (Everest, 1997).

GETTING THERE
By car: the simplest access to the Valle de Ordesa is via the E07/N330 Huesca-Biescas, followed by the C140, Biescas-Torla via the Cotefablo Pass, from where you can drive into the park.

For the Añisclo, Escuaín and Pineta valleys take the C138, Ainsa-Bielsa, and side roads that branch off toward these valleys.

During Oct-Apr weather conditions, particularly snow levels, should be checked because often the park is inaccessible by car during these months.

Ramonda myconi has a purple flower and dark-green crinkly leaves

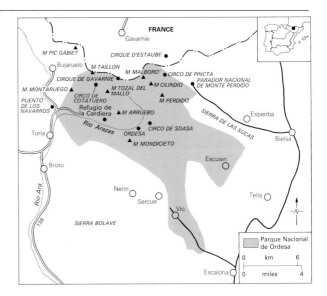

By rail: one daily service runs from Madrid to Sabiñánigo and on to Jaca, and *Regional* services run on the Zaragoza to Canfranc line.
By bus: in July and August there are 2 buses daily between Sabiñánigo and Torla operated by Uberbus, T: (974) 21 32 77. From Torla during these months there are buses every 15 min to the park. Call T: (974) 24 33 61 for more information.

WHERE TO STAY
Torla has a variety of places, including the 3-star Hotel Abetos, T: (974) 48 64 48, F: 48 64 00, and the 2-star Hotel Ordesa, T: (974) 48 61 25, F: 48 63 81. There are several, also, in Sabiñánigo, including the Parador de Bielsa, T: (974) 50 10 11, F: 50 11 88.
Outdoor living: not permitted inside the park, but you can bivouac using a tent just for the night — provided you strike it the next morning — in the Ordesa valley above 2,100 m (6,890 ft), in the Añisclo valley above 1,800 m (5,905 ft), in the Escuaín valley above 1,800 m (5,905 ft) and in the Pineta val-

The flowers of *Geranium cinereum* may be lilac, white and strongly veined, or a deep reddish-purple

ley above 2,500 m (8,200 ft).
Refuges: there are many in the park, on both the Spanish and French sides. In the Circo de Goriz there is the Refugio Delgado Obeda, T: (974) 34 12 01, open all year. The Brecha is the

29

site of a Franco-Hispanic *refugio*, Turracoya. North-west of the Vignemale glacier is the Refugio Oulettes de Gaube, which is one of the most modern in the Pyrenees. The Refugio Baysselance nearby is open July-Sept. The Refugio Brecha de Rolando is open in summer and has an out-building open all year. South-east of Gavarnie is the Refugio Paílla, open Sept-Easter.

There are some rough shelters in Duascaro, Celcilaruego, Rivereta, Cadiera, Carriata, Cotatuero, Frachinal and Loaso.

ACTIVITIES

Walking/climbing: from the Parador Nacional de Monte Perdido, a short walk takes you to the spectacular Circo de Pineta. The Añisclo valley also has its own access route: the regional road that branches off

---

Medieval monks enjoyed the tranquil isolation of San Juan de la Peña

the Ainsa-Bielsa highway toward Nerín. The normal starting point for Ordesa is the village of Torla, on the road leading north from Ainsa along the Ara valley. Most of the trail-heads for the main excursion routes are located near the visitor information centre here. There are dozens of possible trails, though for good reasons the hike to the Circo Soasa — about 5-7 hrs of easy walking — remains the most popular.

An easy ascent to the *fajas* of the Ordesa valley is provided by a series of *clavijas* — iron rods driven into the stone to provide footholds in some of the more slippery places: the first of these were installed years ago by a Torla blacksmith at the behest of an English hunter. One set of 13 *clavijas* leads to the Circo de Cotatuero, which rivals the Circo Soasa as a natural amphitheatre. The Circo Soasa marks the eastern terminus of the Ordesa valley, but a trail leads further up into the massif, to the

Refugio de Goriz, which serves as a base-camp for the more strenuous assaults on the higher reaches of Monte Perdido.

The trail to Cotatuero, on the other hand, leads on to the Refugio de la Cardiera and to the famous Brecha de Rolando, the mythical breach in the rock hewn by the mighty Roland with his great sword, Durandal. The Brecha is on the French frontier: walking due north will bring you to the Cirque de Gavarnie and finally down to Gavarnie itself, the first village in France. Following the ridge toward the north-west will take you to Vignemale, one of the last glaciers in the Pyrenees and still an imposing sight though it has been gradually melting away for many years. Behind it rises the Petit Vignemale 3,032 m (9,945 ft), very popular with experienced climbers, offering almost every conceivable kind of technical challenge.

From the Refugio de Goriz it takes about 2½ hrs to reach the Lago Helado ('frozen lake'), which has not, however, been living up to its name in recent years. Another ½ hr brings you to the summit of Monte Perdido, highest of the three sisters, Las Tres Sorores. Expert climbers are also fond of the Añisclo valley as it offers some of the park's most demanding ascents.

Mountaineering club: Federación Aragonesa de Montañismo, p16.
Mule rides: available around the Ordesa valley. Ask for details at the information centre.

FURTHER INFORMATION
Tourist office: Huesca, p16.
Park office: Parque Nacional de Ordesa y Monte Perdido, Pl. de Cervantes, 5, Huesca, T: (974) 24 33 61, F: 24 27 25.
Weather information: Información Meteorológica, T: (906) 36 53 22.

The mists of legend turned Basques of the forest of Roncesvalles into the Saracens of the *Chanson de Roland*

San Juan de la Peña & Canfranc

Mountain fastness in western Aragón, and nature valley harbouring rare bird life
Sitio Natural de Interes Nacional
264 ha (652 acres)

I've always thought that San Juan de la Peña (Saint John of the Crag), south-west of Jaca, is one of the world's great hiding places. This monastery in the mountains has long ago lost its monks and has become a romantic destination for nature-lovers. Tucked away under the brow of an enormous cliff, it overlooks an isolated valley in one of the outer ranges of the Pyrenees. To the north the view is bounded by the snow-capped peaks on the French border. The surrounding forests are ideal for unstrenuous hikes and pleasant rambles as far as the nearby town of Jaca.

The early kings of Aragón selected this spot as their royal burial ground: its very remoteness would protect their tombs from desecration. Here, too, according to tradition, the 11th-century king, Ramiro I, entrusted 'the sacred chalice of the Last Supper' — the Holy Grail, in other words — to the monks of San Juan for safe keeping. Its presence in this castle-like community of friars could well have given rise to the legend recounted in the 12th-century French grail sagas, which speak of the distant castle of Munsalvaesche — the wild mountain, *monte salvaje* — where the grail is piously guarded by a company of knights. It is an elusive and inaccessible place, not unlike San Juan de la Peña: 'Those who seek it find it not. It is only found unsought. Munsalvaesche its name.' The monks of San Juan de la Peña did, in fact, possess an ornate jewelled chalice, consisting of two sardonyx bowls joined by a beautifully-worked gold 'cage' and handles, which is now under lock and key in the treasury of the cathedral at València.

The Río Aragón which flows past Jaca is the main artery of

another important valley for nature lovers: Canfranc. It also includes the two tributary valleys of the Ríos Lubierne and Estarrún. Canfranc extends all the way to the French border and is bounded on the east by the Tena valley with its Río Gállego and a line of high peaks; on the west by another range of mountains and the Valle de los Angeles; and on the south by the Peña Oroel (1,769 m/5,805 ft). The northern portion of the valley includes the ski resorts of Astún and Candanchú, on the slopes of the Tuca Blanca peak (2,323 m/7,620 ft).

The flora and fauna of these valleys are famous for their variety and abundance. About a thousand species of flowers grow in the fields and meadows adjoining forests of fir and

---

The round-leaved sundew, *Drosera rotundifolia*, is threatened by the disappearance of its boggy moorland habitat

beech that also include maple and hawthorn. Herbalists come here for the spectacular *Adenostyles alliaviae* ssp. *hybrida*, with its 2-m (6½-ft) stem and large silvery leaves.

The isolation of San Juan de la Peña makes it ideal for birdwatching. Although the Spanish imperial eagle and black vulture are mentioned as occurring here, these may be accidental records. Today the cliffs and buttresses that line the valley are a noted haunt of lammergeiers, as well as griffon and Egyptian vultures, while short-toed and Bonelli's eagles are both regularly seen. Here, too, are the sadly declining lesser kestrels, summer visitors that nest gregariously in church towers and old buildings, as well as more naturally in cliff holes. Other species include the delightful black-eared wheatear, cirl and rock buntings and the blue rock thrush.

Before you go *Maps:* IGN 1:25,000 and 1:50,000 Nos. 143, 144, 175 and 176; IGN 1:200,000 Mapa Provincial of Huesca.
Guide-book: Jaca-Canfranc, Cuadernos de Aragón (Trazo Editorial).
Getting there *By car:* from Pamplona take the N240 to Puente la Reina de Jaca, then C134 to Jaca. From Huesca, the E07/N330 leads directly to Jaca, the gateway to Canfranc, and to the monastery of San Juan de la Peña and the surrounding Sierra de la Peña. The E07/N330 continues from Jaca north to the French border and Candanchú. The C125 south from Jaca, then HU230 to the west, brings you to San Juan de la Peña, by way of a little-used and scenic route. The shorter, more prosaic route, is via the C134 west from Jaca for about 21 km (13 miles), then south on the HU230; the distance between Jaca and the monastery is 30 km (19 miles).

By rail: there are services from Zaragoza via Huesca to Jaca and Canfranc. The journey from France through the mountains to Jaca, via Canfranc, is spectacular.
Where to stay: there is accommodation available in Candanchú, Canfranc and Jaca. Try the 3-star Hotel Tobazo, T/F: (974) 37 31 25, in Candanchú; the 3-star Albergue de Santa Cristina, T: (974) 37 33 00, F: 37 33 10, and Hotel Villa de Canfranc, T/F: (974) 37 20 12, and Casa La Truca, T: (974) 37 31 04, in Canfranc-Estación; the 3-star Hotel Canfranc, T: (974) 36 31 32, F: 36 49 79, and 2-star Hotel Conde Aznar, T: (974) 36 10 50, F: 36 07 97, and many others, in Jaca. The 'new' monastery of San Juan de la Peña has a hostel with 5 rooms; it has no telephone and is frequently full.
Further Information *Tourist Offices:* Fernando el Católico, 3, 22888 Canfranc, T: (974) 37 31 41, and Avda. Regimiento de Galicia, 2, 22700 Jaca, T: (974) 36 00 98, F: 35 51 65. *Mountaineering club:* Federación Aragonesa de Montañismo, p16.

Roncesvalles

Historic battlefield descending to deep ravine, on the French border

In this celebrated valley, in the year AD778, the rearguard of Charlemagne's army, led by the legendary Roland, were massacred by infuriated Basques as they tried to slip back into France. Near the battlefield at Roncesvalles there is one of the great oak forests of Europe, the wood of Garralda, where you can obtain at least an inkling of what these Navarran Pyrenees must have looked like in Charlemagne's day. And if you descend from Roncesvalles into the deep ravine called Valcarlos, the old trees seem to leap out at you through the mist and the clouds like the ghosts of Roland's warriors.

This part of northern Navarra has a whole series of fertile valleys that, for the most part, run perpendicular to the main thrust of the Pyrenees — notably the valleys of Aezcoa, Salazar and Roncal with their respective rivers, the Irati, Salazar and Esca. The encircling mountains are rarely higher than 1,500 m (4,920 ft), although the higher peaks afford some splendid panoramic views: Mount Orhí, on the French border, allows you to enjoy a truly international view from a towering 2,017 m (6,617 ft).

The Coto Nacional de Kintoa Real, one of the most westerly nature reserves in the Pyrenees, is centred on Monte Adi (1,459 m/4,785 ft), just west of Roncesvalles. It comprises 5,982 ha (14,780 acres) of mountain woodlands just south of the frontier with France. The French-Spanish border becomes rather capricious and meandering at this point, owing to the unpredictability of the watershed valleys.

Modern life has made some inroads into this ancient landscape. The existence of a television booster antenna marrs the wildness of its heights. Nevertheless, the peak of Orzanzurieta (1,567 m/5,141 ft), just east of Roncesvalles, is a tremendously impressive spot on which to be whipped by the hurricane-like winds that hurl dense clouds across the sky.

Before you go *Maps:* IGN 1:25,000 and 1:50,000 Nos. 90,

91, 116 and 117; IGN 1:200,000 Mapa Provincial of Navarra. *Guide-book:* Carlos de Hita, *Pirineo Navarro y Montes Vascos* (Anaya, 1998).

Getting there *By car:* the line of retreat taken by Charlemagne is still the main north-south route through this part of the Pyrenees. The N135 runs from Saint Jean Pied-de-Port in France to the border post at Arnéguy and then south-west to Pamplona via Roncesvalles and Auritz-Burguete.

The main east-west road is the so-called Ruta Alpina, a secondary road that runs parallel to the Pyrenees, from C135 just south of Auritz-Burguete to Escároz, located in the Salazar valley.

By bus: there is only 1 bus a day running between Pamplona and Roncesvalles July-Aug. It departs in the afternoon Mon-Sat, and in the morning Sun.

Black woodpeckers tend to nest in remote forests of beech or pine

Call Montañesa, T: (948) 22 15 84, for more information.

Where to stay: Roncesvalles itself has 2 1-star *hostales*, La Posada, T: (948) 76 02 25, and the Casa Sabina, T: (948) 76 00 12. Auritz-Burguete has the very attractive Hotel Loizu, T: (948) 76 00 08; Garralda the small Hotel Auñak, T: (948) 76 40 58, F: 76 43 22; while Isaba, Ochagavía and Luzaide-Valcarlos have any number of *casas rurales*, small hotels and *albergues*. In Uscarrés, a little to the south, the Hotel Casa Equiza, T: (948) 47 01 20, boasts typical decor and a sauna.

Outdoor living: the Asolaza, T: (948) 89 30 34, at Isaba, is open all year with capacity for 400 people.

Activities *Walking:* much of this area is ideal for hiking and camping, or simply driving from village to village, stopping to take strolls through the most inviting forests and meadows — in the Coto Nacional de Kintoa (Quinto Real), for instance.

A cross-country trail leads from Orzanzurieta to the vast oak forest that fills much of the area in the Garralda-Garaioa-Olaldea triangle. Another notable excursion begins just to the north of this forest, at the village of Orbaitzeta, where a path follows the Río Irati into the Aezcoa valley. If the weather holds, you can work your way from valley to valley until you reach the banks of the Río Esca.

Further information *Tourist offices:* Palacio de Vallesantoro, C/ Alfonso el Batallador, s/n, 31400 Sangüesa, T: (948) 87 03 29, (Easter-December only); Pamplona, p16.

Mountaineering club: Federación Navarra de Montañismo, p16.

33

CHAPTER 2

Northern Spain

Turn off the lights and step out of your car in a remote mountain pass in the Cordillera Cantabrica at night and you will realise that man's primeval fear of the dark is closer to the surface than you thought. Often without even the faintest glimmer of starlight, sometimes enveloped in low, swirling clouds, you are struck first by the complete and utter silence. Then the sense of being totally alone in that soundless, sightless vacuum.

Some of my most vivid memories of the mountains of northern Spain are of night creatures rarely seen during the day: a hare zigzagging frantically in the headlights; a pair of wild cats skulking in the bushes, staring at me arrogantly with luminous eyes; a badger ambling about sleepily; a chestnut-coated mink, not the fur-farmed American beast, but the untamed and truly scarce animal which is native to Europe.

I doubt if anyone can claim to know these mountains of the Cordillera Cantábrica well. Far off the beaten tourist track, the Cordillera is one of the largest areas of wild terrain remaining in Europe. South of the Costa Verde, from the shores of Galicia eastwards to Bilbao and inland to the foothills of the Meseta, lie wave after wave of mountain ranges covering some 3½ million hectares (over 8½ million acres). Like the Pyrenees, they form an almost impenetrable barrier. The Cordillera Cantábrica has insulated these northern lands from the mainstream of Spanish events, and from effective domination from Madrid. It is hardly surprising, therefore, that the traditions and culture

The Picos de Europa are the highest point in the Cordillera Cantábrica, the 500-km (300-mile) mountain chain that spans northern Spain

here are somewhat different.

The Cordillera is a national stronghold for the lithe and agile chamois, and somewhat appropriately the curve of these mountains resembles the horn of this creature. From the borders of the Basque country — where the mountains subside into wooded hillocks before soaring upwards again into the Pyrenees — the mountains run westwards on a course more or less parallel with the sea, before curling southwards to meet the Portuguese border at Sanabria. The tip of the horn, fittingly, is represented by the Sierra de la Cabrera ('goatherd'), which effectively divorces Galicia from central Spain, and extends to within 30 kilometres (19 miles) of Zamora.

The rocks of the Cordillera Cantábrica vary considerably in age and composition, but most of the oldest massifs lie in the west, with the younger strata to the east. Throughout these mountains, but especially along the coast, you can see the varying effects of erosion that has followed their birth. The durable quartzites and granites have emerged as prominent peaks and headlands, and the softer slates and sandstones have been carved by river and sea into gentle valleys and sandy coves. Elsewhere, especially along the eastern shores, the limestones have been eroded to form a typical karstian relief featuring spectacular siphons and blowholes, which throw up foaming spouts of sea-water at high tide. Inland, these karstian formations are best developed in the Picos de Europa, the highest point of the Cantabrican chain.

The tilt of the mountains is by no means constant throughout northern Spain; Galicia slopes northwards or westwards towards the Atlantic Ocean, and to the east Cantabria has a pronounced list towards Castille and the Meseta. In between is the province of

Asturias with its central longitudinal depression, bordered by the Cordillera Cantábrica to the south, and the Sierra de Cuera to the north. The pattern is further complicated by the chasms of great rivers: most cut northwards to discharge into the Atlantic, but others wend their way southwards. The great Ebro, for example, originates in the mountains of western Cantabria; it is a mountain stream in the upper reaches before carving a bed across the northeast corner of Spain in a series of leisurely meanders, to form a huge delta on the Mediterranean coast. Similarly, the Río Esla flows across the northwestern Meseta before joining the Duero on the Portuguese borders and heading towards Porto.

Many of the rivers which cut through the Cordillera coincide with ancient crossing points from the Meseta to the sea: the principal western passes are El Puerto de Pajares, between Oviedo and León, and Piedrafita, in the mountains of El Bierzo on the pilgrims' route from León to Santiago de Compostela. In the east, the Pas valley from Burgos and the Río Besaya from Palencia have provided access to Santander since the eleventh century. These highways were without doubt a hive of activity for mule trains carrying the wool of the *merino* sheep of the Meseta for export to Flanders.

The Cordillera Cantábrica is thought to be one of the earliest areas of Europe to be settled by palaeolithic peoples in the early stages of the last Ice Age, and evidence of their existence can be found along the length and breadth of these mountains. There are megaliths and dolmens at Peña Tú, for instance, located to the south-east of Llanes on the Asturian coast, and cave paintings such as those at Altamira, thought to be between 10,000 and 25,000 years old.

There are various theories that these people were the ancestors of the Basques, whose language, *euskera*, is one of the oldest in the world and has no affinity with any existing tongue. In their heyday, the Basques were superlative sailors and fishermen, venturing as far afield by boat as Labrador and Newfoundland.

Bronze and Iron Age settlements abound throughout the Cordillera, as the nomadic peoples settled down to a pastoral, and later arable, existence. These small, fortified villages, known as *castros*, are mostly located in the mountains, although Castor de Coaña is one example that lies rather closer to the coast, in western Asturias, on the Río Navia. Each wave of Romans or Moors saw the natives retreat to their mountain fortresses; although no invader had any degree of success in taming these mountains, a ten-year bloody battle between the legions of Augustus Caesar and the native Asturians has been well-documented, as have the celebrated battles of Covadonga and Liébana in the 8th century, which saw off the Arab invaders. In times of peace, the native peoples decamped to the more friendly coastal lands, and into the fertile basins of the Duero and Ebro valleys. As a result, for almost ten centuries the mountains have been like a deserted outpost, with a fragmented population and an antiquated agricultural system. But that isolation hasn't kept them completely from the modern world.

Sadly, the splendid, floristically rich hay meadows are gradually being converted to weedy pastures and what little woodland remains is being cleared to make way for extensive grazing lands. The native *lacha* breed of sheep is being replaced by other varieties, and the indigenous races of cattle are almost extinct. It is rare now to encounter the small, sweet-faced *casina* cow in the mountains of Asturias, or the wide-horned, grey *tudanca* of Cantabria, except in isolated settlements, confined to the most inhospitable terrain.

But for the most part northern Spain presents the same face to the world as it did in medieval times; tiny homesteads in perfect harmony with the harsh environment. Along the coast there are craggy, inhospitable cliffs that stretch for miles, with settlements confined to sheltered river mouths, or *rías*, where fishing, timber exportation and hazelnuts are the prime economic activities. In Galicia, the *palloza gallega*, a small oval house with a thatched roof, is still the dominant type of dwelling in mountain villages, and in Asturias, the *hórreo* — a square, stilted barn, used to store maize and potatoes and completely rodent-proof — is a common feature throughout.

Few fragments of the original forests persist today, having been largely replaced by secondary grassland and heathland communities. Beech woods are the most characteristic and natural vegetation type, especially high up on north-facing slopes. One of the largest areas stretches between the passes of Pandetrave and Panderruedas, separating the towering Picos de Europa from the main bulk of the Cordillera Cantábrica. The southern slopes of the Cordillera are clothed with Pyrenean oak, and the Mediterranean enclaves of the Liébana and Ebro valleys are dominated by evergreen species such as holm, cork and holly oaks. South of Oviedo there are extensive groves of the introduced sweet chestnut, but rather more worrisome are the monotonous, sterile plantations of non-native eucalypts and pines, although recent environmental policy means that new plantations are now few and far between.

But the general absence of intensive farming methods and the lack of artificial fertilizers and pesticides here have preserved some of the most botanically diverse Atlantic grasslands in the world. Even the roadsides are veritable treasure troves: here a lizard orchid, there a patch of sky-blue speedwell, or perhaps pink-purple sainfoin.

In the upper realms of the mountains there lurks a wealth of sub-alpine and alpine plants which are endemic to the Cordillera Cantábrica. Amid dwarf juniper and blazing masses of brooms and gorses, heathers and greenweeds, you can find delicate saxifrages and columbines that bloom nowhere else in the world.

The coastal zone is no less botanically rich, boasting blue-purple sheets of sea lavenders in the tidal salt marshes, together with glassworts, sea purslane and sea asters. The inaccessible rocky cliffs shelter rock samphire, sea spleenwort and golden samphire, and the dune systems support such denizens as sea holly, sea daffodils, and a wealth of early-flowering orchids.

Northern Spain has been described as one of the few surviving regions of Europe where the original post-glacial mammalian fauna remains virtually intact. Wolves and bears still roam the forests, both so isolated from the populations of central Europe that they have evolved into separate Spanish races. There are only five or six hundred wolves left in Iberia today; of these, most are in Galicia, and a good number can be found in the Cordillera Cantábrica, especially to the west.

Other large mammals include the chamois, which in the middle of the last century was threatened with extinction here, but today, after careful conservation measures, numbers some 3,000 in the Picos de Europa national hunting reserve alone. The *asturcón* wild horse, however, has not been so fortunate, with only a handful of pure-bred animals surviving, mostly in the *reserva nacional* of Sueve. Of the three species of deer that live in these mountains, only the roe deer is truly indigenous; the native red deer population died out at the beginning of the century and has since been re-introduced, while the fallow deer requires frequent infusions of new blood to maintain numbers.

All manner of birds frequent northern Spain, but the most characteristic is the capercaillie. Again, so isolated from the other European populations that it has evolved into a separate race, this cumbersome bird here lives in deciduous beech woods rather than coniferous forests. Birds of prey abound here, too: golden, Bonelli's, booted and short-toed eagles circle in the warm up-draughts of the valleys, and griffon and Egyptian vultures scour the upland pastures for carrion. The vultures are most frequently seen from the major north-south roads where southward-flowing rivers have cut deep gorges as they descend to the Meseta. The diversity and abundance of small birds is not great, but the species involved are typically montane and seldom found elsewhere in Spain. The coastal salt marshes provide wintering grounds for a variety of waterfowl and waders, as well as welcome feeding areas for those on migration.

The rivers of the Cordillera and Galicia teem with fish, especially those bound for the Atlantic, which are the spawning grounds for salmon. There are sea trout and brown trout in abundance in the rivers of western Asturias, while the smaller streams and marshlands provide a home for a wealth of amphibians, and lizards scuttle from underfoot on even a short stroll through the countryside.

BEFORE YOU GO
Maps: Michelin 1:400,000 Nos. 441 and 442.

GETTING THERE
By air: the 2 main airports are at Santiago de Compostela (Lavacolla International Airport) and Bilbao (Sondika). There is another international airport at Oviedo, and Santander, San Sebastián and Vitoria have domestic airports.
By sea: P & O European Ferries operates a service between Portsmouth and Bilbao, and Brittany Ferries operates a service plying between Plymouth or Portsmouth and Santander.
By car: from France, the main route is the Autoroute Côte Basque, which runs along the Golfo de Vizcaya to San Sebastián, and turns into the Autovía del Cantábrico on its way to Bilbao and Santander.

From Madrid, the E5/NI takes you to Burgos. From there either take the N623 due north to Santander, or continue along the NI to San Sebastián, taking if you wish the A1/E5/E80 autopista (toll road) to just past Miranda de Ebro, from where you can branch north on the A68/E80 *autopista* to Bilbao. The NVI, from Madrid to Galicia, goes to Lugo in the heart of the region and on to A Coruña (La Coruña) on the north-western coast. Work is proceeding, and is already completed in many sections, to construct the A6 *autopista* parallel to the NVI. The E70/N634 winds along the northern coast connecting the cities of Asturias, Cantabria and Galicia.
By rail: there are regular services connecting northern Spain with France and a network of lines running

through the region, including the narrow-gauge FEVE line. Regular RENFE services also run on the Madrid to Santander line, via Palencia and Valladolid; Madrid to the Galician coast, via Valladolid and Zamora; Madrid to Gijón, via Palencia and León; and Barcelona to Bilbao and San Sebastián, via Zaragoza.
By bus: there are regular services run by numerous private bus companies connecting the towns and cities of northern Spain, and in many cases they provide the only means of public transport to the wild areas. Where names and numbers are not noted, contact the local tourist offices for more detailed information.

WHEN TO GO
From Oct-Apr most of the high passes are completely snowbound. July and Aug are

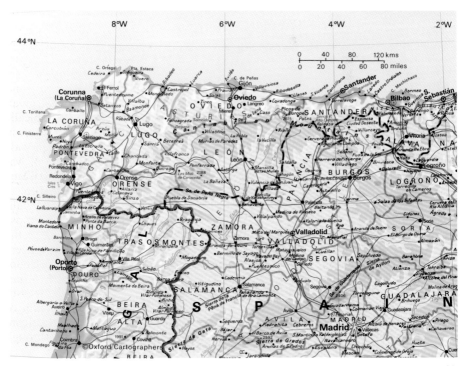

39

the hottest and driest months, but day-time temperatures rarely exceed 25°C (76°F). The closer to the coast, the less extreme the temperature variations are: on the southern side of the mountains the nights can be bitterly cold, even in May.

WHERE TO STAY
Beyond the normal tourist areas – the coastal resorts – accommodation is not as abundant as in other parts of the country. Recently, *casas rurales* have become very popular, and there are many in the region. Ask at tourist offices for detailed lists and suggestions. Most smaller villages have a *fonda*, or you may be able to find a room by asking at the local bar.

ACTIVITIES
Mountaineering clubs: Federación Asturiana de Montañismo, Aptdo de Correos, 1572, Oviedo, T: (98) 525 23 62; Federación Cántabra de Montañismo, Sánchez Diez, 1, 1°, 39200 Reinosa, T: (942) 75 52 94; Federación Castellano-Leonesa de Montañismo, Polideportivo Municipal Canterac, Avda. Circunvalación, s/n, 47012 Valladolid, T/F: (983) 22 64 00; and Federación Gallega de Montañismo, Rua Celso Emilio Ferreiro, 9, 36203 Vigo, T/F: (986) 42 43 31.
Caves: at Altamira, near Santillana del Mar; Castillo and Pasiega at Puente Visgo, south of Santander; and Pindal, to the west of San Vicente de la Barquera. Also the extensive galleries of Tito Bustillo at Ribadasella, one of the world's most important cave systems for prehistoric paintings.
Skiing: the major ski resorts of northern Spain are:
Asturias (98): Valgrande-

Pajares (Puerto de Pajares), 595 71 23;
León (987): Puerto de San Isidro, 73 11 16, and Leitariegos, 49 03 50;
Cantabria (942): Alto Campóo, 77 92 22;
Burgos (947): La Lunada, 12 00 09;
Orense (988): Manzaneda, 30 97 47.

FURTHER INFORMATION
Bilbao (94): tourist office, Pl. Arriaga, s/n, 48005, T: 416 00 02, F: 416 81 68. Red Cross, T: 423 03 55, F: 423 31 29.
Burgos (947): tourist office, Pl. Alonso Martínez, 7, 09003, T: 20 31 25, F: 27 65 29. Red Cross, T: 21 23 11, F: 22 93 80.
León (987): tourist office, Pl. de Regla, 3, 24003, T: 23 70 82, F: 27 33 91. Red Cross, T: 25 25 28, F: 21 69 69.
Lugo (982): tourist office, Pl. España, 27-29 (Galerias), 27001, T: 23 13 61. Red Cross, T: 23 16 13, F: 24 19 08.
Orense (988): tourist office, Curros Enríquez, 1, Edificio "Torre", 32003, T: 37 20 20. Red Cross, T: 22 24 84, F: 22 74 19.
Oviedo (98): tourist office, Pl. de Alfonso II el Casto, 6, (Plaza de la Catedral) T: 521 33 85. Red Cross, T: 25 06 11.
Palencia (979): tourist office, C/ Mayor, 105, 34071, T: 74 00 68, F: 70 08 22. Red Cross, T: 70 05 07, F: 74 35 34.
Santander (942): tourist office, Pl. de Velarde, 5, 39001, T: 31 07 08, F: 31 32 48. Red Cross, T: 36 08 36, F: 36 37 63.

FURTHER READING
Frank Barnett and Chris Gill, *Spain's Hidden Country – a traveller's guide to northern Spain* (Telegraph Publications & Brittany Ferries, 1987); Carlos Cavasco Muñoz de Vera, *Cornisa Cantábrica* (Editorial Everest, 1984); Nina Epton, *Grapes and*

Granite (1960); Nina Epton, *Spain's Magic Coast* (Weidenfield & Nicholson,1965); Kate O'Brien, *Farewell Spain* (Virago, 1937); *Insight Guide: Northern Spain*, ed. Roger Williams (ADA Publications, 1998).

Orduña & Sierra Salvada

Varied landscape of limestone buttresses, forested slopes and pastureland south of Bilbao

Approaching from the south you reach the 900-m (2,950-ft) Puerto de Orduña without any real sense of height: the surrounding countryside is gently undulating pastureland dotted with young pine plantations. The Mediterranean feel of the flora gives no hint of the closeness of the Bay of Biscay and the Atlantic Ocean.
   I rounded an insignificant bend and felt the earth drop away beneath the wheels of the car. The road down to the 8th-century town of Orduña switchbacks alarmingly, each new bend providing a slightly different vista: the dense beech woods growing on the steep north-facing slopes, the monument to the Virgen de la Antigua on the distant Cumbre de Txarlazo to the west. Two interesting butterflies are found here. The woodland brown (*Lopinga achine*), a large, golden-brown creature with a row of ocellated markings along the outer edge of each wing, is confined to just 3 small localities in the Iberian peninsula. The Spanish race is

that of *murciegoi*, and flies between 600-1,200m (1,950-3,900ft). The second butterfly is the chequered skipper (*Carterocephalus palaemon*), a species characteristic of light woodland.
Before you go *Maps:* IGN 1:25,000 and 1:50,000, Nos. 86 and 111; and 1:200,000 Mapa Provincial of Alava, Guipúzcoa and Vizcaya.
Guide-books: José R. de Madaria, *La Ciudad de Orduña* (Colección 'terras vizcainos' No.74, Serie Roja, 1981).
Getting there *By car:* from Bilbao, take the BI625 south to Orduña. From Burgos take the NI to Pancorbo, and then the BI2625 north; as the road winds down from the pass you get a panoramic view of the town of Orduña.
By rail: Orduña lies on the tortuous Logroño-Miranda de Ebro-Bilbao line, which follows the Nervión valley, and does a complete anti-clockwise circuit around Orduña itself.
By bus: there are regular services from Vitoria-Gasteiz to Orduña, operated by La Unión, T: (945) 26 46 26.
Where to stay: accommodation is scarce around here: you would do best to head for Vitoria-Gasteiz where, amongst others, the 3-star Hotel General Alava, T: (945) 22 22 00, F: 24 83 95, can be recommended. Nearby camp-sites are at Ameyugo, T: (945) 34 43 55, on the NI Burgos-Vitoria road just before the junction of the BI2625, which turns north to Orduña; and El Desfiladero, T: (945) 35 40 27, at nearby Pancorbo.
Activities *Walking:* Orduña is within 10 km (6¼ miles) of one of the highest mountains in the Basque country: Peña Gorbea 1,475 m (4,840 ft), near the village of Undurraga on the N240.
Further information *Tourist offices:* Avda. Gasteiz, s/n, Vitoria-Gasteiz, T: (945) 16 15 98, F: 16 11 05, or Bilbao, p40.

Las Marismas de Santoña

This reserva natural *is a coastal wetland in the shelter of Monte Buciero, attracting migratory birds and a diversity of marine life*
Ramsar, ZEPA
3,500 ha (8,600 acres)

The sparkling rivers that stream down from the heights of the Cordillera Cantábrica and the lesser mountains of Galicia

The shelduck, more familiar on North Sea coasts, is also a breeding bird of the Santoña marshes

eventually wend their way to the Atlantic coast, where they form numerous estuaries, or *rías*, amid marshes and flood-plains. Despite the ever-increasing flow of waste products and pollutants into the once-crystalline waters of the mountain streams and ocean, there remain some *rías* which are of immense importance to wildlife.

From the highest point of Monte Buciero, Alto de Peña Ganzo, some 400 metres (1,300 feet) above the sea, you can look across the whole of the *marismas*, or marshes, of the bay of Santoña. Winding through the maze of narrow creeks and salt marshes is the Río Asón, the main river feeding this coastal wetland, which starts life as a spectacular waterfall in the Puerto del Asón, some 25 kilometres (15 miles) south-west of the bay. Sheltered from the often violent Atlantic storms by the huge limestone bulk of

41

Monte Buciero, the river attracts sun-seekers during the summer and flocks of migratory wildfowl and waders in winter.

Among the birds of special significance are spoonbills, which frequently break their long migration here to feed and recuperate; the only other Spanish locality with appreciable numbers is the southern wetland of Doñana. In recent years, Santoña has found favour with shelduck, another bird which was formerly regarded as a Doñana speciality. Santoña is the principal site for wintering birds on the north coast, visited by avocet, grey plover, greenshank, curlew and dunlin among the marshes, and puffins, razorbills and guillemots on the open sea and around the cliffs of Monte Buciero.

This mountain exhibits typical Cantabrican evergreen oak scrub and forests, along with many Mediterranean species. Higher up, the mountain is almost completely devoid of vegetation. Most of the native fauna here has disappeared, due to loss of habitat, hunting and general persecution. Today, the most frequent large bird is the raven, although peregrines have started to re-establish themselves in the area as the natural balance of the woodland is slowly regained.

BEFORE YOU GO
Maps: IGN 1:25,000 and 1:50,000 Nos. 35 and 36; and 1:200,000 Mapa Provincial of Cantabria.
Guide-books: José Luis Gutiérrez Bicarregui, *Datos Culturales, Turísticos, Históricos y Otros Aspectos* (Santoña, 1983).

GETTING THERE
By sea: a ferry service runs frequently between Santoña and Laredo in the summer, but less frequently in the winter.
By car: Santoña is situated on a small coastal peninsula which can be reached by several turnings off the N634 Bilbao-Santander road.
By bus: several buses a day run from Santander along the coast. There are also bus connections with the Santander-Bilbao FEVE train line, from Cicero station or Gama.

WHEN TO GO
The best time to visit Las Marismas de Santoña is Sept-May, as the site is particularly important for migratory birds. Autumn is better as the weather is very unreliable along this Atlantic coast in the spring. When the tide is coming in, the birds are forced to the higher ground within the marshes, and are thus more easily visible amongst the web of creeks and islands; it is best to time your visit so it coincides with high tide. Stormy weather drives the birds into the shelter of the bay to feed and roost, and you will be amply rewarded if you brave the elements at these times. Wellington boots are more or less essential. A leaflet showing the recommended observation points is available from the tourist office.

WHERE TO STAY
There is no shortage of accommodation in Santoña, Laredo and Colindres. However, they tend to be full in the summer months, so book ahead. Try the 3-star Hotel Castilla, T: (942) 66 22 61, F: 66 24 51, in Santoña; the 3-star Hotel Cosmopol, T/F: (942) 60 54 00, in Laredo; and the 1-star Hostal Residencia Montecarlo, T: (942) 65 01 63, F: 65 00 75, in Colindres. Along the peninsula, closer to Santander, are the following attractive options: the Posada el Solar, T: (942) 50 52 92, and Casa Galizano, T: (942) 50 51 32, in Galizano; La Posada de Langre, T: (942) 50 52 36, in Langre; and the Casa Mies de Villa, T: (942) 51 00 73, in Somo.

Outdoor living: there are many sites in the vicinity, including that on the renowned Playa de Berria, the beach lying just to the west of the Santoña estuary itself, open 1 June-15 Sept with space for 270, T: (942) 66 22 48, and a large site, Playa Arenillas, T: (942) 86 31 52, at Islares.

ACTIVITIES
Ruins: at the southernmost tip of the Santoña peninsula, opposite Laredo, you can still see the remains of a massive fort constructed by the French during the Peninsular War. Such was the strategic importance of this site that Santoña was known as the 'Gibraltar of the North'.
Another feature of the area is the penitentiary of El Dueso, magnificently located between Monte Buciero and Playa de Berria.
Viewpoint: Faro del Caballo, on the seaward face of Monte Buciero, is reached by means of 684 steps hewn into the limestone.

FURTHER INFORMATION
Tourist offices: C/ Santander, 5, bajo, 39740 Santoña, T: (942) 66 00 66; Alameda de Miramar, s/n, 39770 Laredo, T: (942) 61 10 96; and Santander, p40.

Las Sierras Palentinas & Alto Campóo

The quiet, untouched sierras of the eastern Cordillera Cantábrica include some of the highest mountains in the region

Stretching from the Ebro dam south of Santander, to the León-Palencia borders south of the Picos de Europa, this eastern section of the Cordillera Cantábrica has a rich and varied landscape, vegetation and wildlife. The western part of the area comprises the Reserva Nacional de Fuentes Carrionas: 47,755 hectares (112,000 acres) of palencian mountain ridges, culminating in the peak of Curavacas (2,525 metres/8,282 feet).

The massif of Fuentes Carrionas, the most westerly, is almost unmarked by roads,

High in the Picos de Europa, summer brings out many wild flowers, including the long-stemmed leopard's bane in the foreground

except for shepherds' tracks and forest trails. The main crossing point between the Picos de Europa and the Meseta, the Puerto de Piedrasluengas, at the head of the Liébana valley, is a complex jumble of calcareous limestones and silicious materials. In springtime the montane pastures in the col are covered with Lent lilies (*Narcissus pseudonarcissus*), meadow saxifrages (*Saxifraga granulata*), cowslips and violet mountain pansies (*Viola bubanii*). From the top of the pass you can see the towering pinnacles of the Picos de Europa to the north, the southern plateau, and the square-topped outline of Peña Labra to the east. If you head north-east from Piedrasluengas, you reach the gorge of the Río Nansa, now almost devoid of water due to the construction of a hydro-electric station, but nevertheless stunningly beautiful.

Further east is the more densely populated valley of Campóo, at the head of which lies Pico de Tres Mares (literally, 'three seas'). The mountain marks the point where five rivers are born and then head towards the three seas of the Iberian peninsula: Ríos Nansa and Saja flow northwards to the Bay of Biscay; Ríos Areños and Pisuerga join the

Duero, and meet the Atlantic coast at Porto; and the Río Híjar runs into the Ebro, and then on to the Mediterranean.

The endangered almond-eyed ringlet butterfly (*Erebia alberganus barcoi*) has been recorded on the slopes of Pico de Tres Mares and the area around Reinosa. This is the only colony in Spain, and is considered to be a different race from the rest of the European populations: it flies in only one brood per year, in late June or early July, over grasslands between 1,000-1,200 metres (3,280-3,940 feet), and the larvae feed off various mountain grasses.

The great Ebro river is born at the tiny village of Fontibre (literally, 'Fuente Ebro') just to the west of Reinosa, and encounters a dam some 10 kilometres (6¼ miles) to the east. The resulting reservoir is 20 kilometres (12½ miles) long, the largest area of fresh water in Cantabria; no less than 12 villages are concealed beneath its waters. At its northernmost point lies the spa of Corconte, which is famed for its healing powers. The Ebro reservoir is too high to attract large numbers of breeding birds, but has great crested grebe and is a useful stopover for a variety of migrant bird-life.

The Campóo valley proper is a gentle landscape spliced between the Sierra de Peña Labra to the south and the Sierras del Cordel and Híjar to the north. It is rather unusual for a valley in the Cordillera Cantábrica in that it is orientated east-west rather than north-south, and consequently is subjected to the full force of the continental climate of the Spanish interior. The haymeadows are few and far between, needing irrigation in the dry season. For the most part, the valley consists of montane pastures, grazed by Swiss cattle and horses.

What woodland there is in Campóo is either Pyrenean oak (*Quercus pyrenaica*) or the highly Mediterranean species, the Lusitanian oak (*Q. faginea*), both providing shelter for an occasional bear or wolf. Griffon vultures are common here too, and booted eagle can often be seen circling overhead.

From Espinilla it is now possible to take a new road to the south over an old Roman route. The banks along the roadsides contain soil of all shades from ochre to crimson, salmon pink to that shade of rose that decorates old ladies' faces.

BEFORE YOU GO

Maps: IGN 1:25,000 and 1:50,000 Nos. 81, 82, 83, 107 and 108; and 1:200,000 Mapa Provincial of Cantabria & Palencia.

Guide-books: Federación Palentina de Montañismo, Fuentes Carrionas (Palencia, 1973); Guía del Macizo del Alto Carrión (Palencia, 1978).

GETTING THERE

By car: take the N611 Santander-Palencia road to Reinosa, then the C625 to Espinilla followed by the C628 which ends near Alto Campóo.

By rail: the Santander — Palencia train stops at Reinosa, Puerto de Pozaza and Aguilar de Campóo.

WHERE TO STAY

Reinosa offers a selection of accommodation; try the 3-star

Hotel Corza Blanca, T/F: (942) 77 92 50. In Aguilar de Campóo try the 3-star Hotel Valentin, T: (979) 12 21 25. Hotel rooms are relatively scarce in this area, but compensated for by an enticing array of *casas rurales* and *posadas*. Try the Posada de Santa María, T: (979) 12 20 00, in Aguilar de Campóo; the Casa de las Campanas, T: (979) 12 01 18, in Salinas de Pisuerga; Casa El Mochuelo, T: (979) 18 10 11, in Santa María de Nava; and Hotel El Convento, T: (979) 12 36 11, in Santa María de Mave. Tourist offices can give full listing.

Refuges: there are a number of refuges in the Campóo valley; ask at the tourist office in Aguilar de Campóo for details.

Outdoor living: you can camp almost anywhere as long as you are discreet about it. The

Monte Royal camp-site at Aguilar de Campóo, T: (979) 12 30 83, is open all year round.

ACTIVITIES

Walking: from the village of Fontibre there are several signposted paths leading to the source of the Río Ebro. Many pleasant walks follow the banks of the streams near Fontibre and traverse the woods of birch, oak and beech.

Skiing: the ski resort of Cantabria is: **Alto Campóo** (942): Brañavieja-Reinosa, 77 92 22.

FURTHER INFORMATION

Tourist offices: Pl. de España, s/n, 34800 Aguilar de Campóo, T: (979) 12 20 24; and Santander, p40.

Mountaineering clubs: Cántabra and Castellano-Leonesa, p40.

Picos de Europa

Parque Nacional de los Picos de Europa, a mountain range comprising 3 towering limestone massifs divided by deep gorges and including the former national park of La Montaña de Covadonga

ZEPA

64,660 ha (159,778 acres)

Daybreak! Suddenly there they were, a cluster of frosted peaks floating above a sea of misty cloud on the far horizon: los Picos de Europa. From the decks of a ferry approaching Santander those who venture to rise with the sun will be treated to an unforgettable sight, assuming of course that the notorious Atlantic climate doesn't intervene with an untimely cloud-bank or rainstorm. The glittering teeth of these mountains were supposedly the first sight of *terra firma* for land-starved European fishermen as they returned from trawling their nets in the northern seas. Standing on the deck of the ferry you can understand how they felt.

Like the backbone of some great supine beast, the Cordillera Cantábrica runs along the north coast of Spain, from the Pyrenees to the Portuguese border. Continuing the analogy, the Picos de Europa is like a slipped disc, displaced to the northern, seaward side of the 'spine' although still linked intimately with it through the mountain pass of San Glorio.

This is the green side of Spain. Only 15 kilometres (9 miles) from the Costa Verde, the Picos de Europa receives most of its weather from the Atlantic; the climate is cool and moist, the valleys lush, and mists occur so frequently that travellers may never see the tops of the mountains.

In contrast to the slates and shales of the Cordillera Cantábrica, the Picos de Europa consists of pale limestones, laid down in the Lower Carboniferous. Localized glacial activity during the Ice Ages created the typical frost-shattered topography of today, with its ancient hanging valleys and glacial *cirque* lakes. There are huge circular hollows, known as *hoyos* or *jous*, in the mountain plateaux: lunar landscapes filled with the shattered limestone rubble, relics of former Ice Ages. Percolating ground waters and underground streams have created huge caverns and galleries decorated with stalagmites and stalactites. You can enter them via sinks or swallow-holes, known as dolines, which can extend vertically for hundreds of metres.

The Picos de Europa comprises three towering massifs separated from one another by steep gorges through which flow the southernmost salmon rivers in Europe. Together they resemble a great bat, spread-eagled and

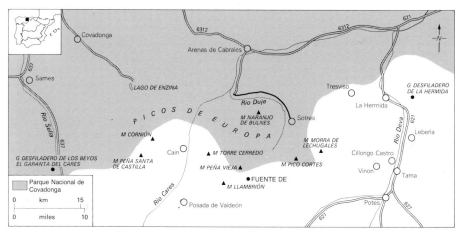

These hay meadows at Las Vegas in the Picos de Europa provide a haven for wild flowers and butterflies

facing the sea; the central massif forms the oval torso while the more slender, uplifted wings are represented by the western and eastern mountain ranges. The western boundary is the Desfiladero de los Beyos, a narrow ravine carved out by the Río Sella. The adjacent massif, Cornión, which includes Peña Santa de Castilla (2,596 metres/8,515 feet), receives much of the rain and snow carried by depressions over the Atlantic. Urrieles, the central massif, is the most awe-inspiring; it includes a number of peaks over 2,600 metres (8,500 feet) high — notably Torre Cerredo, at 2,648 metres (8,687 feet), the highest peak in Cordillera Cantábrica, Llambrión and Peña Vieja. But the star is Naranjo de Bulnes (2,519 metres/8,262 feet). This almost conical block of

limestone, known to the local people as Picu Urriellu, is something of a Spanish Matterhorn and was not finally conquered by man until 1904.

Urrieles is divided from Cornión by the most spectacular gorge in the Picos de Europa: la Garganta Divina, formed by the fast-flowing Río Cares. The walls are almost sheer, rising in places to over 2,000 metres (6,500 feet); these cliffs are a favourite haunt of that elusive bird, the wallcreeper. If you look up from the depths of the gorge you may see a group of griffon vultures drifting lazily across the narrow band of blue sky, and peregrine falcons, crag martins and the occasional golden eagle may also be spotted. La Garganta Divina stretches for some 12 kilometres (7½ miles) from Caín in the south to Puente Poncebos. This is one of the most famous walks in the Picos de Europa, along a narrow mule track that has been carved from the wall of the gorge, high above the spray of the thundering river. You cross from side to side over fragile bridges, in some places walking inside the mountain itself, where the roar of the river becomes just an echo.

The gorges of the Picos de Europa are so sheltered from climatic extremes that many of the trees and shrubs clinging to their walls are typically Mediterranean. Wild jasmine and barberry grow among the glossy evergreen foliage of strawberry trees and Spanish laurel, and the turpentine tree, a close relative of the pistachio, spreads its leaves in the sunniest spots, together with figs, walnuts and wild olives.

Andara is the smallest and easternmost of the massifs. The peaks are less imposing, and are certainly less well-explored. The massif is separated from Urrieles by the Río Duje and from lesser mountains towards Santander by the Liébana valley, home of the Río Deva. Spring comes earlier to this valley; because it lies in the rain-shadow of the Urrieles peaks, the weather is rather warmer and sunnier.

Covadonga, in the western massif, was the site of a decisive battle fought in AD718, in which the Spanish turned back the Moorish invaders, reputedly with divine help: an avalanche crushed the Muslim forces. From here the Christian reconquest of Spain began. Covadonga, according to King Juan Carlos II, is 'the primary and eternal source of the nation'. In 1918, exactly 1,200 years after the Battle of Covadonga, the Parque Nacional de La Montaña de Covadonga was created, to commemorate 'the moment in which we consider Spain to have been conceived'. The park covered almost the whole of the western massif, but was expanded in 1995 to include all 3 massifs and is now called the Parque Nacional de los Picos de Europa.

There are botanical treasures high in the Picos de Europa, but my own idea of heaven is their gloriously colourful haymeadows. Managed in a traditional manner since they were first reclaimed from the primeval forest, these meadows are among the most floristically rich Atlantic grasslands in Europe. Over 40 species of orchid have been recorded here, including the evocatively named pink-butterfly, lizard, man, woodcock, fly and bee orchids. Dark, exotic tongue orchids, towering white asphodels and Pyrenean lilies decorate these meadows, while the montane grasslands are renowned for their daffodils, dog's-tooth violets and fritillaries that burst into flower at the edges of melting snowfields. The tiny Asturian hoop-petticoat daffodils form yellow-studded sheets in the *vegas* in early summer. This is how I imagine the Elysian fields to be.

If you venture even a short way into the mountains, you will undoubtedly encounter the king of that realm: the chamois. Now present in quite large numbers, these wonderfully agile creatures spring up almost vertical cliffs and balance on the most inaccessible ledges. Wild boar forage for underground tubers in the deciduous woodlands, but are wary of intruders; the best time to see them is at the onset of cold weather in the autumn, when they come into the villages to forage for potatoes in the fields. The highly endangered Pyrenean desman (a kind of mole), for which the Picos de Europa is an international stronghold, has declined more in the last 25 years than in all the previous centuries, due mainly to increasing human interference with and destruction of the natural environment.

Pride of place among the birds must go to the raptors, or birds of prey. Spain remains the principal country in Europe for birds of prey and these mountains are renowned as one of their strongholds. The rocky cliffs and gorges are the favoured haunts of golden eagles and both griffon and Egyptian vultures, while short-toed and booted eagles soar in the thermal updrafts over the passes in search of their prey. Hen harriers inhabit the rough heathland areas, goshawks and sparrowhawks patrol the woodlands and buzzards are ten-a-penny. Nesting on the rocky ledges in the heart of the peaks, kestrels swoop overhead and occasionally a peregrine dives past you like a dark arrow.

Smaller forest birds include pied flycatchers, black redstarts, tree pipits, nuthatches and short-toed treecreepers, black woodpeckers as well as their great, middle and lesser spotted cousins, and no less than six

Magnificent beech woods clothe the slopes of the Covodonga national park from 800-1,500 m (2,600-5,000 ft), some 40 m (130 ft) high

different species of owl.

The high peaks are favoured by a number of specialized montane birds, including snow finches, alpine accentors and rock thrushes, while flocks of choughs and alpine choughs swirl tirelessly overhead. Bee-eaters, hoopoes and golden orioles are not uncommon in the southern and eastern reaches of the Picos de Europa, and red-backed shrikes can be seen in many of the valley meadows.

The butterflies that occur in these mountains represent over a third of the entire European fauna. In addition, there are several races which occur nowhere else in the world, and many threatened and endangered species. Rare and vulnerable species include the scarce swallowtail (*Iphiclides podalarius feistamelii*), a Spanish and North African race, and the Spanish argus (*Aricia morronensis*). More specific rarities include the Asturian race of the Gavarnie blue (*Agriades pyrenaicus asturiensis*), a silvery-grey lycaenid whose type locality is the Picos de Europa.

The variety of wildlife present in Picos de Europa is apparently endless. The local people take pride in their history, landscape and natural heritage, and they are always willing to extend their utmost hospitality to you. The sight of such mountains in any weather is enough to uplift the heart and delight the soul, but the utter tranquility of Picos de Europa is what draws me back time after time; that sense of being alone in the wilderness and at one with nature.

BEFORE YOU GO
Maps: IGN 1:25,000 and 1:50,000 Nos. 55, 56, 80 and 81; and 1:200,000 Mapas Provinciales of Cantabria, Asturias and León.
Guide-books: Robin Collomb, *Picos de Europa — Northern Spain* (West Col, 1983); Teresa Farino, *Landscapes of Northern Spain — Picos de Europa* (Sunflower, 1996); Robin

The dog's-tooth violet opens its deep-pink flowers as soon as the mountain snows have melted

Walker, *Walks and Climbs in the Picos de Europa* (Cicerone, 1989).

GETTING THERE
By sea: Brittany Ferries operates a twice-weekly service from Plymouth to Santander, departing Mon and Wed, from Apr to mid-Sept, Sun and Wed off-season, T: (0990) 36 03 60.
By car: the Picos de Europa can be approached from the main Oviedo-Santander road, the N634, heading south down either the N621, Unquera-Potes road, or the N625, Arriondas-Cangas de Onís road.

The main roads in the Picos de Europa circumnavigate the mountains and are confined to the river valleys; no metalled thoroughfares for vehicles traverse the 3 massifs.
By rail: from Santander the narrow-gauge FEVE line runs to Oviedo through some of the most beautiful scenery on the entire length of Spain's Atlantic coastline. If you alight at Unquera, you can get a bus into the heart of the Picos de

Europa. From Bilbao, the same line will take you to Santander.
By bus: there is a daily service each way, operated by Grupo Alsa, between Santander, T: (942) 22 16 85, and León, T: (987) 26 05 00, stopping at Unquera, Potes and Portilla de la Reina. Autobuses Palomera, T: (942) 88 06 11, runs services between Santander, Potes and Fuente Dé.

WHERE TO STAY
There is a wide range of accommodation throughout the region: in Cangas de Onís, the 2-star Ca Pasera, T: (98) 594 02 23, F: 594 02 13; in Potes, the 2-star Hotel Infantado, T: (942) 73 09 39, F: 73 05 78, or 2-star Hostal Picos de Europa, T: (942) 73 00 05, F: 73 00 60; in Fuente Dé, the Parador, T: (942) 73 66 51, F: 73 66 54, and 2-star Hotel Rebeco, T: (942) 73 66 01, F: 73 66 00; just outside Fuente Dé, the Hotel/Apartamentos Nevandi, T: (942) 73 66 13, F: 73 66 08; in Camaleño, the 3-star Hotel Jisu, T: (942) 73 30 38, F: 73 03 15; and in Cosgaya, the similarly rated El

In spring and summer chamois live around the tree line but in summer climb higher to feed on grasses and alpine herbs

Oso, T: (942) 73 30 18, F: 73 36 36.

Outdoor living: there are several official camp-sites, one of the best of which is Camping Naranjo de Bulnes, 1 km (½ mile) east of Arenas de Cabrales on the lower reaches of the Río Cares, T: (98) 562 50 81.

Ask at the tourist offices for a list of places where you are allowed to camp within the park; you may have to obtain a permit.

Refuges: Size and facilities vary from Cabaña Verónica at 2,325 m (7,628 ft), a 6-person hut, to the relative luxury of 70 beds and a restaurant at Aliva, 1,667 m (5,469 ft). For up-to-date information on which huts are open contact the Federación Asturiana de Montañismo, and also the Federaciónes Cántabra & Castellano-Leonesa (see below).

ACTIVITIES

Walking: a fairly tough, 2-day walk is that from the Refugio de Vega Redonda to the Refugio de Vega Huerta and back again, taking you through the Macizo Occidental; this route follows several paths, through fields and lakes, and provides brilliant views and scenery. It takes at least 1 hr to walk from the end of the road — at Vega de la Piedra — to

Refugio de Vega Redonda.

Another classic walk is through the Cares gorge, a walk of 24 km (15 miles) there and back through a sheer limestone gorge, along a path hewn out of the rock high above the thundering river; you can approach either from Caín or Poncebos and the return journey takes about 6 hrs.

Guides: climbing guides are available at Posada de Valdeón, Potes, Cangas de Onís and Sotres.

Viewpoints: from Mirador del Tombo at Cordiñanes, Valle de Valdeón, there is a superb view over the central massif; an even better vantage point is Mirador del Puerto de Panderruedas, 1,450 m (4,760 ft), in the south-west. Mirador de la Reina looks towards the sea from the road between the monastery at Covadonga and the famous glacial lakes on the Vega de Enol. Mirador del Corzo is situated on the road between Potes and Riaño, and looks south-east.

There are several notable viewpoints which are a little way off the main roads. A brisk stroll (or short car ride) north of the Puerto de San Glorio takes you to the Mirador de Llesba and the *monumento al oso* — a life-size statue of a brown bear. One last viewpoint, from where there is

a superb view of the Cordillera Cantábrica and the eastern massifs of the Picos de Europa, is that at the top of the Teleférico: the Mirador del Cable. The only thing that spoils it are the crowds of people in peak season.

Cable-car: a swift 3-min trip in the Teleférico from Fuente Dé takes you up to a wilderness of shattered limestone, saving you an 800-m climb in the process.

Caves: at Buxu, just west of Cangas de Onís, where palaeolithic paintings can be seen.

Fishing: excellent trout and salmon fishing in the clear rivers of the Picos de Europa; these are the southernmost spawning grounds for salmon in Europe. Contact the tourist office for seasons and permits, and the fishing club Federación Asturiana, C/ Julián Claveria, 11, Oviedo, T: (98) 529 86 10, for more information.

Monasteries: the Monasterio de Santo Toribio de Liébana is near Potes; the chapel and church are interesting, and there is also a magnificent view over the Liébana valley. The basilica at Covadonga is built on the site where the legendary King Pelayo fended off the Moors in AD718; the road to the basilica leads on to the glacial lakes of Enol and Ercina, some 1,100 m (3,600 ft) above sea level.

Riding: horse treks are available and can be arranged by Turismo Ecuestre Picos de Europa, at Turieno, near Potes, T: (942) 73 21 44.

FURTHER INFORMATION

Tourist offices: Avda. de Covadonga, 33550 Cangas de Onís, T: (98) 584 80 05, F: 584 85 63; Ayuntamiento, 39470 Potes, T: (942) 73 07 87, and Santander, p40.

Mountaineering clubs: Asturiana, Leonesa and Cántabra, p40.

49

Somiedo & Pajares

Remote parque natural in Asturias, a haven for the typical vertebrate fauna of the Cordillera
ZEPA
54,700 ha (135,200 acres)

Lying south-west of Oviedo, the capital of Asturias, and straddling the crest of the Cordillera Cantábrica, is the Parque Natural de Somiedo. The ancient Palaeozoic rocks, well-faulted in a north-south direction, have weathered to provide fertile valleys and slopes, and consequently the area was favoured by early settlers as far back as pre-Roman times.

There is much evidence of Roman civilization here in Somiedo, notably at Saliencia, which was one of the most important fortresses of the Emperor Augustus in the north of Spain. More famous today, though, are the lakes of Saliencia. There is said to be treasure hidden at the bottom of the lakes, guarded jealously by *xanas*, or nymphs, of Asturian mythology. The lakes, of glacial origin, are imprisoned between the twin peaks of the Peña de la Cueva (1,681 m/5,515 ft) and El Canto de la Almagrera (1,758 m/5,766 ft), and until recently were inaccessible except on foot.

The northern slopes of the Puerto de Pajares to the east are mantled with extensive beech and oak forests, the southern slopes with secondary heathland and pastoral communities. These latter, especially on bare, slaty areas, are home to the delightful crucifer (*Teesdaliopsis conferta*)

— an endemic of the Cordillera Cantábrica — and support other such interesting species as violet mountain pansy, pyramidal bugle (*Ajuga pyramidalis*), leafy lousewort (*Pedicularis verticillata*) and the white-flowered aconite-leaved buttercup (*Ranunculus aconitifolius*), none of which are found in Spain away from this northern area.

To the east of the pass, in the sub-alpine snow-melt areas, the verdant pastures are dotted with dog's-tooth violet (*Erythronium dens-canis*), amplexicaule buttercups (*Ranunculus amplexicaulis*) and two tiny daffodil species, the Asturian daffodil (*Narcissus asturiensis*) and angel's tears (*N. triandrus*). Two other species occur in this mountain pass that are found only on the extreme western edge of Europe in Ireland and along the Atlantic seaboard of Iberia: large butterwort (*Pinguicula grandiflora*), an attractive, purple-flowered carnivorous plant, and St Dabeoc's heath (*Daboecia cantabrica*), a heather-like small shrub heavily laden with pink, urn-shaped flowers.

The absence of roads in Somiedo has ensured that the typical vertebrate fauna of the Cordillera has remained undisturbed and the Somiedo natural park is one of the Spanish strongholds of the Iberian brown bear. This animal must surely be one of the most threatened mammal species in Spain, with a total population of between 85 and 120. Other animals which are typical of Somiedo include red and roe deer, chamois, wild boar and capercaillie.

Before you go *Maps:* IGN 1:25,000 and 1:50,000 Nos. 52, 53 and 76; and 1:200,000 Mapa Provincial of Asturias.

Getting there *By car:* from the

N634 Oviedo-Luarca road, just before Cornellana, take the C633 south to Pola de Somiedo. From the Puerto de Somiedo down to La Vega de los Viejos, the road is closed Dec-Mar. The alternative is to follow the C633 to Aguamestas, then turn off right to Pigüeña. From the south, approach along the C623 from León.

By bus: Alsa, T: (98) 596 96 00, F: 596 96 91, e-mail alsa@las.es and www.alsa.es, operates a twice daily — morning and afternoon — service between Oviedo and Somiedo.

Where to stay: it is difficult to find accommodation in this remote area. Try the 2-star Hotel Castillo de Valdés Salas, T: (98) 583 22 22, F: 583 22 99, in Salas, or the 1-star Hotel Calzada Romana, T: (98) 576 23 24, in Belmonte de Miranda. In Somiedo itself there is the 2-star Hotel Valle del Lago, T: (98) 576 39 39.

Activities *Walking:* from Pola de Somiedo, north of the Puerto de Somiedo, follow the river to Lago de la Cueva, Lago Negro and Lago del Valle, a walk which takes about 4 hrs. Another option is to approach the lakes from the pass. This does take a little longer, though, and is a more strenuous walk.

Peña Ubiña, to the east, is the most interesting mountain in this region for walking. There are several refuges in the vicinity; get in touch with the Federación Asturiana de Montañismo, Aptdo de Correos, 1572, Oviedo, T: (98) 525 23 62.

Further information *Tourist office:* Pl. de la Campa, s/n, 33860 Salas, T: (98) 583 09 88; and Oviedo p40.

Rocky outcrops and scant scrub in Las Médulas suggest the drier south

El Bierzo

Including the Sierra de Ancares, Las Médulas de Carucedo, Degaña and El Bosque de Muniellos (the last 2 are part of western Cordillera Cantábrica) Mountain range; red-rock landscape; hunting reserve

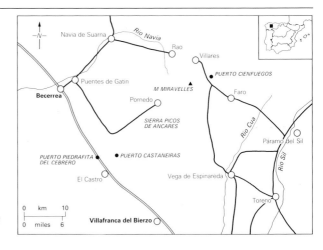

To get to the southern foothills of the Sierra de Ancares, follow the meandering road from the sleepy market town of Cacabelos, through small plots of flowering tobacco plants, tumbling vines and orchards, until the fertile lowlands are left well behind and the wilderness begins.

This southern face of Ancares has a dry and inhospitable aspect; patches of pale eroded soil show through the sparse, shrubby heath and blackened tree stumps testify to the frequent fires that rage across these slopes. Many of the plants bear vicious spines or produce pungent oils to deter grazing animals. Narrow-leaved and sage-leaved cistus bloom amid a bewildering variety of gorses, heathers and brooms. There are stunted evergreen oaks and every so often tall trunks of the most typical and prized tree of these mountains: the sweet chestnut. In the summer in these grasslands you can lie in the sun and listen to the calls of a thousand grasshoppers, or stroll through the flowers preceded by the flashing blue or red wings of these insects.

The Sierra de Ancares extends over some 53,000 ha (131,000 acres) of mountainous terrain which, although lacking the ruggedness of the Picos de Europa, holds a certain quiet

beauty all its own. The outlines are less severe, the contours more rounded — a legacy of the extreme antiquity of the rocks here. Often you will find yourself in a place that feels as if it had never been seen before.

This forgotten land teems with animal life, especially in the western part of the range, which is known as Cervantes (literally, 'the land of the red deer'). Despite the name, it is the roe deer which is most abundant here, although red deer and fallow deer are also found. Their smaller relative, the chamois, was hunted to extinction by soldiers stationed nearby during the Civil War, and is only now becoming re-established from other colonies in nearby areas of Cordillera Cantábrica.

The woodlands provide the best habitat for the typical species of the Sierra de Ancares. That between Suárbol and Piornedo, for instance, comprises lichen-covered oaks on an outcrop of granite, together with holly, bilberry, bracken, Cantabrian broom and alder buckthorn. Other woods here feature beech as a major component, together with hazel, silver birch, yew,

sycamore and the ubiquitous sweet chestnut. In the cover provided by these primeval habitats live wild boar, genets, beech martens, wildcats, red squirrels and foxes, as well as the most characteristic bird of these mountains, the capercaillie. The last native brown bear was killed in Monte Buixicedo some 50 years ago, but occasionally animals wander into the area from Somiedo, to the east. Wolves still thrive in the Sierra de

The capercaillie is restricted to woodlands of the Western Cordillera

52

Ancares, their main prey – the roe deer – being wildly abundant.

Almost due north of the rounded contours of Ancares lies the region of Degaña and El Bosque de Muniellos. Degaña, one of the smaller hunting reserves of the Cordillera Cantábrica, totalling only 8,274 ha (20,450 acres), has managed to maintain its small brown bear population despite a drastic reduction generally in the numbers of this animal in recent years. This is largely due to the heavily forested nature of the reserve, which includes the beech wood of Navariegos. Another attraction is several unspoiled glacial lakes on the southern border of the reserve – Las Lagunas de Fasgueo – but the north-eastern section has been somewhat scarred by coal-mining activities.

El Bosque de Muniellos is one of the largest oak woods in Europe; it is made up of some 3,000 ha (7,400 acres) of superlative natural vegetation and lies between the *puertos* of Connio and Rañadoiro – the latter pass is the birthplace of the Río Muniellos, a tributary of the Narcea. The highest point of the Muniellos is La Bobia de Teleyerba (1,685 m/5,530 ft), from which radiate 3 valleys: Candanosa, which contains 4 glacial lakes; Las Berzas, also known as Las Gallegas; and La Cerezal. The

rivers flowing through these valleys are supplied by a wealth of clean, crystalline streams.

The woodland canopy is comprised of pedunculate and Pyrenean oak (*Quercus robur* and *Q. pyrenaica*), birch, alder and hazel, with a dense understorey of holly, hawthorn and strawberry tree. The autumn fruits of these shrubs attract large numbers of passerines and small mammals, and consequently the predatory vertebrates are also well-represented. As in Degaña, brown bears are frequent, together with wolves, wildcats and foxes. Avian predators include goshawk, sparrowhawk, peregrine, kestrel, golden, short-toed and Bonelli's eagles, although the latter are scarce. Chamois and roe deer are also common, as are wild boar, and this dense woodland represents the most ideal place in the whole Cordillera Cantábrica for the reproduction and survival of the capercaillie.

By some strange miracle, in this day and age, the woodland has been little interfered with. Its status, now that it is owned by the State, is close enough to that of a national park: its official designation is Coto Nacional de Muniellos. But what is important is that considerable care is being taken to ensure that the trees are regenerating, and to control hunting and poaching in the

The great yellow gentian grows in pockets of marsh and damp grassland in hilly regions

woodland.

To the north of Degaña, and east of Muniellos lies another great woodland, this time of beech, which surrounds the Monasterio de Huermo. This is the largest beech forest in Asturias, although it has no legal protection.

On the opposite side of the Ancares, separated from its sunny slopes by the Río Sil and the market town of Ponferrada, lie the Montes Aquilianos and the Sierra del Teleno. At the western end of this narrow mountain chain you come across a landscape scene more typical of the African desert: the weather-scarred cliffs of Las Médulas de Carucedo.

The shy, nocturnal genet can easily be mistaken for a cat, but in fact is a close relative of the mongoose

In the late afternoon sun, Las Médulas appeared to be on fire. The pillars and pinnacles of ruddy-coloured rock have been etched into extraordinary shapes and forms by wind and water, and, strangest of all, by human hand. In the 1st century AD when this part of Spain was under Roman rule, these mountains were mined for gold. Canals were built to bring water from the Río Cabrera, some 28 km (17 miles) away, and underground galleries were dug until the whole plateau, as it then was, became riddled with holes. Gradually the upland was reduced to a series of peaks, which today rise from a sea of sweet chestnut trees. The mines have long since been abandoned, but a labyrinth of galleries remains to be explored. Of these the Mina de Orellán and the Galería de Yeres figure among the most famous and extensive.

What really struck me, as I sat looking down on this incredible landscape, was the juxtaposition of man-made and natural sights and sounds. The noise of swifts' wings ripping through the air close to my head was strangely mirrored by the rasping of the scythes as the local people harvested their wheat and barley in the valley below. And the dome-shaped stacks of straw gradually taking shape around their central poles looked rather like the convex peaks of Las Médulas — in both their colour and their form.

Before you go *Maps:* IGN 1:25,000 Nos. 100, 126, 157 and 158 and 1:50,000 Nos. 99, 100, 125, 126, 157 and 158; IGN 1:50,000, Sierra de Ancares; and Mapa Provincial of León. *Guide-books:* Alfredo Sánchez Carro, *El Parque Natural de Ancares* (Editorial Everest, 1985); David Gustavo López, *Las Médulas* (Editorial

Nebrija, 1983); Angeles Sanjosé Arango, *Comarca del Bierzo* (Helenika, 1998).

Getting there *By car:* from León take the N120 to Astorga and the NVI (or A6) to Ponferrada and/or Pedrafita do Cebreiro; alternatively, take the C623 to Villablino, turning right on to the AS15 and first left on the small road to Degaña, the O733. *By rail:* takes you as far as Ponferrada and Lugo, from where there are bus connections to El Bierzo. *By bus:* 2 bus lines take you into the heart of the Ancares: Lugo to Degrada and Ponferrada to Candín, (bus station T: (987) 40 10 65).

Where to stay: try the Parador de Villafranca del Bierzo on the main Ponferrada-Lugo road, T: (987) 54 01 75, F: 54 00 10; *casas rurales* Casa Carolo, T: (982) 36 71 68 and Casa Galego, T: (982) 16 14 61, in Pedrafita do Cebreiro, and Cantina Mustallar, T: (982) 15 17 17, at Piornedo de Ancares. Ponferrada, the nearest town of any size, has the 4-star Hotel del Temple, T: (987) 41 00 58, F: 42 35 25, and numerous other places. *Outdoor living:* south of the Ancares, but well situated if you plan to visit Las Médulas as well, is Camping El Bierzo at Villamartín de la Abadía, T: (987) 56 25 15, open June-Sept and with space for 240. *Refuges:* the Albergue del Club Ancares at Degrada lies between the peaks of Mustallar and Peñarrubia.

Access: a permit is needed to visit Muniellos and only 20 people per day are allowed access. Apply a minimum 1 week/maximum 3 months in advance to the Consejera de Medio Ambiente y Urbanismo del Principado de Asturias, T/F: (98) 581 26 17.

Activities: Ancares is made up of 2

The clear blue water and shining white sands of Las Islas Cíes remain unspoiled by man

main conservation areas: the region in Galicia now known as the Parque Natural de Ancares, which was formerly a national hunting reserve; and the part of León known as the Reserva Nacional de los Ancares-Leoneses — 38,300 ha (94,600 acres) of hunting reserve for red deer and roe deer; formerly bear and capercaillie were also legal prey here.

Climbing: contact Federación Castellano-Leonesa, p40.

Fishing: there are numerous stretches of river good for fishing. Permits and season information can be obtained from the tourist offices. More information can be had from the local fishing club, Federación Castellano-Leonesa, Avda. José Antonio, 25, bajo, León, T: (987) 22 53 51.

Tours: you can arrange Land Rover excursions through the mountains from Degrada, Castillo de Doiras, Candín and Vega de Espinareda. Ask at the tourist offices for details.
Further information *Tourist offices:* León and Lugo, p40.

Islas Cíes

Archipelago just off the north-western coast by the city of Vigo; an important parque natural *for marine breeding birds* ZEPA
433 ha (1,070 acres)

First impressions are supposed to be the most important. It was mid-July and raining when I left Vigo. Mist had closed over the hills that ring that city's estuary and I could not even see my destination.

I was lucky to visit Las Islas Cíes on a rainy day. I wandered for hours among the eucalyptus trees without ever seeing another person. I spent a happy half-hour following a sparrowhawk from tree to tree in a small Monterrey pine forest on Punta Muxeiro; despite having been planted the woodland was full of native shrubs and herbs, such as sage-leaved cistus and heath lobelia, and the fragrance on this wet day was wonderful. Another half-hour was spent watching the shags diving for fish in the choppy waves around a rock near Playa Cantareira; at any one time there was an equal number of avian spectators perched out of reach of the sea, like so many penguins waiting patiently on an ice-floe.

If I had approached the islands from the western side, I might have formed a very different opinion. Here the granite cliffs receive the full force of the Atlantic Ocean; although the cliffs tower above the sea, the waves have carved out numerous caves at the base, some of which are enormous.

Las Islas Cíes are made up of three main islands, from north to south, Isla del Norte, Isla del Faro (these two linked artificially by a road and sand bar) and Isla del Sur o de San Martín. They lie at the mouth of the Ría de Vigo, some 14½ kilometres (nine miles) from the city itself. It amazes me that they remain so unspoiled despite being so close to 300,000 people. The archipelago also includes many smaller islets and rocky outcrops. The four main ones are El Beriero o Agoeiro, Viños, Popa Fragata and Pinelón da Cortella; the former lies 1.3 kilometres (just under one mile) from the southern island, is topped by a small tower, and supports only about ten plant species on its very barren surface.

Since the declaration of Las Islas Cíes as a *parque natural* in 1980, there has been no access to the whole precipitous western side of Isla del Norte, the cliffs which harbour the highest density of nesting gulls and shags. Similarly, there is no access to the triangular Isla del Sur, and consequently optimal conditions exist for wildlife.

The botanical highlight of Las Islas Cíes is the beach and sand-dune vegetation. The Galician rarity *camariña* (*Corema album*) thrives on both Rodas and Figueiras beaches; this dwarf shrub is endemic to the Iberian peninsula and produces separate male and female plants. With it flourish sea rocket, saltwort, sea knotgrass, cottonweed, sea immortelle and the sea daffodil.

Much of the interior of the islands consists of pine and eucalyptus plantations, boasting an understorey of European gorse, blackthorn, bracken and Pyrenean oak. Here and there the monotonous green is relieved by the pink of round-headed leek, sky-blue sheep's-bit, purple foxgloves and white asphodels. Native tree species are few and far between, but a number of ornamental and orchard trees persist in abandoned domestic gardens. It is strange that the heaths and lings so common in similar habitats on the mainland are virtually absent here. A total of 260 plant species has been recorded on Las Islas Cíes, of which 232 are of European origin.

There is little fresh water on the islands and the sole amphibian found here is the black-and-gold fire salamander, only seen after rain or at night. Of the reptiles, both Bocage's wall lizard and the Iberian wall lizard occur (endemic to north-west Spain and Portugal), as well as the larger, blunt-headed ocellated and Schreiber's lizards.

Birds command most attention in Las Islas Cíes — and justly so. At the height of the breeding season, even the most inattentive day-tripper could not fail to notice the clamour of the gulls as they fight for nesting space on precarious ledges in the cliff-faces. The most important marine breeding birds here are herring gulls, now called yellow-legged gulls in Iberia, and lesser black-backed gulls (occupying their most southerly colony in the world), as well as shags and guillemots. The cave- and cliff-nesting shags had decreased to 300 pairs by 1981; this colony, much the largest in the Iberian peninsula, is one of the prime reasons for the establishment of the natural park.

Of even greater significance, though, is the Iberian guillemot that breeds here. It is on the verge of extinction on Las Islas Cíes, with only two or three pairs returning to nest each year. Not only is this tiny enclave endangered, but the bird is very rare on the entire Atlantic coastline, and thus merits the greatest possible protection, although Iberia is right at the southern edge of the bird's range.

There is also an abundance of pelagic bird life, although these species do not nest here. Gannets are a frequent sight, accompanied in winter by razorbills, puffins and kittiwakes. Although migrant sea-birds such as Manx, Cory's and great shearwaters may be seen off-shore in late summer, these birds are more regularly found off Cape Finisterre to the north.

Between two and four thousand ducks winter in the Ría de Vigo every year mostly mallard, wigeon, pochard and common scoter — and these are a frequent sight in the more sheltered bays of the islands in bad weather. Grey herons can also be seen fishing, and in 1977 a group of 25 flamingoes visited in winter. Waders which winter in the area include a few bartailed godwits and grey plovers, along with turnstones and oystercatchers; the latter used to breed here, but have not done so for a number of years. It is thought that the only shore-nesting bird on the islands is the Kentish plover.

BEFORE YOU GO
Maps: IGN 1:25,000 and 1:50,000 Nos. 222, 223 and 261 and IGN 1:10,000 *Parque Natural de las Islas Cíes*.
Guide-books: Estánislao Fernández de la Cigoña-Núñez, *Islas Cíes, Parque Natural de Galicia.*

GETTING THERE
By sea: the only way to get across to Las Islas Cíes from Vigo is by taking a ferry from the Estación Marítima de Ría. Boats sail only from the end of June until the end of September.

WHERE TO STAY
There is no shortage of accommodation in Vigo. Try the 4-star Hotel Ciudad de Vigo, T: (986) 22 78 20, F: 43 98 71; 3-star Hotel Lisboa, T: (986) 41 72 55, F: 48 26 48, or the 2-star Hotel Junquera, T: (986) 43 48 88, F: 22 06 90. For listings on the islands contact the tourist office.
Outdoor living: there is a campsite, Isla Cíes, on the Isla Cíes, T: (986) 43 83 58. It is open from mid-June to mid-Sept and has space for 800 people. Camping is forbidden elsewhere on the island.

ACTIVITIES
Bird-watching: Observatorio del Faro do Peito (Isla del Norte) for watching the shag colonies; and Observatorio de la Campana (Isla de Faro) for observing herring gulls and shags.
Fishing: for permits and information contact the tourist office, or Federación Gallega, C/ Doctor Gasalla, 29, Lugo, T: (982) 21 62 21.

FURTHER INFORMATION
Tourist office: Estación Marítima de Transatlánticos, s/n, Vigo, T/F: (986) 43 05 77.

CHAPTER 3

North Meseta

The central plateau, or Meseta, covers nearly half the entire area of Spain. It is a high tableland with an average altitude of 700 metres (2,300 feet) in the northern portion, 600 metres (2,000 feet) in the south. Surrounding it is a series of mountain ranges that separate the Meseta from the Costa Verde, the Ebro valley, the Mediterranean and the valleys of Andalucía.

The Meseta is a vast and curiously deceptive region. I have flown over it many times and wondered where the people were hiding; from the air much of it resembles a trackless desert without roads, rivers or villages. But the picture changes dramatically as soon as you travel across the Meseta at ground level. Farmhouses and wheat-fields make their appearance; the brown and grey earth is veined with narrow roads and cart tracks. In summer much of the land is sunbaked to the consistency of terra cotta but there are also some surprisingly fertile regions that have clearly benefited from the use of modern agricultural technology. Yet the Meseta still has more than its share of half-wild lands that are suitable only for sheep-grazing — or for wanderers and nature-seekers looking for remnants of pre-technological Spain. Its very emptiness strikes me as one of its principal attractions, but I know from experience that not everyone shares my predilection for such landscapes. A friend from New York once asked me to recommend a place in the Castilian countryside which he could visit on a daytrip from Madrid, and I gave him the name of a

An eroded gorge near Zaragoza bakes in the summer heat. Although inhospitable-looking, this is a likely habitat for birds such as rock thrush and black wheatear

small decaying town in the midst of a wonderfully bare region of wheat-fields. When I saw him again some months later he took me to task for having wasted his time on this out-of-the-way destination. 'What do you see in it?' he asked me, looking thoroughly mystified. 'There isn't anything there!'

The northern Meseta is separated from the southern by a long, irregular chain of mountain ranges, the Sistema Central, that runs diagonally just to the north of Madrid, stretching from the Sierra de Peña de Francia in the west to the Sierra de Ayllón in the east. This is no mere range of hills. Indeed, to my mind there are no more dramatic mountains in Spain than the Sierra de Gredos, which forms a giant escarpment above the valley of the Río Tiétar, about 140 kilometres (87 miles) west of Madrid. From the southern rim of the Gredos, at well over 2,000 metres (6,500 feet), you can look out across a vast expanse of farms and forested hills, some 1,700 metres (5,500 feet) beneath your feet. In the mountain meadows the ecosystem is alpine, and ibex spring from ledge to ledge; in the Tiétar valley the flora is semi-tropical, with palms and lemon trees. A four-hour climb along a footpath will take you from the sub-tropical plains to the snow-covered mountains. There is skiing in the Gredos during the winter months and serious mountain climbing at all times of the year, but this is also an immensely rewarding region for travellers who want to wander on foot through a superb massif which, except for one or two familiar points, is still largely unknown to international tourism.

In the outlying western reaches of this mountain range you will feel yourself at the edge of the known world. Pilgrims visit the shrine of the Madonna atop the Peña de Francia, but ordinary tourists never come this way. Perhaps it was the sense of isolation which induced the emperor Charles V to retire to Yuste when he abdicated his throne in favour of his son: he could hardly have found a more remote corner of Spain.

The Sierra de Guadarrama, the eastern continuation of the Gredos, lies just above Madrid and is thus crowded with *madrileño* skiers during the winter and holiday-makers during the summer. These cool, green peaks have always served as the summer 'hill stations' of the sweltering inhabitants of the capital. Even the kings and their royal families used the Guadarrama as an escape hatch. While wandering through its high-altitude forests you might do well to visit the 140-hectare (350-acre) garden of La Granja de San Ildefonso, the royal pleasure park that contains the world's finest sculptured fountains. Felipe V loved capturing the cold springs that pour down from these mountains, and this was his way of improving on nature — 26 fountains that incorporate hundreds of sculptures, ponds, cascades, sprays and *jets d'eau*. Although surrounded by wild Spain, this is Baroque Spain with a vengeance, and not even Versailles can hold a candle to it. In the baths of Diana, for example, 20 naked nymphs dance attendance on the goddess of the hunt, while her tame lions roar out great streams of water and cascades splash down a series of marble tiers. There is a fountain that leaps 40 metres (130 feet) into the air; the *fuente del Canastillo* weaves a basket of interlacing jets; a sea-god drives his horses through the fountain of *la Carrera de Caballos*; Apollo slays the python, which bleeds a foaming stream of water. Despite this magnificent variety, Felipe V, who was easily bored, was never entirely satisfied with his fountain-filled garden. One day he paused before one of his aquatic extravaganzas and exclaimed: 'Thou hast amused me three minutes and hast cost me three millions!' When visiting yourself, be sure to check the schedule of days and hours when the fountains are turned on for visitors.

The Sierra de Ayllón, still further to the east, lies off the beaten track and boasts some of the finest rural landscapes of northern Spain. One of the Sierra's chief talking points is the beech forest known as the Hayedo de Tejera Negra, but for me its special fascination lies in its rolling hills and flower-bedecked hay meadows. The whole region was once more densely populated than it is today, and in the middle of some peasant village you'll suddenly come upon the ruins of a medieval church of truly magnificent proportions.

Apart from these central mountains the northern Meseta usually runs to wheat-fields and vineyards, sheep pastures and low hills covered with forests of poplars, pine, beech and oak. The walled city of Avila suggests itself as a natural base of operation in the southern part of this zone, with Salamanca as a possible alternative. Soria, Valladolid and Zamora are the principal cities of the central region, and the two ancient capitals, Burgos and León, dominate the northern portion.

The classic way to see the countryside of northern Castilla between Logroño and Ponferrada is to follow the way of the medieval pilgrims, the Camino de Santiago. I first walked along the pilgrims' road in the 1960s and found it indescribably beautiful. It was early summer and the nights were still chilly, but in the morning the whole chorus of resident and visiting birds were in full voice, and as the day warmed up the crickets formed an impromptu orchestra. We wandered through wheat-fields, marched along remnants of old Roman roads and crossed rivers by means of medieval bridges. Often the villages *en route* still had hospices and monasteries — vestiges of the first great 'mass tourism' enterprise in the western world — and in some cases the monasteries were still inhabited by monks who were busy doing more or less the same things their predecessors had been doing a thousand years before.

It struck me at the time that this re-tracing of an ancient route was just as adventurous as striking out on your own through an uncharted wilderness; indeed, this particular admixture of nature and history is more akin to what one can find in India than in Europe. As Walter Starkie writes in *The Road to Santiago*, 'a reflective pilgrim on the road to Santiago always makes a double journey...the backward journey through Time and the forward journey through Space'. When the historical dimension is added to this journey, and to the whole experience of walking through fertile fields and semi-deserts, across rolling hills and deeply scarred *arroyos*, every step the pilgrim takes 'evokes memories of those who passed that way century after century'.

It used to be that people would trudge all the way to Santiago de Compostela and back, hanging up their tattered shoes in their local church as proof of their piety — to say nothing of their endurance. Today few people will go as far as this and many hikers are content with covering just a small part of the Camino (a sign of the short attention span prevalent in the 20th century). If I had time for only one segment I would probably choose the 90 kilometres (55 miles) between Nájera and Burgos — a superb and thoroughly characteristic sector of the Camino that leads from one of the old royal cities of

Navarra to the erstwhile capital of Castilla. The route traverses a variety of plains and hills, including the oak-forested mountains of Oca, and takes in a dozen medieval towns and villages: Santo Domingo de la Calzada with its 12th-century cathedral; Villafranca de los Montes de Oca, with its 600-year-old hospice for pilgrims; and Valdefuentes, which was once a mountainous hiding-place for both monks and bandits (the monks left the more interesting memento, the ruined monastery of San Félix de Oca).

All along the Camino there are opportunities for observing the flora and fauna of the northern Meseta. Certainly you'll see the white storks nesting in the church towers, but it is more difficult to spot some of the endangered species of the region: the peregrine falcon, whose hunting dives have been

clocked at 400 kilometres (250 miles) per hour; or the eagle owl, known locally as the *buho real* or the *gran duque*, the most powerful of all European birds of prey. Smaller birds, however, are well provided for in the ecosystems of the northern Meseta, and they also abound in the monastery gardens along the Camino. At Santo Domingo de Silos, John Gooders once recorded storks breeding in the bell tower and rock buntings nesting in the buildings themselves; spotless starling and melodious warbler in the gardens; yellow wagtail in the water-meadows of the nearby valley, with woodchat shrike, golden oriole and serin in the poplars that grow there; rock thrush above the treeline; and in the crags above the valley, griffon and Egyptian vultures, alpine swift, crag martin and chough. He also found the eagle owl, red-necked nightjar and the wallcreeper, 'which should not be in this part of Spain at all'. Perhaps it, too, had decided to become a pilgrim on the road to Santiago.

Among the olive trees of Sierra de Peña de Francia, the pattern of pastoral life has remained unchanged for centuries

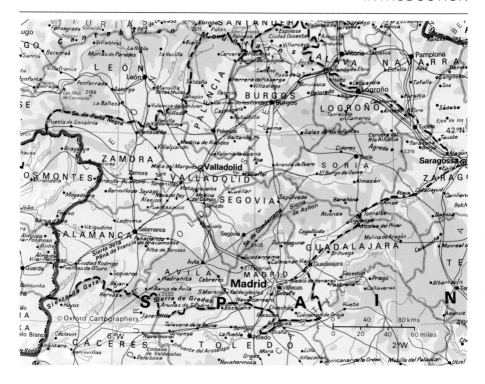

BEFORE YOU GO
Maps: Michelin 1:400,000 Nos. 441 and 442.

GETTING THERE
By air: Madrid is well connected by air to all European capitals and other parts of the world, as well as being the centre of the Spanish internal network. Valladolid has the only other airport in the North Meseta.
By car: the motorway network radiates from Madrid like the spokes of a wheel, providing high-speed access to the main cities of the North Meseta. However, by far the best way to travel in this region is on the secondary and tertiary roads that take you through the more remote places.
By rail: there are excellent connections between Madrid and the cities of the northern Meseta such as Aranda de Duero, Burgos, León, Logroño, Palencia, Soria, Salamanca, Valladolid and Zamora. For information call RENFE in Madrid, T: (91) 328 90 20, or check the schedules on RENFE's web-site, www.renfe.es.
By bus: an elaborate network of local companies covers most of the cities, towns and villages of the Meseta. For destinations from Madrid call the Estación Sur, T: (91) 468 45 11. For destinations from points beyond Madrid check with the local tourist office.

WHEN TO GO
The temperatures in Madrid, which lies at about 600 m (2,000 ft) above sea level, are extreme. Here and throughout the region, expect freezing winters and burning summers, when temperatures often rise above 38°C (100°F). For more moderate weather, go in spring or autumn.

WHERE TO STAY
For accommodation, refer to the entries for individual exploration zones or contact the regional tourist offices.

ACTIVITIES
Mountaineering clubs: Federación Madrileña de Montañismo, Apodaca, 18, 1º derecha, 28004 Madrid, T: (91) 593 80 74, F: 448 07 24, e-mail: federacion@fmm.es, www.fmm.es; Federación Castellano-Leonesa de Montañismo, Polideportivo Municipal de Canterac, Avda. Circunvalación, s/n, 47012 Valladolid, T/F: (983) 22 64 00.
Fishing: for information on permits and seasons contact the local tourist offices or the following fishing club: Federación Castellano-

63

Leonesa, Avda. José Fernando, 48, 1°, 39010 Santander, T: (942) 23 55 89.
Skiing: the main ski resorts in the northern Meseta are:
Madrid (91): Navacerrada, 852 14 35, and Valdesquí, 852 04 16;
Segovia (921): La Pinilla, 55 03 04.

FURTHER INFORMATION
Avila (920): tourist office, Pl. de la Catedral, 4, 05001, T: 21 13 87, F: 25 37 17. Red Cross, T: 22 48 48, F: 25 19 16.
Burgos (947): tourist office, Pl. Alonso Martínez, 7, 09003, T: 20 31 25, F: 27 65 29. Red Cross, T: 21 23 11, F: 22 93 80.
Guadalajara (949): tourist office, Pl. de los Caídos, 6, 19001, T: 21 16 26. Red Cross, T: 22 11 84, F: 23 20 43.
León (987): tourist office, Pl. de la Regla, 3, 24003, T: 23 70 82, F: 27 33 91. Red Cross, T: 25 25

28, F: 21 69 69.
Logroño (941): tourist office, Paseo del Espolón, s/n, 26071, T: 26 06 65, F: 25 60 45. Red Cross, T: 22 52 12, F: 20 04 00.
Palencia (979): tourist office, C/ Mayor, 105, 34071, T: 74 00 68, F: 70 08 22. Red Cross, T: 70 05 07, F: 74 35 34.
Salamanca (923): tourist office, Casa de las Conchas, C/ Compañía, 2, 37002, T: 26 85 71, F: 26 24 92. Red Cross, T: 22 10 32, F: 22 84 82.
Segovia (921): tourist office, Pl. Mayor, 10, 40001, T: 46 03 34, F: 46 03 30. Red Cross, T: 44 02 02, F: 44 14 03.
Soria (975): tourist office, Pl. Ramón y Cajal, s/n, 42003, T/F: 21 20 52. Red Cross, T: 21 26 40, F: 22 89 77.
Valladolid (983): tourist office, Oficina Municipal, C/ Correos, s/n, 47001, T: 37 20 85 or 35 47 31. Red Cross, T: 35 33 18, F: 35 72 64.

Zamora (980): tourist office, C/ Santa Clara, 20, 49014, T: 53 18 45, F: 53 38 13. Red Cross, 52 33 00, F: 51 18 42.

FURTHER READING
Alistair Boyd, *The Companion Guide to Madrid and Central Spain* (London, 1974);
Robin Collomb, *Gredos Mountains and Sierra Nevada* (Reading, 1974);
Santiago García, Ed., *Libro de la Naturaleza: Castilla y León* (Junta de Castilla y León/Ediciones Leonesas, 1990);
Ernest Hemingway, *For Whom The Bell Tolls* (New York, 1940);
Domingo Pliego Vega, *Excursiones para Colegios por las Sierras de Madrid* (Desnivel, 1992);
Walter Starkie, *The Road to Santiago: Pilgrims of St James* (London, 1957).

Sierra de Gredos

This parque regional *is a massive range of mountains running west from Madrid, one of Spain's major strongholds for birds of prey*
86,238 ha (213,098 acres)

There was no path as such, only a few stone markers placed at desultory intervals atop some of the more prominent boulders. Very gradually I was ascending a broad valley strewn with great rocks that had fallen from the flanking heights, their rough-hewn surfaces covered with lichen in delicate shades of green, yellow and pink. There was hardly a cloud in the sky but with a pleasant breeze and the temperature perfect for walking. As a counterpoint to the omnipresent sound of birds there was the sweetly tangy fragrance of thyme and laven-

der; clearly all was right with the world. Finally, I crossed the main brook flowing down the centre of the valley, ascended a steep slope and reached the high southern ridge, my aim for the last hour. To my left rose the peaks of Los Campanarios (2,152 metres/7,059 feet). But suddenly there was nothing beneath my feet except a yawning abyss that fell away for more than 1,000 feet (300 metres).

I had discovered the not-so-discreet charm of the Gredos, the majestic range of mountains lying athwart the centre of Spain like a titanic rampart. Until recently, the beauties of the Gredos were a fairly well-kept secret, known mainly to hunters, mountaineers and cross-country skiers. During the past decade, however — since the building of a road to a place appropriately known as the Plataforma — the very centre of the range has been opened up to just about anyone capable of putting one foot in front of the other. As a result, there are summer Sundays when the path up the highest mountain (Pico Almanzor; 2,592 metres/8,500 feet) is almost as crowded as the Ramblas of Barcelona.

The Circo justifies all the superlatives that have been written about it; that (and the relative ease of the three-hour climb that takes you there) is one of the reasons why so many weekenders make the trip. It's worth noting, however, that this is virtually the only place in the Gredos where you'll find a surfeit of people.

To the east, the crooked elbow formed by the Río Alberche on its way to meet the Tajo divides the Gredos from the Sierra de Guadarrama; to the west, the trench of Aravalle separates the Gredos from the Sierra de Béjar (sometimes regarded as the western extension of the Gredos). The peaks of the Sierra grow progressively higher from east to west — Cerro Guisando, 1,320 metres (4,330 feet); El Cabrero, 2,188 metres (7,176 feet); La Mira, 2,348 metres (7,700 feet); Almanzor, 2,592 metres (8,500 feet) — then they decline before ending abruptly with the majestic Covacha, overlooking the Sierra de Tormantos at 2,399 metres (7,870 feet). Like second-year Latin, the Gredos are usually divided into three parts: the Eastern Massif, between the Peña del Cadalso and the Puerto del Pico; the Central Massif, which includes Almanzor, a favourite haunt of griffon and black vultures; and the Western Massif, comprising the mountains west of the Puerto de Tornavacas.

The black stork, unlike the white, nests in forest treetops far from human habitation

The most striking differences, however, are not between east and west but between the northern slope of the Sierra and the south face, which plunges so abruptly from the highest peaks (over 2,100-2,500 metres/6,900-8,200 feet) to the 300 metres (980 feet) of the Tiétar valley. The north side of the Gredos consists of hills that rise by easy steps from 1,400 metres (4,600 feet).

Although the altitude is not especially great, the Cordillera happens to lie in one of the coldest zones in Spain, and temperatures resemble those of much more alpine regions. Curiously, the northern slope supports a sub-alpine flora, with great stands of pine (especially in Hoyos de Espino, Navarredonda, Hoyo Casero and the whole

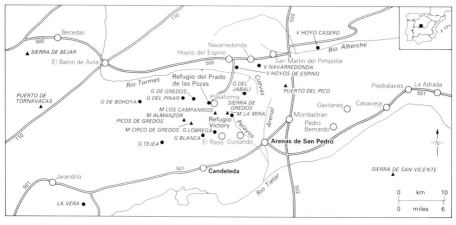

Eastern Massif), large tracts of *Genista purgans* and the rich meadows that a Brown Swiss cow would instantly recognize as home, while the southern slope borrows its sub-tropical flora from the Valle del Tiétar and La Vera (the so-called 'Andalucía of Avila'), what with holm oaks, olives, citrus trees and such. In the Gredos, in other words, the sure-footed botanist can have the best of both worlds.

The Central Massif begins at Arenas de San Pedro, the real capital of the Sierra de Gredos — a much-besieged town whose history is written into its coat of arms: 'Always burning and always faithful'. It stands at the confluence of the rivers Arenal and Cuevas, and is surrounded by an immense circle of mountains.

In the Central Massif some 23,000 hectares (57,000 acres) are set aside as a *coto*

The Río Arbillas begins life as a shallow, rocky stream near Arenas de San Pedro in the central part of the Sierra de Gredos, then flows south to join the Río Tiétar

nacional, but hunting is strictly controlled and only a few selected animals are culled every year. Originally this was a royal preserve, the Coto Real de Gredos, established by Alfonso XIII in 1905 as a means of saving the local ibex from extinction. Successive governments have succeeded so well in this endeavour that the ibex population is currently estimated at 5,000, and you can hardly walk through the high Gredos without seeing them at close range.

Three hundred metres (980 feet) above La Apretura — a narrow defile between the Galayos and Risco Enebro, where a high waterfall marks the birth of the Río Pelayos — rises the peak of La Mira (2,343 metres/7,685 feet). Here you can often see numbers of ibex with their young in the high meadows called *cervunales*. La Mira is known as the best observation point of the entire range; the ruined tower on its summit is a relic of an old optical telegraph station which sent and received messages at enormous distances thanks to its immense field of view.

The Gredos can be enjoyed in innumerable ways that are not always overly strenuous. In every part of the Cordillera there are ancient towns and villages from which you can make short excursions into the neighbouring fields and meadows. In the central Gredos, near Arenas, there is the Cerro de Guisando (1,303 metres/4,274 feet) and one of the oldest thoroughfares in Spain, the 'Pass of the Horses', connecting Toledo and Valladolid. Nearby stand the mysterious stone bulls that must have belonged to some Celtic rite — the famous Toros de Guisando. The Río Tiétar rises some distance to the east, and you can make an idyllic detour through the villages of its valley, keeping an eye — and an ear — out for the warblers that frequent this area, including Cetti's melodious, Orphean and Dartford warblers. Other birds found here include quail and stonecurlew, bee-eater, spotless starling, golden oriole and the azure-winged magpie.

Above all, however, the Sierra de Gredos is known as one of the major strongholds of birds of prey in the whole of Spain. Here the rare and endangered Spanish imperial eagle may be seen soaring on flat, broad wings. It

In the Coto Nacional de Gredos, ibex live above 2,000 m (6,500 ft) on mountain crags, feeding on tufts of grass and lichens

has developed a white crown and mantle that extends across the forewings, making identification simple for a bird of prey. These are denizens of large forested hillsides, although they soar over the mountain tops as easily as the vultures.

Also with a stronghold in Gredos is the equally elusive Bonelli's eagle, a cliff and buttress nester almost as large as the Spanish imperial. Here, too, are golden, short-toed and booted eagles, so that all five Spanish eagles may possibly be seen in a single day. The road between Avila and Arenas via the Puerto del Pico is a good starting point but the more remote valleys should also be explored.

Eagles apart, Gredos has both red and black kites, goshawk, chough and, hidden away on its most remote cliffs, the highly elusive black stork. Vastly outnumbered by their white cousin, these are mainly forest birds which cross the straits of Gibraltar to winter in sub-Saharan Africa.

The relatively high rainfall and the mild winters of the Sierra de Gredos have produced a thick cover of Pyrenean oak (*Quercus pyrenaica*) and maritime pine (*Pinus pinaster*) woodlands, especially in the area of Arenas de San Pedro.

One of the more interesting species endemic to western-central Spain is *Echium lusitanicum* ssp. *polycaulon*, which has soft, hairy stems and leaves to guard against ultra-violet radiation, and small, pale blue flowers. Similarly, the Spanish lupin (*Lupinus hispanicus*) is known only in Portugal and western Spain; its pale cream flowers turn lilac-pink as they mature.

The highly acidic soils of the granite uplands support a wide range of heathland scrub species, such as gum cistus (*Cistus ladanifer*), poplar-leaved cistus (*C. populifolius*) and *C. psilosepalus*. Leguminous shrubs include the silver-leaved *Genista florida*, and the two broom species, *Cytisus multiflorus* and *C. striatus;* the former has white pea-like flowers, the latter the more characteristic yellow blooms.

In the Scots pine woods at Hoyocasero, the pale yellow race of the alpine pasque-

67

flower (*Pulsatilla alpina* ssp. *apiifolia*) is found. Later on, the colour in these woods is provided by two crimson peony species and the less conspicuous but deliciously scented lily-of-the-valley (*Convallaria majalis*). This forest is most renowned for the huge summer-flowering knapweed, *Leuzea rhaponticoides*, with purple florets extruded from a husk-like calyx; this is its type locality. Also occurring here are St Bernard's lily (*Anthericum liliago*), martagon lily (*Lilium martagon*) and the endemic pink, *Dianthus laricifolius*, which is restricted to central Spain.

Other interesting plants in the Sierra de Gredos include the highly localized composite *Hispidella hispanica*, with flat yellow flowers with purple hearts, and a star-of-Bethlehem (*Ornithogalum concinnum*) more usually found in Portugal, as well as the blue-and-white columbine *Aquilegia dichroa*, known from mountains in north-west Spain and Portugal. Two species endemic to the Sierra de Gredos range itself are the pale yellow-flowered snapdragon, *Antirrhinum grosii*, and *Reseda gredensis*, with slender white-flowered spikes; the only other known locality for this latter plant is the Sierra de Estrêla in Portugal, again in mountain pastures. One of the more attractive grassland species which may be found here is the storksbill *Erodium carvifolium*, with flowers of deep crimson, two petals

The short-toed eagle is a specialist hunter of snakes and lizards

larger than the other three.

The Spanish argus butterfly (*Aricia morronensis navarredondae*) is a race specific to the Sierra de Gredos. Other races in Spain include *ramburi* from the Sierra Nevada; *elsae* from Riaño, south of the Picos de Europa; and *ordesiae* from the Valle de Ordesa, in the Pyrenees. The type locality of *Aricia morronensis* is the Sierra de Espuña.

BEFORE YOU GO
Maps: IGN 1:25,000 and 1:50,000 Nos. 530, 531, 554, 555, 556, 557, 578 and 579; IGN 1:200,000 Mapa Provincial of Avila.
Guide-books: Carlos de Hita, *Sierras de Gredos y de Bejas* (Anaya, 1998); Gerardo Sánchez Peña, *Entre Guadarrama y Gredos* (Catanata, 1997).

GETTING THERE
By car: from Madrid take the E90/NV to Navalcarnero, then the M507 to its junction with the C501. There, strike off westwards to Arenas de San Pedro by way of the Tiétar

valley. This route brings you to the south side of the Central Massif. Approaching from the north, take the A6/NVI to Villacastín and then drive south-west on the N110 to Avila. Continue along the N110 to El Barco de Avila, or branch off south on the N502 to Arenas de San Pedro.
By rail: there are numerous services to Avila from north and north-west Spain, and from all other places via Madrid. From Avila, take a bus to Arenas de San Pedro or El Barco de Avila (see below).
By bus: from platforms 43-48 at the Estación Sur in Madrid, Doaldi, T: (91) 530 48 00, runs

frequent daily services to and from Arenas de San Pedro, T: (920) 37 17 55. From platforms 13-15 at the same bus station CEVESA, T: (91) 539 31 32, operates a more limited service to and from El Barco de Avila (and on to Béjar, Salamanca).

WHERE TO STAY
There is a wide choice, including two paradores. The Parador de Gredos, T: (920) 34 80 48, F: 34 82 05, just east of Navalconda de Gredos, is the first ever built and offers superb views of the Central Massif from the north. South of the range, towards its western end, the Parador

Jarandilla de la Vera, T: (927) 56 01 17, F: 56 00 88, occupies the restored castle of the Condes de Oropesa.

Many of the small towns have *hostales* or *pensiones*. Alternatively, try the 3-star Hostería Los Galayos, T: (920) 37 13 79, in Arenas de San Pedro or the 3-star Hotel Manila, T: (920) 34 08 44, F: 34 12 91, in El Barco de Avila. In Avila itself, there is the Parador de Avila, T: (920) 21 13 40, F: 22 61 66, or the 4-star Meliá Palacio de los Velada, T: (920) 25 51 00, F: 25 49 00, for modern comfort in an ancient building; or else try the old-world charms of the 2-star Gran Hotel La Hostería de Bracamonte, T: 25 12 80.

Outdoor living: permitted throughout the *coto nacional* and at official sites such as Los Galayos, T: (920) 37 40 21, in Guisando, open all year; the Gredos, T: (920) 20 75 85, in Hoyos del Espino, open from May-Oct and the Prados Abiertos, T: (920) 38 60 61, in

Hispidella hispanica thrives on the arid mountain slopes of the Gredos

Mombeltrán, open 1 June-15 Sept.

Refuges: sometimes in semi-ruined condition but still used at a pinch. The better ones are carefully tended by sponsoring mountaineering clubs: Albergue José Antonio Elola, on the Laguna Grande, property of the Federación Española de Montañismo; Refugio Victory (2,000 m/6,600 ft), at La Apretura, at the foot of La Mira and Los Galayos; Refugio de La Mira (2,250 m/7,380 ft), in the meadow of Los Pelaos, 800 m (2,600 ft) from the peak of La Mira, in poor condition; Refugio-Hermitage of Nuestra Señora de la Nieves, in the Collado Alto, Guijo de Santa Bárbara. The refuge in the Prado de las Pozas is in very poor condition. All the other refuges indicated on existing maps, including the Refugio del Rey in Majasomera, are in ruins.

ACTIVITIES

Walking: this is beautiful country for nature walks, although there are relatively few hiking trails. Apart from the old *trocha real* built by Alfonso XIII as a footpath from Candeleda to the Venteadero across the Central Massif, there are marked trails only up the Gargantas de Gredos, del Pinar and de Bohoyo, and one which starts at El Raso (near Candeleda) and leads up the Garganta de Chilla to the pass known as the Portillo Bermeja, just below Almanzor.

Climbing: good rock climbing. By the village of Guisando a forest path traverses the Nogal del Barranco and ascends to La Apretura; the refuge here is used as a base-camp for climbing the nearby Galayar, an imposing array of granite 'needles' that rise from a 300-m (980-ft) base to an average of

over 2,000 m (6,600 ft). Among the more daunting needles are Punta Amezua, Aguja Negra, Diedro de la María Luisa, Risco de la Ventana (which offers the best view of Galayar) and the fiendishly difficult Torreón.

Candeleda, just south of the Central Massif, makes an ideal starting point for those who want to assault the highest peaks from the lowest base. Several paths lead from the village into the mountains; points of interest include the natural swimming pool formed by the Garganta de Santa María Luisa and a Roman bridge, the Puente del Puerto.

The following clubs provide detailed information on many walks and climbs in the region: Federaciónes Madrileña and Castellana-Leonesa de Montañismo, p63.

Caves: the Cuevas de Aguila, T: (920) 37 71 07, are 4 km (2½ miles) south of the village of Ramacastañas. Open daily, in the summer 10:30 am-1 pm and 3 pm-7 pm; the rest of the year they close an hour earlier.

Fishing: excellent trout fishing in the waters around Arenas de San Pedro; check with the local tourist office for permits and seasons or contact the local fishing club, Federación Castellano-Leonesa de Pesca, Avda. José Antonio, 25, bajo, León, T: (987) 22 53 51.

Riding: one way of seeing the Cordillera is on horse-back. Local stables such as Almanzor Turismo Ecuestre, T: (920) 34 80 47, in Navarredonda de Gredos, and La Esmeralda, T: (920) 34 91 35, in Hoyos del Espino, offer tours of peaks, passes, mountain lagoons and areas of perpetual snow.

FURTHER INFORMATION
Tourist offices: Arenas de San Pedro, T: (920) 37 23 68, and Avila, p64.

Sierra de Guadarrama

A continuation of the Central Cordillera, to the north-west of Madrid, famous for its forests, streams and nesting birds of prey

The Sierra de Guadarrama with its uplands of wild herbs lies 56 km (35 miles) from Madrid

The Guadarrama appears on topographic maps as a sort of gable above Madrid. It rises from the central plateau and stretches across Castilla for about 100 kilometres (60 miles), from the Puerto de Somosierra to the peak of San Benito, situated between the mighty watercourses of the Tajo and Duero, separating Castilla-La Mancha and Castilla-León. In summer, coming up from the sweltering Meseta on either side of it, you are greeted by the cool, almost alpine air of a range of mountains rich in forests and spring water. Here Felipe V, the first Bourbon monarch of Spain, built the summer palace, whose gardens contain the world's greatest array of fountains and *jets d'eaux*, La Granja de San Ildefonso.

The sierra was known in ancient times as Mons Carpetani — the sentinel and protector of Madrid — although the effect it has on the city's climate is less than beneficial. Northerly gales sweep down from the heights of the Guadarrama in winter, causing intense cold and often bringing snow, while in summer the ridge intercepts the moisture carried by the Atlantic air currents, keeping the city hot and dry. Madrid in August has more than once been likened to a cement oven.

Those areas that are not easily reached by car are still in the ecological golden age. Off on the less accessible peaks, with their forests and fields full of thyme, rock-roses and lavender, it is the wild animals that predominate: roe deer, wild boar, foxes, otter, badger — even wolves and eagles uphold their end of the ecological balance.

The Sierra de Guadarrama is subdivided naturally into three separate zones converging at Siete Picos ('seven peaks'), between the passes of Navacerrada and Fuenfría. The western one begins in the Sierra de la Mujer Muerta ('the dead woman') and runs south-west toward the Risco San Benito. The eastern region is formed by Cabezas de Hierro ('iron heads'), Cuerda Larga ('long string [of peaks]') and La Najarra, as far as the Morcuera pass. The north-eastern salient forms a spine of 2,000 metres (6,600 feet) or more between the Valsaín valley,

with its Río Eresma, and the valley of the Río Lozoya. These forested peaks create a watershed for the Lozoya, Guadalix, Manzanares and Guadarrama rivers, which are all tributaries of the Tajo, while the Eresma, Pirón, Cega and Duratón, born in the same massif, eventually flow into the Duero.

The highest peak is Peñalara (2,430 metres/7,970 feet), decorated at the summit by a megalith, and the most famous pass, Navacerrada, which links Segovia and Madrid. The general appearance is less rugged than the Sierra de Gredos, but the Guadarrama is almost as high. This mountain chain is renowned for its numerous nesting birds of prey, including black and griffon vultures; golden, booted, Bonelli's and Spanish imperial eagles; goshawk; red and black kites; and honey buzzard.

There are extensive Scots pine forests on

the mountains' northern and southern slopes, with the shrub layer typically comprising *Genista florida* and another legume, *Adenocarpus telonensis*, as well as juniper and tree heather. The pine forests abound with herbs revelling in the more humid micro-climate in the shade of the trees, and include three toadflax species (*Linaria nivea, L. incarnata,* and *L. triornithophora*), a cut-leaved ragwort (*Senecio adonidifolius*), Spanish bluebells (*Hyacinthoides hispanica*), woodrushes, bedstraws, and the sweet-scented, spherical pink flowerheads of a mountain valerian (*Valeriana tuberosa*). The dry, acid soils above the forest level are a strong-hold of the broom *Cytisus purgans.*

There are no villages within the sierra: except for the recently built ski resorts, the human settlements were all, for good reason, built in the peripheral valleys. It seems that only hermits and bandits could cope with the rigours of Guadarrama, but they certainly made the most of it.

Of course, many of the most spectacular views of the sierra can be enjoyed without any of the muscular exertions that can make the going tough. But the motorized visitor to these hills would be missing the hard-won hiker's pleasure afforded by this rugged range of mountains.

BEFORE YOU GO
Maps: IGN 1:25,000 and 1:50,000 Nos. 483, 484, 485, 486, 506, 508, 509, 511, 532 and 533; IGN 1:200,000 Mapas Provinciales of Madrid and Segovia; and IGN 1:50,000 Sierra de Guadarrama.
Guide-books: C. Enríquez de Salamanca, *Por la Sierra de Guadarrama* (Madrid, 1981); Carlos de Hita, *Las Sierras de Guadarrama y Ayllón* (Anaya, 1998); Juan Pedro Velasco Sayago & José Luis Huertás, *Excursiones por la Provincia de Segovia* (Disnivel, 1995).

GETTING THERE
By car: the southern slopes of the Guadarrama are just 50 km (31 miles) from Madrid, from where there are two main routes: the A6/NVI Madrid-Galicia, turning north on to the N601 towards Navacerrada; and the C607, which heads almost due north from Madrid before turning west towards Navacerrada. The C607 also affords access to Manzanares el Real and Miraflores de la Sierra, continuing to Rascafría via the Puerto de la Morcuera. From Segovia the heart of the Sierra can be approached on the N601, which follows the valley of Valsaín to the Puerto

de Navacerrada.
By rail: Cercedilla, the village just below the pass of Navacerrada and the Siete Picos, is a stop on the Madrid-Segovia line. From there, a funicular ascends to the Puerto de Cotos, with a stop at Navacerrada; this is a most beautiful train ride.

WHERE TO STAY
Accommodation, at every level, is plentiful. Try the 3-star Hostal Nueva Venta Arias, T: (91)852 11 00, at the

Navacerrada ski resort, the 4-star Hotel Arcipreste de Hita, T: (91) 856 01 25, F: 856 02 70, at Navacerrada, or the 4-star Hotel Santa María de El Paular, T: (91) 869 10 11, F: 869 10 06, and the 2-star Hotel Los Calizos, T/F: (91) 869 11 12, at Rascafría. San Lorenzo de El Escorial, with its wonderful monastery, has the 4-star Victoria Palace, T: (91) 890 15 11, F: 890 12 48, and quite a few other places. Segovia, with its world-famous Roman aqueduct, has the 3-

The imperial eagle builds its bulky nest in tall, often isolated trees

star Infanta Isabel, T: (921) 46 13 00, F: 46 22 17, and Los Linajes, T: (921) 46 04 75, F: 46 04 79.

Outdoor living: The Camping Acueducto, T: (921) 42 50 00, just outside Segovia, opens 1 June-30 Sept, and holds 420 people.

Refuges: a whole series of refuges are scattered through the Sierra: the Albergue de Club Alpino Español, A. de la R.S.E.A. Peñalara, A. del Club Alpino Guadarrama, A. 'Dos Castillas', A. 'Cumbres' and Residencia José Antonio are all near Navacerrada at about 1,800 m (5,900 ft). The Albergue Coppel 1,870 m (6,140 ft) is at Puerto de Cotos, the Refugio Zabala 2,100 m (6,900 ft) near the Laguna de Peñalara, the Refugio de Navafría in the Puerto de Navafría and the Refugio Diego de Ordás in the Valdesquí.

ACTIVITIES

Walking/climbing: the Valle de la Acebada, with its streams and pine forests, offers some beautiful walks. The route along the ridge of the Sierra de Guadarrama runs from Cercedilla to Espinar over 5 major summits, offering stunning views. Taking approximately 9 hrs one-way, you can end up at the Espinar railway station on the Segovia-Madrid line.

Historic trails: the ancient trail from Miraflores de la Sierra, on the southern slope of the range, to the Monasterio El Paular ('the poplar') in the Valle de Rozoya is a 5-hr hike used for centuries by the Carthusian monks for whom Juan I built the first *chartreuse* in Spain.

Another historic hiking route crosses the Malagosto (or Reventón) pass which, in the Middle Ages, was the main route between Castilla-La

Mancha and Castilla-León.

Fishing: the Río Angostura is a well-known trout stream. For information regarding permits and seasons contact the tourist office, or the fishing club Federación Madrileña de Pesca, Carrera de San Jerónimo, 18, Madrid, T: (91) 522 86 51.

FURTHER INFORMATION

Tourist offices: C/ Floridablanca, 10, 28200 San Lorenzo de El Escorial, T: (91) 890 15 54; Madrid and Segovia, p64.

La Cuenca Alta del Manzanares

Parque regional
4,000 ha (9,900 acres)

La Cuenca Alta del Manzanares contains an amazing range of granite and limestone mountains that have been gradually eroded into a breathtaking variety of abstract shapes. If the park were located deep in rural Spain it would probably be regarded as a geological wonderland – which it is – but since the Pedriza del Manzanares (as it is generally known) lies only 50 km (31 miles) from Madrid it has become a popular weekend excursion area for *madrileños* who seem quite unaware that this is more than just an attractive picnic area.

Bounded by the Sierra de los Porrones, the peak known as La Maliciosa and the range called La Cuerda Larga, the *parque regional* divides into 2 distinctive zones: the Pedriza Anterior and the Circo Posterior, which are separated by the hills known as the

Collado de la Dehesilla and the Hoya Calderón. Vegetation is sparse and some areas could be used as backdrops for a film on lunar life. On the lower slopes grow dwarfed holm oaks; in the higher reaches, juniper, holly and the newly planted pines of the state forestry service, notably in the Sierra de los Porrones and the Cabezas de Hierro.

But it is the bare rocks that steal the show from the flora and fauna, such as it is. The Yelmo, for example, is a huge mass of bare-scrubbed limestone in the shape of a helmet (or, for that matter, a bald pate) which rises straight into the air for 150 m (500 ft); on a clear day it can be seen from the northern outskirts of Madrid. Or there is the crumpled escarpment known as Las Buitreras ('the vultures' roost'), whose highest caves and fissures are stained white with the *guano* of the many pairs of griffon vultures that build their nests in them. The whole massif is shot through with cracks, cavities and caves, with giant boulders poised dramatically as if to crash into the abyss at any moment, and limestone 'statues' resembling Rodin's 'Balzac' or even the heroic entanglements of Gustav Vigeland.

The Río Manzanares snakes through the adjoining valleys, blithely unaware that it has been responsible for creating one of the world's great outdoor art galleries. It receives help from tributary streams such as the Garganta, Cuervo, Majadilla and Hoya Calderón. Once the Manzanares has united all these waters, it enters the Garganta de la Camorza, flows past the Peña Sacra, rushes through the village of Manzanares and forms an artificial lake at the Embalse de Santillana.

Many steep paths lead upward

through the rocks from the Arroyo de la Dehesilla, and if you follow one of them to the heights of La Pedriza you encounter dozens of strangely contorted rock formations. Fallen rocks sometimes block the way, and occasionally there are bramble thickets to be circumvented, but small meadows also make their appearance; in the springtime they are covered with wild flowers such as irises and narcissi.

Before you go *Maps:* IGN 1:25,000 and 1:50,000 Nos. 508 and 509; IGN 1:200,000 Mapa Provincial of Madrid.

Getting there *By car:* the simplest way to get there from Madrid is on the A6/NVI road to Collado-Villaba, continuing on the M608 north to Manzanares; 1 km (½ mile) past the village an access road leads to the control post at the gates of La Pedriza.

By bus: there is a regular service from Madrid to the village, but no public transport to the gates of the park.

Where to stay: try the 1-star Hotel El Tranco, T: (91) 853 00 63, in Manzanares el Real. Nearby, try the 4-star Arcipreste de Hita, T: (91) 856 01 25, F: 856 02 70, in Navacerrada, or the 3-star Hotel Galaico, T: (91) 951 03 04, F: 851 03 03, in Collado-Villalba.

Outdoor living: permitted only in the special camping zone near the Embalse de Santillana.

Refuges: there is a small refuge within the park, beyond the Canto Cochino.

Access: avoid visiting the park at weekends and fiestas, when the number of admissions is limited by the park wardens.

Activities *Walking/climbing:* until fairly recently it was quite difficult to get to the heart of La Pedriza; the only access was an unpaved track that follows the Río Manzanares and leads

74

up to the chapel on the Peña Sacra, and a footpath that leads through the Garganta Camorza to the Pradera de los Lobos ('meadow of wolves') and Canto Cochino.

Nowadays you can drive to the Canto Cochino in a matter of minutes, thanks to the paved road that crosses the Collado de Quebrantaherraduras ('the horseshoe-breakers pass'). On the far side of this settlement are paths that lead beyond civilisation, to the Peña Siro, the imposing peaks of El Pájaro ('the bird'), Las Buiteras and El Cocodrilo ('the crocodile'); in the further distance lies the summit of Las Torres ('the towers').

For detailed climbing information contact the Federación Madrileña de Montañismo, p63.

Further information *Tourist office:* Madrid, p64.

Sierra de Ayllón

30 km (19 miles) south of Ayllón, containing the parque natural *of Hayedo de Tejera Negra*

The Sierra de Ayllón begins a long way south of the medieval walled city it is named after, which is one of the historic show-places of the province of Segovia. Much of the Sierra, in fact, lies in the province of Guadalajara, but large tracts of land in the Sierra used to belong to the feudal rulers of Ayllón, 30 km (19 miles) to the north, and hence the name.

Perhaps the most convenient base for a reconnaissance tour of this still unspoiled and half-forgotten Sierra is the village of Galve de Sorbe, a sleepy com-

munity of shepherds and wheat farmers at the eastern edge of the Sierra de Ayllón. The village and its ruined hilltop castle belong to Guadalajara — and also to another world. Architecturally speaking it is still in the Middle Ages, and life goes on as it did before the machine age, with farmers cutting hay with scythes and bringing in the harvest on the backs of their mules.

You can walk for miles into the open countryside, past hamlets half in ruins, through flowering meadows and into forests that ascend the adjoining low hills and gently-rounded mountains. The highest point in the range is the Pico del Lobo (2,273 m/7,457 ft). From the naturalist's point of view, the most important part of the Sierra is the Hayedo de Tejera Negra, a *parque natural* made up of a 1,391-ha (3,440-acre) beech forest. The park lies within the township of Cantalojas and includes portions of the Sorbe river valley and the valley of the Río Lillas. Its northern limit is the Pico de la Buitrera ('the vulture's peak'), which is just over 2,000 m (6,600 ft) above sea level. The beeches, however, are confined to the cooler, wetter slopes of the Sierra, from 1,300-1,800 m (4,300-5,900 ft). Elsewhere in the same range are 2 other significant stands of beech trees — the Hayedo de Puerto de la Quesera and the Hayedo de Montejo.

Before you go *Maps:* IGN 1:25,000 and 1:50,000 Nos. 432 and 459; IGN 1:200,000 Mapas Provinciales of Segovia and Guadalajara.

Guide-books: Miguel Angel López Miguel, *Guía del Macizo de Ayllón* (Madrid, 1982).

Getting there *By car:* Cantalojas, the village nearest the Hayedo de Tejera Negra, is just south of the C114, almost half-way between Ayllón and

The Sierra de la Demanda rises above the valley of the stately Río Najerilla in the wine region of Rioja

Atienza. Within the park, a forest road leads from Cantalojas to the *parque natural*, 12 km (7½ miles) from the village, though it may be impassable after heavy rains or winter snowfalls.

By bus: twice-daily service between Madrid and Campisábalos, operated by Autocares Samar (Estación Sur, in Madrid, T: (91) 468 48 39; and Estación de Autobuses, C/ Dos de Mayo, 1, Guadalajara, T: (949) 21 66 00), stops at Galve de Sorbe and Cantalojas.

Where to stay: try the 2-star Pensión Nuestra Señora del Pinar, T: (949) 30 20 29, in Galve de Sorbe.

Further information *Tourist office:* Guadalajara, p64.

Sierra de la Demanda

Sierra running east-west with mountains rising to 2,000 m (6,600 ft)

La Rioja has the best wine and some of the most magical places in Spain. Driving south from Nájera, where the remains of some medieval kings of Navarra lie in a church (equipped with its own cave), I stopped off to see another historic cave, on a hillside in the Cerro de San Lorenzo, where the 6th-century hermit, San Millán de la Congolla, passed 40 years saying prayers and performing miracles. His cave, known as the Suso monastery, holds his empty sarcophagus,

the dry bones of some monks and a row of magnificent Moorish arches.

A little further on, the rolling hills of grape-vine and wheat suddenly come to a stop, and a line of peaks 1,000 metres (3,200 ft) higher than the hills rears up and blocks the way. This is the Sierra de la Demanda, whose 2,000 m (6,600 ft) mountains are as imposing as they are unexpected. You pass 2 villages that cling to the slopes of the outermost peaks in the range, then the road plunges into a shadowy wood of birches, beeches, poplars and pine. For 15 km (9 miles) you won't meet a soul along this forest track, which has the Pancrudo mountain (2,072 m/6,798 ft) looming over it: the track leads to the most important stand of beech trees in the province of La Rioja. If you wanted to get

75

lost, you could hardly find a wilder and less inhabited spot in the Iberian peninsula.

The Sierra de la Demanda runs from east to west: San Lorenzo (2,271 m/7,451 ft) is the highest peak in La Rioja, and San Millán (2,131 m/6,980 ft), the highest mountain in the neighbouring province of Burgos. This is a very old range — over 500 million years — and for this reason the peaks are more rounded than usual.

Ideally, this is a region for quiet hikes and for wandering from village to village through unbroken forests. Toward the east the forests thin out and give way to *matorral*, but even the scrub country contains many points of interest to the naturalist. The road along the Río Najerilla towards Anguiano, for instance, is a tangle of broad-leaved shrubs over the shales of the Sierra. The lilac-striped flowers of the pale toadflax (*Linaria repens*) resemble miniature rabbits' heads, although the stems that bear them can reach up to a metre (3 feet) in height. The Lusitanian pink (*Dianthus lusitanus*) forms cushions of grey and pink beneath the silver-leaved, yellow-flowered bushes of *Genista florida*.

At Enciso, just beyond the eastern edge of the Sierra de Camero Viejo, on the Río Cidacos (about 50 km east of the Sierra de la Demanda), you can follow in the footsteps of the dinosaurs: the so-called Ruta de los Dinosaurios exhibits a series of dinosaur tracks made about 130 million years ago.

Before you go *Maps:* IGN 1:25,000 and 1:50,000 Nos. 201 202, 239 and 240 and 1:25,000 Nos. 201, 202 and 239; IGN 1:200,000 Mapas Provinciales of Burgos and La Rioja. *Guide-books:* Leopoldo Valdivielso Gómez, *Las Sierras de la Demanda y de Neila* (Federación Española de Montañismo, 1982).

Getting there *By car:* 2 roads cross the Sierra de la Demanda from north to south. From the N120 Logroño-Burgos you can either turn south at Nájera on to the C113, which follows the valley of the Najerilla to Villavelayo, or turn off at Santo Domingo de la Calzada, and follow a secondary road along the Oja river valley to Ezcaray and the peak of San Lorenzo, which lies at the heart of the Sierra. An alternative is the Logroño-Soria road, which takes you to Villanueva de

Cameros through the Iregua valley.

By bus: from Logroño, Autocares Martínez, T: (941) 21 19 18, operates services to the Valles of Iregua and Leza; Riojacar, T: (941) 24 35 72, operates services to the Valle del Oja and on up to Ezcaray; and Julio Jiménez, T: (941) 22 42 78, runs buses to San Millán.

Where to stay: interesting choices here: the Parador de Santo Domingo de la Calzada, T: (941) 34 03 00, F: 34 03 25; the Hostería Monasterio San Millán, T: (941) 37 32 77, F: 37 32 66, in San Millán; the 3-star Hotel San Fernando, T: (941) 36 37 00, F: 36 33 99, in Nájera; and the 3-star Hotel Echauren, T: (941) 35 40 47, F: 42 71 33, and Albergue de la Real Fábrica, T: (941) 35 44 74, in Ezcaray. In Logroño, try the 4-star Carlton Rioja, T: (941) 24 21 00, F: 24 35 02, or a host of smaller places.

Activities *Walking:* the Sierra de la Demanda is a very pretty area with many walks, ranging from the gentle to the strenuous. For information, check with the tourist offices.

Further information *Tourist offices:* Burgos and Logroño, see p64.

Sierra de Peña de Francia

The isolated western edge of the Central Cordillera which stretches east from Béjar to Ciudad Rodrigo

These so-called 'French' mountains are the westernmost segment of the Spanish central system (the other four parts are Ayllón, Guadarrama, Gredos and Béjar). Por-

tugal lies 50 kilometres (31 miles) to the west, France 600 kilometres (370 miles) to the north-east. The range is called the Sierra de Peña de Francia because in the 11th century, after the Christian reconquest, it was repopulated with settlers from France. This rather attenuated French connection is recalled in such place names as Río Francia, Soto de Francia, and Peña de Francia.

The Sierra de Peña de Francia is off the beaten track in many respects: agricultural development was slow to arrive in this obscure corner of Spain, and for centuries it remained an isolated and rather mysterious region of impenetrable forests and small peasant villages. Today, however, it offers an extraordinary mixture of nature and folklore: vast forest reserves, mountain pastures, villages with half-timbered medieval houses, Stone Age sites decorated with cave paintings, and hunting reserves, where deer, wild boar and small game are abundant.

Between Salamanca and the inner core of the sierra rises an outer range of mountains, of which the highest is Pico Cervero (1,463 metres/4,800 feet). Here meadows and peaks alternate with dense forests like that of La Honfría, in the *municipio* of Linares de Ríofrío, which is traversed only by footpaths and an unpaved forest road. On the southern slope the underbrush is so thick as to make the forests of Las Quilanas almost impassable; they are prime examples of Iberian vegetation in an untouched state of nature. This is the watershed of the Río Quilana, which flows into the Alagón, one of the many rivers in this region which are tributaries of the Río Tajo.

At 1,732 metres (5,682 feet) the Peña de Francia is the highest peak in the sierra, looming above the rest like a giant pyramid and affording superb views in every direction. The towers of the shrine and hospice that stand atop the mountain can be seen for miles around.

Much of the peak is bare granite, here and there sprouting a deep yellow rock daffodil (*Narcissus rupicola*), but the lower slopes are covered with the forests of oak, poplar and fern that are characteristic of the

The Spanish lynx or pardel hunts at dusk, lying in ambush or stalking its prey, mainly rabbits

zone. The surrounding valleys are carpeted in yellow and purple flowers in late spring. Past the memorable medieval village of La Alberca begins the valley of Las Batuecas, a *reserva nacional* of 20,976 hectares (51,832 acres). Carmelite nuns chose this remote spot for one of their convents in 1599. Today their erstwhile retreat, San José de Batuecas, is a monastery for Carmelite monks (who do not admit visitors either). It is said that there are 18 chapels scattered throughout the mountains, and 24 in the valley, but every one I've ever come across is in ruins. There are wolves deep in the reserve, as well as roe deer and wild boar, the Spanish imperial eagle and black vultures.

BEFORE YOU GO
Maps: IGN 1:25,000 and 1:50,000 Nos. 527, 551 and 552; IGN 1:50,000 No. 526; and IGN 1:200,000 Mapa Provincial of Salamanca.
Guide-books: J. M. Cervantes, *La Alberca, monumento nacional* (1981); L. González, *La Casa Albercana* (Salamanca, 1982).

GETTING THERE
By car: from the north, take the E80/N620, Salamanca-Ciudad Rodrigo, turning south on to

the C525 in the direction of Tamames, a village situated on the north side of the Sierra. The eastern approach, from Béjar, is via the C515 to Santibáñez de la Sierra, or you can turn off on to the C512 to Linares de Ríofrío, in the north-east.
By bus: the Adojaju company, T: (923) 12 08 00, operates a limited daily service to and from La Alberca. Departures are from the bus station in Salamanca, Avda. Filiberto Villalobos, 71-85.

WHERE TO STAY
La Alberca has the 4-star Doña Teresa, T: (923) 41 53 08, F: 41 53 09, and several other places; Cepeda, Miranda del Castañar and Sequeros each have places, as does Béjar where you might try the 3-star Hotel Colón, T/F: (923) 40 06 50.

FURTHER INFORMATION
Tourist offices: Paseo de Cervantes, 6, 37700 Béjar, T: (923) 40 30 05; Pl. Mayor, 37624 La Alberca, T: (923) 41 52 91, and Salamanca, p64.

77

Camino de Santiago

*Medieval pilgrims' route that wends its way
along the northern borders of the Meseta
to Santiago de Compostela in Galicia*

Clumps of broom flower enhance a fortress of rock in
the valley of Las Batuecas

The way from Roncesvalles, in the Pyrenees, to Santiago de Compostela in distant Galicia, is a matter of some 800 kilometres (500 miles). In the Middle Ages it was
one of the great pilgrimage routes, which
many people covered on foot and the most
pious on their knees. For centuries there
were miracles and apparitions to be seen at
every turn of the road to Santiago: you

could meet angels, beggars, kings and sta-
tus-seekers — the Plantagenet king Edward I
on horseback, St Francis of Assisi walking
barefoot, and a certain Flemish wayfarer
who is reputed to have carried a mermaid
around with him, in a tub.

You don't meet many pilgrims of the old-
fashioned sort on the Camino de Santiago
nowadays, but more than half a million people travel along the route each year. And it is
still one of the most beautiful journeys in
Europe. The miracle is that so little seems to
have changed since the Middle Ages; that
you can still cover large parts of the route on
unpaved tracks leading through fields and

forests — or occasionally on paved sections of road that were built by the Romans in order to facilitate the movement of their legions through the endless expanse of their Iberian colony. The road enters Spain from France in the high Pyrenees and winds across unforgettable countryside to the western edge of the continent. According to the old chronicles, this was where the bones of the apostle James were discovered early in the 9th century, by a local bishop who was amazed to see bright light emanating from the ground and a star pointing to the spot where the saint lay buried.

When news of the saint's whereabouts reached the rest of Europe, many thousands of devout pilgrims began converging on the cathedral that was built over his tomb — after Rome, this was the holiest place in medieval Europe. It was a spot so sacred, it was 'honoured by miracles never ceasing, and with a plenty of candles from Heaven that burn day and night, and godly Angels who serve without end'. At the beginning of the

Many valleys of the Sierra de la Demanda are planted with mixed woodland, the finest growing here in the Reserva de Cameros

11th century a progressive king of Navarra built a new road from the French border — Roncesvalles to Pamplona, Logroño, Burgos, León and towns further west. Several competing monastic orders, notably the Benedictines of Cluny, established hospices and priories along this 'French road'. Some of their more elaborate hospices had facilities for a thousand guests, and traffic along the Camino reached truly formidable proportions, especially during the summer when the pilgrim season was at its height and the road was jammed with the devout.

They came, led by their dukes and bishops, from France, Britain and Germany; from Italy, the Lowlands and the Balkans. Inevitably, there were a certain number of camp followers 'having neither office nor profession', and these were accused of bringing the pox to Santiago. Yet despite the many hazards it was considered imperative to make the journey. As Dante puts it in *La Vita Nuova*, 'He is no pilgrim who does not make his way to the tomb of St James and return therefrom'.

In the 1960s I travelled the entire length of the Camino, partly by car and frequently on foot, and was enchanted by this slow intensive way of getting to know the northern third of the Iberian peninsula. I travelled with a portable tape-recorder, taking down vestiges of the folk music of this incredibly musical country. Indeed, pockets of ancient music had survived along the more remote stretches of the road, and I was lucky enough to hear peasants in the fields singing the old reaping and threshing songs. A Castilian wheat farmer in his 70s sang an old harvesting song that must have been new in Columbus's day. 'The land is poor and the crop is bad and we have nothing to sing about,' his daughter complained, but the old man went on singing anyway, an endless chant about sailors and kings and how we shall all be equal in the grave.

The Camino of today entails crossing many major urban centres and following long stretches of main road, but some of the open country between is absolutely magnificent. The road descends from the hills of Navarra and crosses the plains of Castilla-León, then negotiates the hill country of Galicia before entering the city of Santiago — a Renaissance town with wall-to-wall streets and a 12th-century cathedral that has a Baroque façade. Such contrasts are commonplace all along the Pilgrims' Way, as old buildings are constantly adapted to new uses, pouring new wine into old bottles.

The pilgrims' road combines glimpses of a vanished medieval way of life, with long rambles through the great outdoors. The route itself is not fixed and offers many alternatives and detours, such as the one to the monastery of Santo Domingo de Silos, for example, which takes you about 50 kilometres (31 miles) south of the 'standard' Camino. As a way of discovering the heartbeat of this astonishing land, there is no more satisfying means than to travel on foot along a portion, if not all, of the Pilgrim's Way, the historic Camino de Santiago.

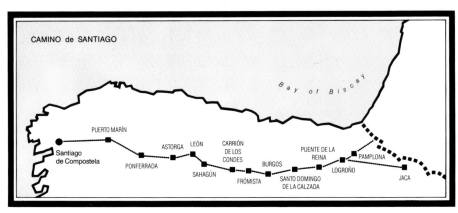

CAMINO de SANTIAGO

BEFORE YOU GO
Maps: IGN 1:600,000 Camino de Santiago, Año Santo Compostelano and IGN 1:1,000,000 Santiago en los Caminos Históricos de la Península Ibérica.
Guide-books: P. Barrett and J. N. Gurgand, *La Aventura del Camino de Santiago* (Vigo, 1982); Eusebio Goicecha Arrondo, *El Camino de Santiago* (Madrid, 1982); Walter Starkie, *The Road to Santiago: Pilgrims of St James* (London, 1957); with notes by Enrique Barco Teruel and drawings by Juan Commerleran (Codex Calixtinus), *Ruta de Santiago* (Barcelona, 1965); Robin Hanbury-Tenison, *Spanish Pilgrimage* (Charnwood, 1992).

GETTING THERE
Traditionally there were 4 main points of departure in France for the Camino de Santiago: Paris, Vezelay, Le Puy and Arles. Pilgrims from the 3 northern cities entered Spain via Roncesvalles; those from Arles travelled by way of Toulouse, Auch and Oloron, entered Spain via the pass of Somport and Canfranc, descended the Pyrenees to Jaca, and joined the main route of the Camino at Puente la Reina, 24 km (15 miles) west of Pamplona, the first major town on the northern route. The other main points of the road are Logroño, Santo Domingo de la Calzada, Burgos, Frómista, Carrión de los Condes, Sahagún, León, Astorga, Ponferrada, Portomarín and, finally, Santiago de Compostela.
By air: these days pilgrims not wishing to walk can fly directly, internationally or internally, to Santiago de Compostela.
By sea: from England, ferries go from both Plymouth and Portsmouth to Santander, although the service varies according to time of year, and from Portsmouth to Bilbao, offering a convenient approach to the Camino.
By car: you can still drive along the ancient routes from France, using the Roncesvalles or Somport passes as crossing points. All the towns and villages along the Camino have road signs and historical markers pointing the way to significant monuments associated with its history.
By rail: from Madrid, RENFE's railway network intersects with the Camino at Jaca, Pamplona, Burgos, León, Ponferrada and, of course, Santiago de Compostela. For RENFE details, see p.63.
By bus: a number of public and private buses connect the major cities of the Camino, so that you can travel the whole route by relays of buses, stopping off in small towns and villages along the way.

WHERE TO STAY
The national Parador chain has converted the following buildings, historically related to the Camino, into very beautiful hotels: the Parador de Santo Domingo de la Calzada, T: (941) 34 03 00, F: 34 03 25; the Hotel San Marcos, in León, T: (987) 23 73 00, F: 23 34 58; and the incomparable Hotel Reyes Católicos, in Santiago de Compostela, T: (981) 58 22 00, F: 56 30 94, which is not only considered to be the oldest hotel in Spain and one of the most emblematic in the world, but fills one side of the Plaza del Obradoiro — perhaps the most beautiful in Spain.
Other hotels along the Camino are: the 3-star Hotel Canfranc, T: (974) 36 31 32, F: 36 49 79, in Jaca; the 3-star Hotel Reino de Navarra Silken, T: (948) 17 75 75, F: 17 77 78, in Pamplona; the 4-star Carlton Rioja, T: (941) 24 21 00, F: 24 35 02, in Logroño; the 2-star Hotel Mesón del Peregrino, T: (948) 34 00 75, F: 34 11 90, in Puente de la Reina; the 3-star Hotel Del Cid, T: (947) 20 87 15, F: 26 94 60, in the centre of Burgos, and the 5-star Hotel Landa Palace, T: (947) 20 63 43, F: 26 46 76, just outside Burgos; the 16th-century Posada de Castrojeriz, T: (947) 37 86 10, F: 37 86 11, in Castrojeriz; the 3-star Hotel Real Monasterio San Zoilo, T: (979) 88 00 49, F: 88 10 90, in Carrión de los Condes; the 4-star Hotel Alfonso V, T: (987) 22 09 00, F: 22 12 44, in the centre of León; the small 2-star Hostería Cuca la Vaina, T/F: (987) 69 10 78, just west of Astorga; the Casa Los Abuelos, T: (987) 69 54 39, in Campo, just east of Ponferrada; the 3-star Pousada de Portomarín, T: (982) 54 52 00, F: 54 52 70, in Portomarín; and the historic 3-star Hostal Hogar San Francisco, T: (981) 57 24 63, F: 57 19 16, just a couple of hundred yards from the cathedral in the ancient centre of Santiago de Compostela.

FURTHER INFORMATION
Tourist offices:
Jaca: Avda. Regimiento de Galicia, 2, 22700, T: (974) 36 00 98, F: 35 51 65; **Pamplona:** p16; **Logroño:** p64; **Burgos:** p40; **León:** p40; **Ponferrada:** C/ Gil y Carrasco, 11, 24400, T/F: (987) 42 42 36; **Santiago de Compostela:** Rua del Villar, 43, 15705, T: (981) 58 40 81.

CHAPTER 4

South Meseta

'**S**o, like a good knight, he decided to add the name of his country to his own and call himself Don Quixote de la Mancha.'

The adventures of Don Quixote hold the same symbolic significance for the southern Meseta as the pilgrims' road has for the northern. La Mancha — originally Al Mansha, 'the dry land' or 'the wilderness' — was the Moorish name for the vast, parched plain that stretches from the mountains of Toledo to the Sierra Morena. Modern maps indicate it as a rather vague stretch of territory south of Madrid and east of Ciudad Real. Historically, it never was a province or any other formal territorial unit, but under the new Spanish constitution the five provinces of Cuenca, Ciudad Real, Toledo, Guadalajara and Albacete have come together as the autonomous region of Castilla-La Mancha, and this is the main administrative component of the great topographical region known as the southern Meseta. This region also includes Extremadura to the west, with its provinces of Cáceres and Badajoz.

Cervantes chose La Mancha as the setting for his masterpiece not only because he knew it very well personally but also because it was then a backward peasant region whose very name was calculated to bring a smile to the lips of his sophisticated urban readers. But the 20th-century La Mancha is very different from the 17th-century one, for what was once a wilderness has become one of the great wheat-growing and wine-making regions of Spain, even though there are hardly any cities to speak of,

The plains of La Mancha stretch to the horizon beyond a group of olive trees on the flat tableland of the south Meseta

only some farm villages and a scattering of six or seven market towns. Although the highway south from Madrid traverses it, tourists rarely bother to stop here as they race through Don Quixote's country on the way through to Jaén in Andalucía.

Needless to say, the true Manchegan would not trade the monotonous landscape for all the hanging gardens of Granada. But as readers of Cervantes are aware, the land is not invariably flat. Here and there the Meseta is broken by a chance row of hills, occasionally topped by the famous windmills that Don Quixote mistook for giants.

' "Take care, your worship," said Sancho, "those things over there are not giants but windmills, and what seem to be their arms are the sails, which are whirled round in the wind and make them turn."

"It is quite clear," replied Don Quixote, "that you are not experienced in this matter of adventures. They are giants and if you are afraid, go away and say your prayers, while I advance and engage them in fierce and unequal battle." '

The windmills of La Mancha are not an ancient and immutable part of the landscape. The first ones had been introduced to Spain from the Low Countries in the 1570s, about 20 years before Cervantes began writing his book, and they represented a great leap forward for Spanish technology. As Lewis Mumford points out in *Technics and Civilization*, windmills were marvels of mechanical efficiency and provided the main source of power for what he terms the eotechnic phase of machine civilization, the 'dawn of modern technics'.

When Don Quixote charged the windmills (there were 20 or 30 at that place) he was, therefore, doing battle with the menace of the machine. There is every evidence in the book to suggest that his mistaking mills for monsters was intentional, for Sancho testifies that 'nobody could mistake them, unless he has windmills on the brain'. Quixote, then, is not just literature's great child, obeying our primordial instinct to stick a probing finger into the electric fan; he is the first of the human-ecologists to challenge the implacability of the machine: 'The wind turned it with such violence that it shivered his weapon in pieces, dragging the horse and his rider with it, and sent the knight rolling badly injured across the plain'.

Of the hundreds of windmills built in La Mancha during the 16th and 17th centuries, only a handful are still in existence, most near the town of Campo de Criptana, where Quixote's encounter is supposed to have taken place. Ever since they stopped turning around the turn of the 20th century they have served a purely decorative purpose. If you want to see a far more authentic collection of windmills, take the road that runs north-west from Campo de Criptana to the town of Consuegra in the province of Toledo.

Three or four really first-rate wines are produced in the vineyards of the southern Meseta. A bottle of Valdepeñas blanco, lightly chilled by being hung in a well, is a proven antidote to the mid-afternoon heat that melts the marrow in your bones.

' "I'll bet," said Sancho, "that before long there won't be a wine-shop or a tavern, an inn or a barber's shop, where the history of our exploits won't be painted up." '

The tourist ministry has gone one better by erecting a monument to Sancho and Quixote in every town and village even remotely connected with their wanderings. There is the tavern of Don Quixote, the inn of Sancho Panza and the wine-shop of Dulcinea. In the village of El Toboso, the inhabitants take great pride in showing you their 'casa de Dulcinea', despite the fact that Cervantes' Dulcinea passes through his book as the great unattainable ideal, the eternal feminine mirage. It is, however, a perfectly good excuse for going to see the village which, though it has only one windmill, is one of the most beautiful in La Mancha: a sleepy community which has been bypassed by just about everything except literary fame.

By following in the footsteps of the ingenious Spanish gentleman, you can wander through some of the wilder and more forgotten landscapes of the southern Meseta. But, as elsewhere in Spain, the real wilderness begins where the mountains commence, at the periphery of the plains and valleys. In the west, the Parque Natural de Monfragüe straddles the banks of the now-dammed Tajo (Tagus) as it flows between two mountain ranges, the Sierra de Gredos and the north slope of the Sierra de Guadalupe, before commencing its descent through Portugal to the Atlantic. In the east there is the Parque Natural del Alto Tajo, which embraces the river's swift-flowing head-waters in Guadalajara province. Further to the south, the Serranía de Cuenca forms part of the Meseta's eastern margin: it is

a mountain range full of mineral springs and the beginnings of streams such as the Río Cuervo, which tumbles over mossy banks and small caves before beginning its long journey to the Guadiela and the Tajo.

By contrast, the nearby Montes Universales are more like a Jules Verne conception of the mountains of Mars or Jupiter; although the Tajo rises here (in the form of a barely discernible trickle), these are noticeably dry mountains, often devoid of topsoil. Thanks to the absence of human habitation, however, it is a region that provides a favourable habitat for eagles, vultures, kites and falcons. The neighbouring Sierra de Albarracín is also full of wild places and mountain villages almost high enough to have you panting for oxygen; this was once part of a tiny Arab kingdom and it still strikes me as a world apart. Unfortunately, it is not enough for a nature reserve to be off the beaten track in order for it to survive; Las Tablas de Daimiel, a wetland ecosystem considered important enough to qualify as the one national park in the southern Meseta, is in danger of drying up, owing to agricultural depletion of the underground waters that used to fill these lakes and marshes to overflowing. Which only goes to prove that nowadays even the wilderness has to be managed.

BEFORE YOU GO
Maps: Michelin 1:400,000 No. 444.

GETTING THERE
By air: Madrid is well served by international flights from Europe and the rest of the world, as well as being the hub of the internal network. València receives international flights from Europe and internal flights.
By car: the only motorways in

this region are the E90/NII Madrid-Zaragoza and the E901/N3 Madrid-València roads. Other roads range from secondary to mountain roads in very poor condition, many of them impassable in winter.
By rail: RENFE's most useful lines in this area are Madrid to Cuenca; Madrid to Albacete; Madrid to Ciudad Real (on the high-speed AVE train); Madrid to Manzanares/Valdepeñas; and Zaragoza to València, via

Teruel. For information, call RENFE in Madrid, T: (91) 328 90 20, or check the schedules on RENFE's web-site, www.renfe.es.
By bus: there are long-distance buses from Madrid, Estación Sur, T: (91) 468 45 11, to the major cities of the southern Meseta. Local bus companies provide services to the towns and villages of the region. Schedules can vary with the seasons, or simply change, so

check with local tourist offices where specific information is not given in the entries for individual exploration zones.

WHERE TO STAY

Paradores are well represented throughout the southern Meseta; the one at Cuenca has marvellous views of the Hanging Houses, *Casas Colgadas*, and the one at Almagro is particularly historic and beautiful.

The best towns and villages in which to find accommodation are listed in the individual entries. For more detailed lists contact the local tourist offices.

ACTIVITIES

Mountaineering clubs:
Federación de Deportes de Montaña de Castilla-La Mancha, Hellin, 60, 02002 Albacete, T: (967) 24 67 21; Federación Aragonesa de Montañismo, Albareda, 7, 50004 Zaragoza, T: (976) 22 79 71, F: 21 24 59.

Fishing: Federación Castellana-Manchega, Travesía Más de Ribero, 13, 45004 Toledo, T: (925) 22 65 38.

FURTHER INFORMATION

Albacete (967): tourist office, "Posada del Rosario", C/ Tinte, 2, 02071, T: 58 05 22. Red Cross, T: 21 90 50, F: 24 29 77.
Albarracín (978): tourist office, Pl. Mayor, 1, 44100, T: 71 02 51.
Aranjuez : tourist office, Pl. de Santiago Rusiñol, web-site: www.ribernet.es/aranjuez.
Cáceres (927): tourist office, Pl. Mayor, 3, 10003, T: 24 63 47. Red Cross, T: 24 78 58, F: 21 05 99.
Ciudad Real (926): tourist

office, C/ Alarcos, 21, 13080, T: 21 20 03. Red Cross, T: 22 97 99, F: 25 44 56.
Cuenca (969): tourist office, Pl. Mayor, 1, 16002, T: 23 21 19, F: 23 53 56. Red Cross, T: 23 01 31, F: 22 94 20.
Guadalajara (949): tourist office, Pl. de los Caídos, 6, 19001, T: 21 16 26. Red Cross, T: 22 11 84, F: 23 20 43.
Madrid (91): tourist office, Pl. Mayor, 3, 28012, T: 366 48 74. Red Cross, T: 533 66 65, F: 553 25 79.
Teruel (978): tourist office, Tomás Nogués, 1, 44001, T: 60 22 79. Red Cross, T: 60 26 09, F: 60 03 86.

FURTHER READING

Alistair Boyd, *The Companion Guide to Madrid and Central Spain* (London, 1974); Fernando Chueca Goitia, *Madrid and Toledo* (London).

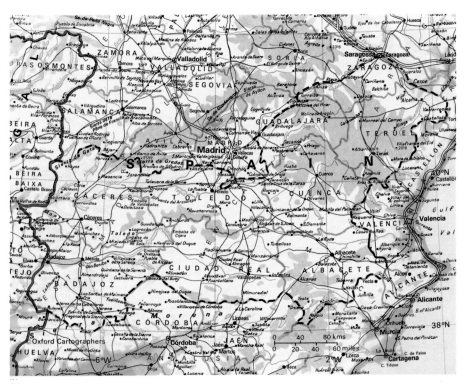

Serranía de Cuenca

Mountain range to the east of Madrid, including the Ciudad Encantada and several protected areas

High above the head-waters of the Tajo rise the peaks of the Serranía de Cuenca, a chain of mountains occupying the north-east corner of the province of Cuenca. They form the western rampart of a major massif that also includes the Montes Universales and the Sierra de Albarracín. A number of subordinate sierras are contained within the Serranía de Cuenca: the Sierra de Tragacete, de los Palancares, de las Cuerdas, de Mira and de Bascuñana. The highest peak in the system is the Cerro de San Felipe (1,839 metres/6,030 feet), near Tragacete.

The range is full of quirks and surprises: hot springs, caves, cliff-hanging villages, an

The Río Cuervo is the most magical of the many rivers that spring from the 'enchanted' rocks of the Serranía de Cuenca

'enchanted city' of natural sculptures and rivers that pour out of fissures in the mountainside. The Ciudad Encantada resembles the ruins of some prehistoric city: huge blocks of limestone, sculpted into weird shapes by erosion, lie scattered through a 2,000-hectare (4,900-acre) forest where you can exercise your imagination by trying to identify 'El Teatro', the 'Roman Bridge', 'The Ships' and whatnot. But apart from this famous tourist attraction, the Serranía de Cuenca will reward patient study and quiet walking tours.

Plants of interest include *Antirrhinum pulverulentum*, a hairy, pale-yellow snapdragon with leathery leaves that grows from rock crevices; *Saxifraga fragilis* (also known as *S. corbariensis*), a cushion-forming saxifrage with glaucous, tough leaves; *Leucanthemopsis pallida*, a composite with silvery-haired leaves from which rise slender flowering stems, each with a pale-yellow bloom; and the strange poppy, *Sarcocapnos enneaphylla*, which creeps across sheer rock faces, a bundle of irregular yellow-white flowers in a nest of blue-green trifoliate leaves.

The Serranía de Cuenca generally is rich in orchid species, with woodcock and late spider orchids (*Ophrys scolopax* and *O. sphegodes*) numbering among the more exotic. There are seven helleborine species from a range of habitats, including the marsh helleborine (*Epipactis palustris*) and the red helleborine (*Cephalanthera rubra*), which is restricted to calcareous woodlands. Burnt-tip orchids (*Orchis ustulata*) and frog orchids (*Coeloglossum viride*) also favour lime-rich soils, as does the violet bird's-nest orchid (*Limodorum abortivum*). Three rare butterflies have been recorded here: the large blue (*Maculinea arion*), the spring ringlet (*Erebia epistygne* ssp *andera*) and iolas blue (*Iolana iolas*).

One day at the village of Beteta — the word means 'splendid' in Arabic — I went looking for one of the local mineral springs that reportedly issues from beneath a chapel-shrine to La Virgen del Rosal, the Madonna of the Rosebush. I finally found it, too, at an abandoned farm near the village, steadily pouring forth its medicinal waters, which were being used further downhill to irrigate an orchard. Nearby there is a second spring, no less therapeutic, of rose-tinted, ferruginous water said to be a cure for anaemia. Higher up on the mountain stand the ruins of the chapel and a tangled forest of pine.

There are mineral springs throughout the region, and even one or two spas that are still in operation, notably the one at Solán de Cabras. The Río Cuervo, which eventually flows into the Guadiela and the Tajo, also begins as a mineral spring; its source high in the Serranía is a far more interesting spot than the source of the Tajo across the way in the Montes Universales. Part of the river comes pouring out of a cave in the mountain; another cascades over a series of rocks and caverns, covering their entrances with a curtain of rivulets. This specially protected area is not far from another of the Serranía's main talking-points, the Parque Cinegético del Hosquillo, which occupies about 1,000 hectares (2,400 acres) in the centre of the immense area known as the Reserva Nacional de la Serranía de Cuenca.

The Hosquillo park, which was founded in 1964, lies within a valley flanked by Cerro Gordo, El Pajarero and El Barranco, and traversed by the Río Escabas; it has become one of the country's main deer-breeding stations and is separated from the rest of the reserve by a high wire fence (park entrance is restricted). Within it live red, fallow and roe deer, brown bears and wild boar; the area is also known for its otters, eagles and griffon vultures. More accessible is the Serranía's *reserva nacional*, adjoining the Montes Universales. It contains superb forests and deep valleys inhabited by deer, boar and several species of raptor; its mountains and ravines are virtually untrodden by tourist feet but known to specialists for their geological and ecological interest.

BEFORE YOU GO
Maps: IGN 1:25,000 and 1:50,000 Nos. 565, 587, 588, 610, 611 and 612; and IGN 1:200,000 Mapa Provincial of Cuenca.

GETTING THERE
By car: the most direct approach is via Cuenca, or you can traverse the mountains from Molina de Aragón or Teruel.
By rail: there are direct services

from Madrid or Valencia to Cuenca.
By bus: bus services from Cuenca to the villages of the Serranía, usually only one a day — sometimes more in the summer — are run by Empresa Campi, T: (969) 22 14 65, to Beteta; Empresa La Rápida, T: (969) 22 27 51, to Cañete; and Empresa Rodríguez, T: (969) 22 64 87, to Tragacete. All start from the bus station at C/ Fermín Caballero, T: (969) 22

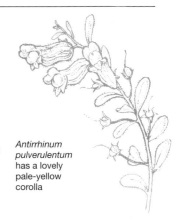

Antirrhinum pulverulentum has a lovely pale-yellow corolla

The large blue flies in June and July high on the bare Montes Universales

70 87. There is an afternoon bus, run by Agreda, T: (969) 22 94 11, from Ramón y Cajal, 57, to the source of the Río Cuervo; but no services to El Hosquillo, which can only be visited with prior permission.

WHERE TO STAY

In Cuenca, some distance from the Serranía, there are numerous places; try the Parador, T: (969) 23 23 20, F: 23 25 34, or the 3-star Leonor de Aquitania, T: (969) 23 10 00, F: 23 10 04, which is in the old town. In the countryside outside Cuenca the 3-star Cueva de Fraile, T: (969) 21 15 71, F: 25 60 47, is a good choice. Beteta, in the north, offers the 2-star Hotel Los Tilos, T: (969) 31 80 98, F: 31 82 99, and Cañete, in the south, has the charming 3-star Hostería de Cañete, T: (969) 34 60 45. The 2-star Balnearios Solán de Cabras, T: (969) 31 30 70, F: 31 31 14, in Beteta, offers an interesting alternative. **Outdoor living:** Camping La Dehesa, T: (969) 31 04 71, in Cañamares, is open over Easter and July-Aug and holds 216.

ACTIVITIES

Walking: paths that traverse the Serranía are not marked but there is plenty of scope here for easy walking through pine forests and strange rock formations. From the mountains above Cuenca, there is a splendid view over the plains of La Mancha.

The best way to see the Ciudad Encantada is to get as far away from the tourists as possible. It is an extraordinary area littered with some gigantic rocks, wind-blown and water-worn into intriguing shapes and forms. The park is some 27 km (17 miles) north of Cuenca, and is open sunrise to sunset. **Caves:** near the small village of Villar del Humo are some interesting palaeolithic cave paintings.

FURTHER INFORMATION

Tourist office: Cuenca, p86.
Mountaineering club: Castilla-La Mancha, p85.

Montes Universales

Birth-place of the Río Tajo; bare mountains, snow-covered for up to eight months of the year

An immensely pompous monument more suited to the Rockefeller Center marks the spot, but no matter: just behind the *nacimiento* (birth-place) of the Tajo lies a wonderful area, a happy tableland for sheep, designed as though by a Japanese master in the art of landscape architecture. Low shrubs grow in dark-green circles against a grey limestone background, like polka-dots in a giant *bata de lunares*, the dress of the *flamenco bailadora*. Here and there a red-roofed shepherd's hut is outlined against the green polka-dots, or an equally cubist sheep corral.

The mountains are bare, wind-swept and beautiful, rising to about 1,800 m (5,900 ft). Above the beginnings of the Tajo looms the massive Muela de San Juan ('St John's Molar'), whose heights are snow-covered for eight months of the year. The former state institution for nature conservation, ICONA, planted pine forests on the Montes Universales, but the most fascinating landscapes are the half-bare mountainsides with their fragrant herbs and wild flowers. They are inhabited by deer, wild boar, hares, rabbits, partridges and large raptors. Here you may find the large blue butterfly (*Maculinea arion*), which has the most famous and well-studied symbiotic relationship with ants (of the species *Myrmica sabuleti*) in Spain: the larval butterflies are carried into the nest by the ants when they reach their final instar, where they spend the winter. This is also one of the few places in the world (apart from Alaska) where I have seen an eagle feasting on a hare, not far from a path regularly used by human beings. For lovers of solitude this quasi-Tibetan landscape is a godsend. **Before you go** *Maps:* IGN 1:25,000 and 1:50,000 Nos. 565, 566, 588 and 589; IGN 1:200,000 Mapas Provinciales of Cuenca and Teruel. **Getting there:** there is no way to get into the mountains by public transport. Auto Transportes Teruel, T: (978) 60 26 80, operates a daily afternoon service between Teruel and Albarracín. *By car:* the Montes Universales can be approached from either Albarracín or Guadalaviar in the province of Teruel, or Tragacete in Cuenca. The Tragacete-Frías de Albarracín road leads through the Montes and past the source of the Tajo; many forestry tracks lead off from this road.

Only one metalled road traverses the Montes, although others lead up to its slopes and then come to a stop. Another road leads from Toril (south of Albarracin) to the villages of Masegoso and El Vallecillo, where carefully tilled fields alternate with wild mountain scenery; the road carries on towards Tragacete, but is unpaved. Half-way between the two villages a road takes you to the falls of the Río Cabriel, beside the Molino de San

Pedro. Nearby stand some of the oldest pines in the sierra, with enormous trunks that are nearly 4 m (13 ft) in circumference.

Where to stay: choose from among the Parador Teruel, T: (978) 60 18 00, F: 60 86 12, the 3-star Hotel Reina Cristina, T: (978) 60 68 60, F: 60 53 63, and a host of others in Teruel; the 3-star Hotel Albarracín, T/F: (978) 71 00 11, and a surprising number of smaller places, in Albarracín; the 2-star Hotel Ballester, T: (978) 70 10 84, or the Casa Julia, T: (978) 70 11 65, in Bronchales; other *casas rurales* are La Sabina, T: (978)

70 51 43, in Calomarde; Casa Vicente, T: (978) 70 10 33, in Pozondón; and Peña el Castillo, T: (978) 70 60 68, in Tramacastilla.

Activities *Walking:* Forestry tracks lead off the Tragacete-Frías de Albarracín road. Paths are not marked. For information about mountaineering, walking routes and cave exploration, contact the local tourist offices or the mountaineering clubs of Castilla-La Mancha and Aragonesa, p85.

Further information *Tourist offices:* Albarracín and Teruel, p86.

Sierra de Albarracín

Rugged reserva nacional *with ancient pine forests and meadowlands near the city of Teruel*

The Sierra de Albarracín always was a world apart, as much in its history as its geography. In Muslim Spain, Albarracín was ruled as an independent kingdom by the family of Aben Racin — hence the name — as a vassal state of the caliphate of Córdoba. Today it is part of the province of Teruel, in Aragón, yet it seems to be a separate enclave, neither quite Aragonese nor Castilian, and it is one of the best places in Spain to see medieval stone villages and hamlets in their original setting of fields, meadows and forests. The sierra extends roughly from the Cuenca border to the town of Gea de Albarracín, but its focal point is the beautiful town of Albarracín itself — an almost perfectly preserved walled city of the Middle Ages.

Tramacastilla, 18 kilometres (11 miles) to the west of the town, is the point of departure for excursions into pine-clad mountains and the valley of Noguera, to the north, or the fieldstone villages of Villar del Cobo and Griegos, both of which claim to be even higher than Trevélez in the Alpujarras (Andalucía), the highest village in Spain. To reach them you pass through some of the steepest ravines and most rugged landscape in the whole of Spain.

Toward Orihuela del Tremedal stretches a great tableland at over 1,600 metres (5,250 feet) that contains ancient pine forests and

The contrasting wildernesses of the Montes Universales (left) and the Sierra de Albarracín (opposite page) are both easily reached from the medieval city of Albarracín.

fertile meadows in which red deer are a common sight. The land gradually rises to the Sierra Alta (1,855 metres/6,085 feet). Here the bare limestone screes take on a mantle of pink-purple in summer from the flowers of the storksbill *Erodium daucoides.* *Ranunculus gregarius*, a yellow buttercup with kidney-shaped leaves in a basal rosette, also grows at this height. More unusual is *Astragalus turolensis*, a milk-vetch normally found in North Africa. This is the only population in Spain of the low-growing, yellow-flowered legume and it supports the larvae of the rare violet-suffused zephyr blue butterfly (of the race *hespericus* in Albarracín). The zephyr blue flies in May on gentle slopes, usually over limestone, between 400-1,100 metres (1,300-3,600 feet) in altitude, and lives in extremely small colonies. Other rare or endangered species of butterfly found in the sierra include the American painted lady (*Cynthia virginiensis*), which thrives on flowery mountain slopes and is thought to breed here; and the Iolas blue (*Iolana iolas*), a large butterfly with silver underwings and lustrous azure upperwings — it has a symbiotic relationship with ants of the genus *Myr-*

mica, often in conjunction with the larvae of the more common long-tailed blue.

From the Sierra Alta there is a panoramic view of the 59,000-hectare (146,000-acre) *reserva nacional* of the sierra, established by ICONA in 1973 as a means of protecting the forest and meadowlands of eleven villages. But the inhabitants of some of these villages are far from happy with the result. The farmers of Guadalaviar and Villar del Cobo complain that the deer are destroying their crops and vegetable gardens. In a referendum on the question, '*Reserva sí, reserva no*', 98 per cent of the villagers voted against it, and the issue remains a political football. The local shepherds point out that the law forbids them to leave their goats untended lest they destroy young pines — but the pines, they say, are being destroyed anyway by young deer. Whatever the rights and wrongs of this situation, a walk through the Sierra de Albarracín is almost like a visit back to the Middle Ages, when peasant communities were still working out what ecological compromises they could make with the natural environment out beyond their doorstep.

BEFORE YOU GO
Maps: IGN 1:25,000 and 1:50,000 Nos. 565, 566, 588 and 589; and IGN 1:200,000 Mapa Provincial of Teruel.
Guide-books: J. Albi, *Albarracín y su Serranía* (Everest, 1976).

GETTING THERE
By car: the most direct approach is from the east, along the Teruel-Albarracín road.
By rail: the nearest train station is Teruel, on the Zaragoza-València line.
By bus: Auto Transportes Teruel, T: (978) 60 26 80, operates a daily afternoon service between Teruel and Albarracín.

WHERE TO STAY
See the Montes Universales fact-pack, p90.

ACTIVITIES
Walking: there is an endless variety of trails in the area.

FURTHER INFORMATION
Tourist offices: Teruel and Albarracín, p86.

The lilac-coloured *Erodium daucoides* colonizes barren mountain scree

Mountaineering clubs: Castilla-La Mancha and Aragonesa, p85.

Alto Tajo

Parque natural *just outside Molina de Aragón*
16,940 ha (41,860 acres)

One evening I drove from Sacecorbo to Molina de Aragón, a distance of well over 100 km (60 miles), and did not meet so much as one other car on the road until I came to the outskirts of Molina. I felt utterly alone, surrounded only by trees and sky, in this glorious natural park of the Alto Tajo — the Upper Tagus.

The Tajo rises, in fact, in the Montes Universales, south-east of the *parque natural*, but when it reaches this part of Guadalajara it already has the strength of a young giant, running swift and clear, forcing its way between immense red-and-ochre limestone cliffs that time has eroded into fantastic, phantasmagorical shapes. It makes long loops through the hills and meets the Río Gallo at Puente de San Pedro; a memorable spot, which has been described as 'one of the fairest sights in Spain'. Collecting fresh tributaries at every turn, it soon acquires such power that it can carry heavy timbers downstream, from Peralejos to the royal river port at Aranjuez. Building rafts of up-country logs and poling them down river used to be the dangerous occupation of the men known as *gancheros del Tajo* — the *gancho* was the long-staved grappling hook they used to shepherd their logs through the narrows — who often lost their lives in the furious onrush of a turbulent river choked with fast-moving logs. Modern technology has since made them redundant but their exploits are still spoken of with awe by the older villagers of the Alto Tajo.

Walking the full length of the upper Tajo can be an unforgettable experience for hikers with thick boots and strong legs. Most of the countryside is as pristine and unspoiled as it was on the eighth day of Creation, with mountains, valleys, meadows and rivers, and countless hiking paths that are rarely trodden by alien feet. Beyond the park is an ancient spa, the Balneario, called La Esperanza ('hope'). At this point, the Tajo enters a reservoir, the Embalse de Entrepeñas, where it ceases to be the swift-running river of the *gancheros*.

Before you go *Maps:* IGN 1:25,000 and 1:50,000 Nos. 488, 489, 513, 514 and 539; and IGN 1:200,000 Mapa Provincial of Guadalajara.
Getting there *By car:* Molina de Aragón is best reached via the N211, which branches off the Madrid-Zaragoza E90/NII at Alcolea del Pinar.
By bus: Autocares Samar, T: (91) 468 42 36, operates services from Madrid Estación Sur, and Teruel, T: (978) 60 34 50, to Molina de Aragón, Bar San Juan, T: (949) 83 01 85.

Public transportation between the villages is limited; far better to use a car.
Where to stay: the charming Molina de Aragón has accommodation ranging from the historic 4-star Hotel La Subalterna, T: (949) 83 23 63, F: 83 23 18, to the Casa Rural Asensio, T: (949) 83 00 52, or www.molina-aragon.com/asensio. Peralejos de las Truchas has a handful of places, including the Hostal del Tajo, T: (949) 83 70 34, and the Pensión El Molino, T: (949) 83 70 72. Zaorejas has the Hostal Martínez, T: (949) 81 61 29, the Pensión Quinto Pino, T: (949) 81 61 02, and a *casa rural*, T: (949) 81 61 16. In Escalera, look for the small, charming Hotel El Descansillo, T/F: (949) 83 12 52, while Cifuentes has two *hostales*, the San Roque, T: (949) 81 00 28, F: 81 07 55, and Las Secuollas, T: (949) 81 00 37. Check the tourist office for more details.
Activities *Walking:* the 2 base-camp towns from which explorations are best undertaken are Cifuentes, just to the west of the park, and Molina de Aragón, not far from the north-east corner.

You can follow the course of the river, starting at the southern extremity of the park and walking northwards until the Tajo swings westward in a great arc. Peralejos de las Truchas (the *truchas* are the mountain trout for which the village is famous) can be reached in a 2-day hike from Molina de Aragón, the county seat, but you may want to set aside an extra day to visit the Barranco de la Hoz ('the sickle gorge'), where high cliffs loom above the poplars lining the Río Gallo. There is a small shrine to the Virgen de la Hoz here, a simple image of the Madonna that stands in a sanctuary that is half-cave, half-chapel.

If you have time for just a single day's excursion, a good place to spend it is at or near Villanueva de Alorcón, which is known for its local peak, La Zapatilla ('the slipper') — an easy climb — and for the waterfall called El Hundido de Armallones, another outstanding bit of scenery. Whichever route you choose, it is advisable to take along a bottle of insect repellent; for some reason, this magnificent landscape is more insect-ridden than most of the rest of Spain.
Further information *Tourist office:* Carmen, 1, 19071 Molina de Aragón, T/F: (949) 83 24 53. *Mountaineering club:* Castilla-La Mancha, p85.

Laguna de Gallocanta

Largest natural inland lake in Spain (1,400 ha/3,500 acres) in the southernmost part of Zaragoza
Ramsar

Situated in an otherwise fairly desolate landscape, this is one of the Iberian peninsula's great bird-watching sites. During the great winter waterfowl

migrations the sky above the lake of Gallocanta is often black with birds; 80 different species have been recorded here, and Gallocanta is particularly noted as one of the major wintering haunts of the European crane. Feeding during the day on the surrounding fields, up to 8,000 of these great birds come to roost each evening from Nov to Feb. By the beginning of March they are on their way northwards along a traditional route that eventually leads them to the southern shores of the Baltic.

The *laguna* is also the main watering-ground in Europe of the red-crested pochard, plus there are hen and marsh harriers in the reed-beds and red kites soaring overhead. Pin-tailed sandgrouse, pigeon-like birds of the arid regions, with needle-like tail feathers that trail somewhat in flight, come to drink, and the whole area is alive with larks.

The number of birds fluctuates dramatically from one year to the next. In 1978 some 200,000 birds were estimated to have used the lake as a stopover point; by 1981 the number had dropped to 50,000.

Located at 1,000 m (3,300 ft) above sea level in the southernmost part of the province of Zaragoza, not far from Daroca, the Laguna de Gallocanta is of geological interest, too. It covers about 1,400 ha (3,500 acres) — which makes it the largest natural inland lake in Spain. It is connected to a subsidiary *lagunazo* at the northern end, and, on the opposite side, to a labyrinthine appendix of reeds and ponds known as the

The waters of the Ruidera lagoons abound in eels and other fish, food for the herons and egrets that stalk the dense reed-beds

Lagunazos de Tornos. The local farmers grow sunflowers and wheat in the surrounding fields, although there is also a lot of dry pastureland and some fields of thyme. The trees that once surrounded the lake have vanished, but there are pines and holm oaks in the nearby hills.

Before you go *Maps:* IGN 1:25,000 and 1:50,000 Nos. 464 465, 490 and 491; and IGN Mapa Provincial of Zaragoza.
Getting there *By car:* from Daroca, take the A211 (towards Molina de Aragón) to Santed; shortly afterwards turn left to the village and *laguna* of

Gallocanta. From Calamocha, south of Daroca on the N334, take the A1507 towards the *laguna* and village.
By bus: the bus service that comes closest is from Daroca to Santed, a few km from the village and *laguna* of Gallocanta. Autobuses Tezaza, T: (976) 27 61 79, runs buses between Zaragoza and Teruel, via Daroca and Calamocha.
Where to stay: Posada del Almudi, T: (976) 80 06 06, F: 80 11 41, in Daroca; 2-star Hotel Fidalgo, T: (978) 70 03 57, F: 73 02 77, in Calamocha; Albergue Allucant, T: (976) 80 31 57, F: 80 30 90, in Gallocanta, or 3-star Hotel Calatayud, T: (976) 88 13 23, F: 88 54 38, in Calatayud.
Further information *Tourist office:* Guadalajara, p86.

The remote region of the Alto Tajo preserves primitive rugged landscapes and an equally primitive way of life

Las Lagunas de Ruidera

Group of eleven lakes centred on the town of Ruidera; parque natural *Ramsar, ZEPA*

Cervantes, in *Don Quixote*, says that there are seven of these small lakes; in actual fact there are eleven. You sense their presence even before you finally see them, after driving through some of the driest countryside in Spain. This, indeed, is Don Quixote country — La Mancha, the sunbaked Arabic 'wilderness' whose heatwaves had a notoriously hallucinogenic effect on the wits. The road from Argamasilla de Alba to Ruidera is lined with poplars and there are gentle undulations in the flat Manchegan landscape, announcing an imminent change of scenery.

At the Embalse de Peñarroya the plain turns into hills and you find yourself in another, friendlier, habitat. The first natural lake along the route is Cenagosa, accompanied by an incessant clamour of birds, for whom this *zona húmeda manchega* is an oasis in the desert (the more so since the Tablas de Daimiel are drying up). The reeds and bullrushes along its shore provide perfect cover for many kinds of duck. A little further on, already accustomed to the cooling air that rises from these unexpected bodies of water, you come across another *laguna*, La Colgadilla, which receives much of its water via subterranean filtration from the great cavecum-storage deposit known as the Cueva de la Morenilla.

Not far from the sleepy village of Ruidera are the two largest lakes, the Laguna del Rey and La Gran Colgada. The fell hand of tourism has lately made itself felt hereabouts in the form of small hotels, camp-sites and private villas. Even so, the birds have not been driven away and ducks, herons and egrets especially flock to these remarkably clear lakes in significant numbers.

The road from Ruidera winds along their banks and gradually ascends from one lake to the next, for each is just a step higher than its neighbour. Just after several small *lagunas* — Batana, Santo Amorcillo and Salvadora — is La Lengua, which is sausage-shaped and full of fish, hence much frequented by anglers. It receives most of its water via a row of small falls and rivulets that pour into it from the next link up in the chain, Redondilla. This, in turn, receives water from San Pedro, whose shore is partly lined with houses and plant nurseries. At last you reach the highest and least visited, the Laguna Conceja, with its marshy shoreline and wooded surrounding hills.

I have spent some extremely pleasant nights on the shores of Laguna Redondilla, and woken up at dawn to hear a philharmonic chorus of birds such as I have rarely encountered anywhere else, even in the remotest of bird sanctuaries. Their vocal enthusiasm is perfectly understandable, for these crystalline lakes are in such stark contrast with the parched *maquis* of the encircling hills.

The name Ruidera is said to derive from the noise (*ruido*) made by the water running from lake to lake, which stretches along a total of 25 kilometres (16 miles), with a dif-

Under cover of the reeds, the great crested grebe builds a nest surrounded by water

ference of 128 metres (420 feet) in height between the southernmost pool, La Blanca, and Cenagosa at the northern end. Geologists have demonstrated that while some of the water runs from one lake to the other along surface streams and cascades, it also flows underground, through layers of clay and gypsum or sandstone.

The protected area of the Parque Natural de Ruidera includes not only the lakes but also the tributary valley of San Pedro, with the ruins of Rochafrida castle and the cave of Montesinos, which plays such an important role in the second part of Don Quixote. The ruins of the castle are perched close to the cave atop a limestone redoubt that overlooks a cultivated field, which must also have been a shallow pool before it was subdued by mules and a plough.

These are literary landmarks. Rochafrida is mentioned in Spanish medieval romances, although it was already in ruins when Cervantes roamed this district as a tithe proctor for the Knights of St John at Argamasilla. Hence Don Quixote must go underground to meet the heroes of his ever-romantic imagination: Montesinos, Belerma, Durandarte. Here he learns that the inhabitants of the cave, Guadiana and Ruidera, together with their seven daughters and two nieces, have been transformed into a river and several lakes by Merlin the magician.

Indeed the traditional explanation is that the lake at the bottom of Montesinos's cave, which is said to communicate with the Laguna de San Pedro via an underground stream, constitutes the real source of the Río Guadiana. The Lagunas de Ruidera, as a group, were reputed to be the head-waters of an eccentric and recalcitrant stream that went underground again after the Cenagosa, only to reappear 40 kilometres (25 miles) to the west, at the Tablas de Daimiel. Some geologists have recently questioned the hypothesis that this really is the subterranean Guadiana, and the argument continues to exercise some of the best scientific minds of Spain.

The great subterranean reservoir, through which the river supposedly flowed westward, has been tapped by the pumps of the wine-growers of Tomelloso, and the wetlands of the Tablas de Daimiel have ceased to be the great national park they once were. But the Lagunas de Ruidera are upstream from the pumps, and thus more precious than ever.

BEFORE YOU GO
Maps: IGN 1:25,000 and 1:50,000 Nos. 762, 763, 787 and 788; and IGN 1:200,000 Mapas Provinciales of Albacete and Ciudad Real.

GETTING THERE
By car: the village of Ruidera is half-way between Manzanares and Albacete, on the N430. Manzanares is on the E5/NIV Autovía de Andalucía, linking Madrid and Andalucía.
By bus: Francisco Gómez, T: (967) 22 32 75, runs one daily bus each way between Albacete and Ossa de Montiel, but there is no public transport to the *lagunas*.

WHERE TO STAY
There are several places alongside the *lagunas*. Try the 3-star Aparthotel Albamanjón, T: (926) 69 90 48, F: 69 91 20, on the Laguna de San Pedro; Hostal Los Leones, T: (926) 69 90 56, on the Laguna Tomilla; and the 2-star Hotel Entrelagos, T/F: (926) 52 80 22, in Ruidera, where there are several other places. Not far away is the 3-star Hotel Ramomar, T: (926) 50 59 94, F: 50 53 65, in Tomelloso, and the historic Hospedería Real Buscón de Quevedo, T/F: (926) 36 17 88, in Villanueva de los Infantes. In Manzanares try the 3-star Hotel El Cruce, T: (926) 61 19 00, F: 61 19 12.
Outdoor living: Camping Los Molinos, T: (926) 52 80 89, in Ruidera is open at Easter and 1 July-15 Sept, and holds 80 people; Camping Los Batanes, T: (926) 69 90 76, is located near the Laguna de San Pedro and holds 1,500 people.

ACTIVITIES
Fishing: permits can be obtained from the tourist offices in Ciudad Real and Albacete. More information from the fishing club Castellana-Manchega, Travesía Más de Ribero, 13, 45004 Toledo, T: (925) 22 65 38.
Cave: the road to Montesinos's cave begins at the Laguna de San Pedro, and takes you almost to its entrance.

FURTHER INFORMATION
Tourist offices: Albacete and Ciudad Real, p86.
Park office: the Centro de Recepción, Lagunas de Ruidera, T: (926) 52 81 16, is open Mon-Sun 10 am-2 pm and 5:30-9 pm.

Tablas de Daimiel

Parque nacional *that was once one of the great wetlands of Europe; 40 km (25 miles) from Ciudad Real*
Ramsar, ZEPA, Biosphere Reserve
1,928 ha (4,764 acres)

The Tablas de Daimiel have achieved an international reputation as one of the most important wetland reserves of Spain. But the fact that the *tablas* were declared a *reserva nacional* in 1966, then a *parque nacional* in 1973, has not managed to save them from the consequences of sweeping ecological and economic change.

As you approach the village of Daimiel from any direction, you pass vast areas of newly planted vineyards that are irrigated with water pumped up from artesian wells.

The shrunken lagoons of the Tablas de Daimiel, once the Venice of La Mancha, were formerly a magnet for red-breasted pochard and other mainly surface-feeding duck

The vineyards are thriving under the blazing sun of La Mancha, and there are signs of flourishing modern farms and agricultural co-operatives. The cumulative result, however, is that the Río Guadiana has been pumped dry and the Cigüela has been both diverted and polluted. In 1982 the Guadiana dried up for the first time; now, the Tablas de Daimiel have almost ceased to exist as a way-station or a breeding ground for wildfowl. At the beginning of summer, there is no sign in the park that this was formerly one of the great marshlands of Europe — only a few stagnant pools remain to suggest that this was not entirely a wilderness of thistles and scrub.

The authorities responsible for the national park have declared an environmental emergency and are attempting to impose water conservation measures that will restore the *tablas* to something approaching their original state.

The Manchegans use the word *tablas* for the shallow lagoons that form when the river overflows its banks in winter. Most of the *tablas* always did dry up during the summer droughts, but there were several la-

goons that survived all year round and saw the birds through until the autumn rains replenished the river. Actually the *tablas* were fed by four sources: the Guadiana, Cigüela, Zancares and Riansares, with the first two providing the lion's share of the water. The Cigüela's slightly salty waters come from the Serranía de Cuenca, whereas the Guadiana emerges from its underground course some 15 kilometres (nine miles) north of the *tablas* to form the pools known as *ojos* (eyes), from which the village of Villarrubia de los Ojos takes its name.

The park's even landscape is composed of five major elements: the *tablas*; the surrounding reed-beds; the *masiegal*, consisting of slightly higher ground covered with saltwort and low scrub; the islands; and finally the small, relatively fertile dales known as *vegas*. Of these the *masiegal* is the one element that has remained untouched by the drought: this is one of the most extensive areas of its type in Western Europe, and walking through it is a decidedly prickly experience.

You can still see the series of small islands dotted throughout the marshes: the Isla de Pan ('bread'), Isla de los Asnos ('donkeys'), Isla de los Generales, Isla de Algeciras, Isla del Descanso ('repose') and so on. To find the *vegas* is more difficult; they occur at the south-west corner of the park's 1,812 hectares (4,480 acres), between the areas known as Prado Ancho and Suerte de Don Felix, and are (or were) subject to brief annual inundations.

If the waters return to Las Tablas, an army of birds will surely put in an appearance once more. Among the breeding group, mallards and red-crested pollards have traditionally predominated. Gadwalls and pochards also used to breed here, and a few pairs of ferruginous duck. The reed-beds of Rosaleo were famous for their purple herons, as well as coots, moorhens, water rails and great-crested grebes.

The long list of wintering birds included pintails and shovellers, as well as contingents of northern mallards and pochards that joined their live-in relatives every year. Black-tailed godwit, snipe and even black kites and imperial eagles also migrated here. The mammals were headed by wild boar, red foxes and large families of otters.

BEFORE YOU GO
Maps: IGN 1:25,000 and 1:50,000 Nos. 737, 738 and 760; and IGN 1:200,000 Mapa Provincial of Ciudad Real.
Guide-books: Enric Balasch and Yolanda Ruiz, *El Parque Nacional de las Tablas de Daimiel* (Planeta, 1998).

GETTING THERE
The Parque Nacional de Las Tablas de Daimiel is situated about 180 km (110 miles) south of Madrid, and 40 km (25 miles) north-east of Ciudad Real, capital of the province of the same name.
By car: motor south from Madrid on the E5/NIV Autovía de Andalucía to Puerto Lápice, then take the N420 south to Daimiel and on to the park's visitor centre 11 km (7 miles) to the north-west.
By bus: no public transport

from Daimiel to the park.

WHERE TO STAY
Interesting options around here. Try the very beautiful 4-star Parador, T: (926) 86 01 00, F: 86 01 50, in Almagro; the eclectic combination of history and art-deco of the Palacio de la Serna, T: (926) 84 22 08, F: 84 22 24, in Ballesteros de Calatrava; or the unusually styled 2-star Aprisco de Puerto Lápice, T: (926) 57 60 25, F: 57 61 50, on the E5/NIV at Puerto Lápice. The very new and modern Confortel Almagro, T: (926) 86 00 11, F: 86 06 18, at Almagro, is also a good base. Daimiel itself has several small places to stay.

FURTHER INFORMATION
Tourist office: Ciudad Real, p86.
Park office: the park's Centro

de Visitantes, T: (926) 69 31 18; open 8 am-9 pm in summer and 8 am-6 pm in winter. There are 3 walking itineraries that allow you to observe the wide array of flora and fauna. The best times for the latter are early morning or late afternoon.

The black-tailed godwit has suffered from the drying-up of the *tablas*

Monfragüe

Parque natural, *about 25 km (16 miles)
south of Plasencia; breeding ground for an
extraordinary 218 vertebrate species
ZEPA
17,852 ha (44,112 acres)*

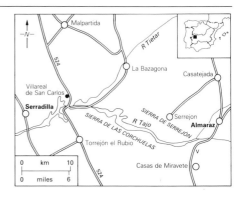

Early one morning I went for a walk
through the cork oak *dehesa* that surrounds the *cortijo*, or farmstead, of Las
Cansinas in the heart of Monfragüe. The
hot sun was already steaming the dew off
the rich tapestry of spring flowers underfoot. The air was filled with the hum of insect wings, hoopoes and golden orioles were
uttering their first notes of the morning and
a woodchat shrike flitted from tree to tree.
Down by the river, a colony of bee-eaters
took wing from an ancient evergreen oak to
soak up the heat of the new day. Then I noticed the short-toed eagle (known here as
águila culebrera, the snake-eagle) perched
on a rocky mound nearby. I crouched down
and studied the broad, grey, almost owl-like
head, with prominent brows and unusually
large eyes; strangely, the toes seemed to be a
normal length! The *águila* never moved,
save to flinch as half-a-dozen azure-winged
magpies dive-bombed it from the branches
of a nearby tree, a situation of David taking
on Goliath if ever there was one.

Later I learned that this bird had been re-
leased, somewhat prematurely, the day before from Las Cansinas, after having been
nursed back to apparent health subsequent
to sustaining an injury in the wild. Since it
was apparently unable to adjust to freedom
just yet, a warden was duly dispatched to
find it. It took him nearly two days to gain
its confidence, at which point we were finally rewarded with the sight of a somewhat
humiliated and indignant bird, blindfolded
and carried by those ferocious talons, head
down like a trussed-up chicken. Freedom
had been cancelled, at least for the time
being.

The Parque Natural de Monfragüe gets

its name from the Castillo y Ermita de
Monfragüe, which overlooks the western
end of the reserve. The castle was built on
the top of the Sierra de las Corchuelas by
the Berbers as a look-out over the ancient
crossing point of the Río Tajo at Puente
Cardenal, and given the name Al-Mofrag.
To the Romans, this difficult, uneven and
somewhat inhospitable terrain was known
as Monsfragorum.

The origin and composition of the rock
formation here is mirrored almost exactly in
the Sierra de Ancares, at the western end of
the Cordillera Cantábrica. The land consists of a Palaeozoic platform, much elevat-
ed and faulted during the Hercynian and
Caledonian orogenies, or upliftings. It now
forms a slightly dissected plateau, which
tilts towards the west and the Atlantic
Ocean. The valleys are composed of slates
of Silurian age, bisected at more or less regular intervals by ridges of quartzite running
in a north-west to south-east direction. The
two most commanding and prominent
ridges are the Sierra de las Corchuelas,
south of the rivers, and the Sierra de Serre-
jón, to the north, just outside the park.

The crystalline parent rocks have weathered slowly, producing dry, acid soils that
are highly erodible, making it very important that the natural vegetation cover is
maintained. Sadly, almost 20 per cent of the
park has been afforested with non-native
maritime pine and eucalyptus. However, the
authorities have now committed themselves
to restoring the more stable *dehesa* and
woodland habitats, which are of infinitely

greater value to wildlife.

Dehesa habitats are restricted to the Iberian peninsula and north-west Africa; they are composed of sparse plantations of cork and holm oak, traditionally harvested for acorns, firewood, cork and charcoal. The high-quality land beneath is used as pasture, a centuries-old practice that is acknowledged as being the best way to use this harsh terrain. Consequently, a totally characteristic fauna and flora has evolved, one that is unknown anywhere else in the world.

The second major habitat is virtually the only remaining original Mediterranean woodland. It is dominated by evergreen shrubs and trees, often species that produce aromatic oils to deter would-be herbivores. Looking down the northern slopes from the Castillo y Ermita de Monfragüe, you can see a wondrous tangle of mastic and turpentine trees, wild olives, laurustinus, strawberry trees, stone pines and the holly (or Kermes) oak. Beneath this green canopy are the cistus which are so typical of Monfragüe — the gum, grey-leaved and popular-leaved varieties — together with pink Spanish heath, fragrant French lavender, yellow-flowered broom and bladder senna.

Two hundred and eighteen vertebrate species breed within the Parque Natural de Monfragüe, and many more drop in on their long migratory journeys. Some 20 species of raptor nest and raise their young

The range of the snub-nosed Lataste's viper extends from Tunisia to the Pyrenees

here, with substantial proportions of the global populations of black vultures and Spanish imperial eagles. Both these species are severely threatened with extinction, and the presence of this last redoubt is one of the prime reasons for the existence of the natural park: the imperial eagles make their homes and breed more successfully here than in their better-known refuge in Doñana.

The black vulture and Spanish imperial eagle nest in the tops of ancient cork and holm oaks, as do goshawks, sparrowhawks, booted eagles and most of the owl species that occur here. Other raptors make their homes on remote rocky ledges, such as the griffon vultures at Peñafalcón, a huge crag by the Puente Cardenal which is also inhabited by their smaller cousins, the Egyptian vultures. Both the common species of kite nest in the park, and can frequently be seen quartering more open ground, controlling direction with a deft twist of their forked tails. Golden eagles, Bonelli's and short-toed eagles, peregrines and both species of kestrel have also found Monfragüe greatly to their liking, as have marsh and Montagu's harriers and those other great masters of the air, the ravens and the choughs.

The assemblage of smaller birds, which is typical of *dehesa* and Mediterranean woodland, must be one of the most colourful anywhere. Hoopoes and woodchat shrikes represent the more conservative members of a clan which includes such brightly plumaged fellows as the bee-eater, golden oriole, azure-winged magpie and roller. With the exception of the last, which is a rather uncommon sight, the other birds are present in such numbers that you can fully immerse yourself in their fluting calls and flashing colours as they go about their business almost — but not quite — indifferent to your presence.

It is the black stork, however, that emerges as the truly memorable bird of Monfragüe. Again, it is a species threatened continually by human activities, and is suffering a great contraction in its former range; that said, some seven pairs choose to return to Monfragüe every summer to rear their young.

Many of these birds can be seen simply by parking at the roadside opposite Peñafalcón and watching the vultures circle overhead to land on the great buttress opposite. Among them may be an eagle, a peregrine or a black stork returning to its nest in one of the clefts near the dammed waters below. Black vultures sometimes join them, but are more common over the oak forests to the south on the road to Trujillo. Eagles, too, are more abundant elsewhere. Try stopping alongside the road after it has crossed the dam to the east where all five eagles and three vultures of Monfragüe may be seen.

One of the special birds of Monfragüe is the black-winged kite. Among the most beautiful and rarest of all European raptors, it nests among the cork oaks to the north and south of the great river systems, but is always difficult to locate. In areas where they occur it is definitely worth the effort of investigating every bird that hovers, for, like the kestrel, these splendid birds spy out most of their food by this technique.

The mammals of Monfragüe are no less exciting, the speciality of the park being the Spanish lynx, although the retiring nature of this animal makes it unlikely that you will

The display of the great bustard (below) is one of the natural wonders of Monfragüe, while Peñafalcón (opposite) is, as the name suggests, home to many birds of prey

see it. No less elusive in the night air are the 15 species of bat found here.

Red deer and the smaller, palmately horned fallow deer are among the permitted targets of game hunters, the authorities reasoning that limited hunting of these sustainable resources will bring in extra money for conservation of other species. The numerous wild boar, *jabalí*, of the *dehesa* are also popular with hunters.

Wild cats, Egyptian mongooses and genets inhabit the Mediterranean woodland, all of them frightened away by the least noise, and otters patrol the *arroyos*, or streams, which lead into the reservoirs. Foxes, badgers, roe deer, polecats and beech martens, as well as the introduced *mouflon*, are also resident in Monfragüe, as is the garden dormouse, a tree-dweller, and the subterranean mole: every niche has been exploited.

The 19 species of reptile that breed in the *parque natural* include such exotic creatures as the Moorish gecko, often seen clinging adhesively to the wall beside a window at night, feeding on the insects which have been attracted to the light. Less frequently encountered is the amphisbaenian or worm lizard, resembling nothing so much as a large, pink earthworm, and occupying a similar territory. Three-toed and Bedriaga's skinks, the latter limited to Iberia in its world-wide distribution, also occur in Monfragüe, their tiny vestigial legs an evolutionary leftover from the days when they resembled true lizards and had not adapted to their current burrowing habit.

Nine species of snake lurk in the undergrowth; three are poisonous — Lataste's viper, the false smooth snake and the Montpellier snake. None is fatal, and the latter two have fangs positioned right at the back of their mouths and so cannot inject their venom unless they have a really good grip. Other, somewhat less threatening, species include the horseshoe whip and ladder snakes.

The wetter habitats of Monfragüe — the reservoirs of the dammed Tajo and Tiétar rivers and their minor tributaries — support an equally diverse animal community, particularly with respect to amphibians and wintering and migratory birds. Great crested

The Moorish gecko is most likely to be seen in villages at night, lured on to walls by street lamps that form brilliant insect traps

grebes and the beautifully marked collared pratincole can be seen during the summer months, the former with its cargo of fluffy chicks aboard, the latter swooping noisily around the mud-flats that become exposed as the water levels drop. These same mud-flats are swarming with house martins during May, as they gather material from which to construct their little mud igloos under the lips of the dams. The wintering avifauna includes cattle egrets, spoonbills and greylag geese, as well as both grey and night herons, stalking though the shallows, while regimental ranks of cormorants perch on the rotting remains of partially submerged trees.

The amphibians at home in the creeks and gullies surrounding the reservoirs include livid black- and yellow-fire salamanders and the khaki-camouflaged marbled newt. Bright green tree frogs perch on their arboreal vantage points, while natterjacks, spadefoots and midwife toads go about their chores. Other species include painted and parsley frogs, and the sharp-ribbed salamander, an ugly, warty creature confined to Iberia, and one of the largest-tailed amphibians in Europe, reaching almost 30 centimetres (12 inches) in length.

BEFORE YOU GO
Maps: IGN 1:25,000 and 1:50,000 Nos. 651, 652, 678 and 679; and 1:200,000 Mapa Provincial of Cáceres.
Guide-books: José-Luis Rodríguez, *Guía del Parque Natural de Monfragüe* (Ediciones Fondo Natural, 1985).

GETTING THERE
By car: from Plasencia southwards, and Trujillo northwards, the C524 leads to Villarreal de San Carlos, home of the park information centre.
By rail: the nearest station is Monfragüe, on the Madrid-Cáceres line (but served only by slow, stopping, *Regional* services). However, it is an extremely isolated location, and not a viable option for visits to the park.
By bus: again, not a viable option for visits to the park.

WHERE TO STAY
Good accommodation close to the park is scarce. The brand new 3-star Hotel Cañada Real, T: (927) 45 94 07, F: 45 94 34, at Malpartida de Plasencia, is the best option. Just a little farther north, in Plasencia, you will find the 3-star Hotel Alfonso VIII, T: (927) 41 02 50, F: 41 80 42. South of the park, just outside Torrejón El Rubio, a new hotel/*albergue* is being built. Torrejón itself has several small places, including the Carvajal, T: (927) 45 50 88, and Pensión Monfragüe, T: (927) 45 50 26. Three *paradores* are also close: Jarandilla de la Vera, T: (927) 56 01 17, F: 56 00 88; Trujillo, T: (927) 32 13 50, F: 32 13 66; and Oropesa, T: (925) 43 00 00, F: 43 07 77.
Outdoor living: permitted within the park in strictly designated areas. Camping Parque Natural de Monfragüe, T: (927) 45 92 33, on the C524 and fairly close to the railway station, is open year round and

holds 369 people.

ACCESS
Within the boundaries of the park is a *reserva integral*, which is closed to the public at all times, so that the rarer Monfragüe birds can breed and rear their young in peace. The exact location of this closed area is unknown, so as not to attract undue attention. Respect all fences within the park — you can get spectacular views of all the bird species from well within the open-access area.

ACTIVITIES
Walking: several tracks and pathways lead to the interior of the park. The route to the summit of Castillo y Ermita de Monfragüe starts at the bridge over the Tajo (Puente Cardenal); from there follow the small winding footpath up to the castle. There is a small cave nearby, which contains a few Bronze Age paintings of archers and goats; you cannot see very much, however, as there is now a grille across the entrance to the cave to protect the drawings.

Southwards from the castle, there is a narrow cleft in the quartzite and sandstone ridge, through which road and river both squeeze, albeit on different levels. A magnificent quartzite pinnacle rises steeply from the water to your right — this is Peñafalcón, one of the most visited and popular sites in the park, largely because of its bird population. At almost any daylight hour the sky teems with birds such as griffon vultures, passing overhead to the Sierra de las Corchuelas. On warm sunny days, if you have your binoculars handy, you will be able to see several of Monfragüe's pairs of breeding black storks, perched on the south side of the rock face and reviewing the scene below them

with a regal air.
Fishing: for a permit to fish the reservoir apply to the tourist office in Cáceres. For more information contact the fishing club, Federación Extremeña, Aptdo de Correos, 463, Plasencia, T: (927) 41 59 86.

FURTHER INFORMATION
Tourist offices: Turismo de Plasencia, Pl. de la Catedral, s/n, 10600 Plasencia, T: (927) 42 38 43, and Cáceres, p86.

The Mediterranean Coast

Spain's Mediterranean coast has had a decisive and incalculable effect on the country's history. It was the 'middle sea' that brought the Greeks, Carthaginians and Romans to this siren shore in ancient times. Later, after the Moorish invaders had finally been ejected, Spain became, for a time, the foremost maritime power in the western Mediterranean. Columbus's discovery of America changed all that: for economic reasons, Spain's interest shifted to the Atlantic, and the Mediterranean became something of a backwater.

But in our own day the sleepy fishing villages and farming communities along this coast have been engulfed by a new but hardly less problematic invasion, this time of northern sun-seekers and holiday-makers, who come to these latitudes for the sunshine and pleasantly warmed salt water they lack at home. Thus many of the once-pristine beaches of the Spanish Mediterranean have been turned into mass bronzing beds, with just enough space beside each over-exposed body to accommodate a bottle of suntan lotion, a paperback best-seller and a pair of sandals. Beyond the beaches rise the serried rows of shoe-box hotels that house the sun worshippers when they're not on the beach: the consensus seems to be that these ho-

The sand dunes, salt-marshes and saline lagoons of the Delta del Ebro, between Barcelona and València, form the largest unspoiled area of the Spanish Mediterranean

tels are not a pretty sight, but that it's too late to do anything about it. Personally I have never begrudged people their well-deserved summer holidays and have witnessed at first hand the agreeable and salubrious influence of the Mediterranean sun on people from more northern climes.

Yet there are wild places, and often they begin just behind the seaside resorts, on the landward side of the mountains that usually form a sort of rampart to the west of the beaches separating the real Spain from the land of the bikini bottom and the beach umbrella. Often it is only a short drive — or even a hike, although not in the broiling August heat if you can help it — from some of the busiest cities of the strand to some of the most deserted landscapes of the sierra. A case in point is the Sierra del Maestrat (Maestrazgo), which begins hardly 30 kilometres (19 miles) from the crowded beaches of Castelló (Castellón) de la Plana and yet belongs among the most forgotten parts of Spain, a Shangri-la of hilltop towns and fortified villages, windswept highlands and vast Mediterranean forests.

Murcia, which used to be one of the poorest provinces of Spain, has become remarkably prosperous thanks to its new-found status as *el huerto de Europa*, the fruit orchard of the European Union. Not far from its capital city rises the Sierra Espuña, a part of the coastal range that contains some astonishingly wild landscapes and a *reserva nacional*. For a real sense of what the Mediterranean hinterland used to be like, you could do worse than to camp out in the Sierra Espuña for a few days.

Those who live on the shores of this great sea have always had good and sundry reasons for climbing the peaks of the nearby mountains. In Roman times there was a temple of Venus on Montserrat, the sacred mountain that rises almost sheer from the lowlands of the Catalan plain to reach a height of 1,237 metres (4,057 feet). Since the 9th century there has been a shrine to the Black Madonna at the same spot, and every year tens of thousands of pilgrims visit the sanctuary and the adjoining Benedictine monastery. But the mountain is also used by climbers from Barcelona and other nearby cities, who practise their rapelling techniques on the fantastically shaped cliffs of the Montserrat massif. Thus, while the monastery is besieged by a constant stream of visitors arriving by car and bus, the adjoining mountains are as daunting and unspoiled as any range in the further interior.

Montserrat can best be seen, incidentally, from the town of Vic (Vich), far to the north of the mountain itself. It is one of the special characteristics of this 'most Catalan of mountains' that it presents a fantastic shape from whichever side it is viewed — a series of irregular silhouettes. From its summit you can see as far as the mountains of Aragón as well as much of nearby Catalunya (Cataluña); on especially clear days you may be able to discern Mallorca on the distant horizon. Two geological cataclysms account for the startling rock formations of this famous range: the first plunged the whole region to the bottom of a vast Eocene lake; the second pushed it up above what is now the valley of the Río Llobregat. Quaternary glacial action sculpted it into a series of bulging cliffs and gorges so that its outlines suggested the name Montserrat: the saw-toothed mountain.

Farther north, between Granollers and Arbúcies and also quite close to the coast, the Sierra de Montseny offers a less dramatic landscape but even more varied opportunities for hikers, campers and climbers. Indeed the whole coastal range behind the Costa Brava of Catalunya has summits and escarpments that afford spectacular views across the wine-dark Mediterranean, from which it is rarely separated by more than 30-40 kilometres (19-25 miles) of coastal plain.

South-west of Tortosa lies a different kind of exploration zone, the Puertos de Tortosa y Beseit (Beceite) — a region of wooded mountains and gentle valleys that is part orchard and part wilderness. This is another of the wholly unknown corners of Spain, and a walking tour of the forests and peasant villages of the Puertos de Beseit might well be combined with a bird-watching excursion to the Delta del Ebro, less than 50 kilometres (30 miles) to the east. The delta is unlike any other region of Spain, except the nearby Albufera de València. Much of it consists of a succession of shallow basins for growing rice, and these, of course, make ideal feeding troughs and swimming pools for wintering birds and passage migrants. For human beings, too, the delta can hardly be bettered as an island of psychological calm light-years removed from the madding beach belt that extends endlessly north and south along almost the entire coast.

From the mouth of the Ebro to L'Albufera, south of València, is only 180 kilometres (110 miles) as the mallard flies, and this famous freshwater *laguna* at the· edge of the Mediterranean also offers an inviting habitat for waterfowl — both for those who like to breed among its reeds and rushes, and for birds who only use it *en passant*. L'Albufera and its environs cannot be said to be truly 'wild', but it does constitute an extremely important bird-watching area and is included here for that particular reason.

Essentially there are two Spains, the wet one and the dry one, and it is all the more remarkable to find these two great wetlands here on the Mediterranean coast, which belongs emphatically to the dry Spain. In both instances, however, the water comes from the upland regions that receive far more rainfall than the coastal strip itself. In any case, the vegetation on this shore has learned to live with what the French call *la grande chaleur*: the hot, dry period from June to September, when virtually no rain falls and the sun burns down for an average of more than ten hours per day. Most plant growth ceases during the hot summer and resumes only when the first rains arrive, normally about the end of October. Which is not to say that the Mediterranean has a dependable rainy season, like the monsoons of India; there may very well be unexpected summer downpours which can wreak havoc with orchards, terraced gardens and the dry river-beds known appropriately as *torrentes*.

These abnormal downpours can also confuse the seeds that are lying in wait for the autumn; if they deceive the grasses into sprouting in July or August, the sun will soon burn them to a crisp and deprive the farmer of the necessary

fodder for the winter season.

When the autumn rains come, everything wakes up from the deep summer sleep that is like hibernation in the northern countries. Almost overnight the earth turns green with vegetation and is decorated with bright red poppies. This is the 'second spring' of the Mediterranean. Some species flower during the late autumn and early winter, and some continue active growth throughout the months when it rains. Most perennials flower in the early spring and the flowering period reaches a crescendo towards the end of April, when a great variety of annuals also decks the lowlands and hillsides. By June they have died down in preparation for summer and most have shed their seeds: only the thistles and members of the mint family are likely to be still in flower.

Withal the Mediterranean shore is renowned for the richness and variety of its plant life, with its remarkable amalgam of the wild and the cultivated, the native species and the exotic. The prickly pear with its spiky green paddles, that are such an atmospheric feature of the landscape, originally came from the New World; Columbus is said to have brought it back from one of his voyages. The century plant, or American agave, another ornamental sentinel in many dry gardens and areas of *maquis*, also came from across the seas. Indeed, palms, cacti, mimosas, eucalypts, oranges and lemons are all foreigners. The all-important olive, too, seems to have made its way westward from Asia. In the classic Mediterranean culture it provides oil for cooking, for putting on to bread and into lamps, and

for every kind of medicinal use, as well as being pickled, both green and ripe; its wood is used for the fire and for carving into bowls and spoons. But no one ever cut down a tree — in ancient Greece cutting down an olive tree was a capital crime. The wood for fuel and carving is obtained from the branches and pieces of trunk that are pruned every year.

Many of the truly native plants (some of them were eventually domesticated during centuries of Mediterranean farming) grew here as long ago as Tertiary times, while the myrtle, oleander, vine and lentisk have all survived the intervening Ice Ages of the Quaternary period. The carob, the sole survivor of some pre-Ice Age family, yields the long brown beans known as St John's bread, as the saint is said to have lived on them in the wilderness. Its fructose-rich filling can, in fact, taste like candy when the bean has ripened to a dark brown, but while green it has an absolutely ghastly taste, and even the sheep won't touch it until it turns brown.

In valleys such as the Puertos de Beseit the whole brilliant spectrum of Mediterranean plant life can unfold during the spring, autumn and winter: the olives and carobs on the terraced orchards; fruit trees of many varieties; palms rising proudly beside the farmhouses and rustling in the wind; the pine woods in the mountains and holm oak forests; the wild flowers scattered among the rocks. The sheer sensuous pleasure of these fruits and flowers, tastes and odours, is enough to make anyone forget the sandy delights of the beaches that lie just down the road.

BEFORE YOU GO
Maps: Michelin 1:400,000 Nos. 443 and 445.

GETTING THERE
By air: the major airport of the Mediterranean coast is at Barcelona; València and Alacant (Alicante) are both, respectively, further south and smaller. All of these have flights to many European cities, as

In Spain, lesser grey shrikes breed in Aiguamolls de l'Empordà and also on the Lleida steppes

well as regular internal flights.
By sea: the main ports of the region are Barcelona and València, both with regular ferry services to the Balearics.
By car: there is easy access to the coast from the French border all the way to Murcia and Cartagena. The Autopista del Mediterráneo (with heavy tolls) runs parallel to the coast and constitutes a fast way of getting to the wild places and away from the numerous tourist centres.
By rail: an excellent service operates along the Mediterranean coast. From Portbou, on the French border, all the way down to Murcia, local and long-distance services connect Girona, Barcelona,

Tarragona, Castelló (Castellón), València, Alacant and Murcia. There are also frequent services from Madrid to Barcelona and on up to Portbou; from Madrid to València, via Albacete and Xàtiva; slower and less frequent services from Madrid to València, via Cuenca; from Madrid to Alacant; and from Madrid to Murcia and Cartagena.

For information, call RENFE in Madrid, T: (91) 328 90 20, or consult the schedules on RENFE's web-site, www.renfe.es.
By bus: regular buses from Barcelona and Girona cover the entire Mediterranean coast north of Barcelona. Here services are mainly provided by 3 companies: Compañía de Ferrocaril San Felio, T: (972) 20 77 70 (Girona); the Línea Regular de Viajeros, between Lloret de Mar, Vidreres and Girona, T: (972) 20 10 18 (Girona) and T: (972) 33 41 42, 33 40 72 and 33 58 32 (Lloret); and Línea Sarfa, connecting Barcelona, Girona and the Costa Brava, T: (972) 20 17 96 (Girona). Numerous companies cover the coasts south of Barcelona; for information, T: (93) 329 06 06 (Barcelona); (965) 22 07 00 (Alacant); (968) 29 22 11 (Murcia); and (96) 349 72 22 (València).

WHERE TO STAY
There are thousands of hotels on Spain's Mediterranean coast, but the wild places behind the beaches and in the sierra tend to be in areas where hotels are few and far between. For accommodation near the exploration zones, consult the individual entries or ask at the local tourist offices (see below).

ACTIVITIES
Mountaineering clubs:

Federació d'Entitats Excursionistas de Catalunya, Ramblas, 41, 1°, 08002 Barcelona, T: (93) 412 07 77, F: 412 63 53, www.feec.es; Federació Territorial Valenciana de Muntanyisme, Mariano Luiña, 9, bajos, 03201 Elx (Elche), T: (96) 543 97 43.
Skiing: the closest resorts for downhill skiing are in the Sierra de Gúdar.
Teruel (978): Valdelinares, 72 80 08; Javalambre, 76 81 81.

FURTHER INFORMATION
Alacant (96): tourist office, Explanada de España, 2, 03002, T: 520 00 00, F: 520 02 43. Red Cross, T: 525 41 41, F: 524 48 11.
Barcelona (93): tourist office, Gran Vía Corts Catálanes, 658, T: 301 74 43, F: 412 25 70. Red Cross, T: 205 14 14, T: 205 62 15.
Castelló (964): tourist office, Pl. María Agustina, 5, 12003, T: 35 86 88, F: 35 86 89. Red Cross, T: 72 48 50, F: 72 48 55.
Girona (972): tourist office, Rambla de la Libertad, 1, 17004, T: 22 65 75, F: 22 66 12. Red Cross, T: 23 01 31,F: 20 88 83.
Murcia (968): tourist office, Alejandro Seiquer, 4, 30001, T: 22 28 00, F: 21 37 16. Red Cross, T: 21 88 93, F: 22 04 51.
València (96): tourist office, C/ Paz, 48, 46003, T: 398 64 22, F: 398 64 21. Red Cross, T: 380 83 81, F: 380 82 92.

FURTHER READING
Carlos Carrasco-Muñoz de Vera, *Catalunya — Guia de la Naturaleza* (Editorial Everest, 1981); Norman Lewis, *Voices of the Old Sea* (Picador, 1996); Rose Macauley, *Fabled Shore* (Oxford University Press, 1986);John & Christine Oldfield, *Landscapes of the Costa Blanca* (Sunflower, 1997); George Orwell, *Homage to Catalonia* (London, 1938).

Aiguamolls de l'Empordà

This parc natural *is one of the last wetland refuges in Mediterranean Spain, 25 km (16 miles) south of the French border*
Ramsar, ZEPA
4,088 ha (10,101 acres)

From the air, the Golfo de Roses, enclosed by the foothills of the Pyrenees, looks as though some huge, mythical sea-beast has bitten a chunk from the land. Although it is one of the least spoiled parts of the tourist-ridden Costa Brava, the area is full of high-rise hotels, and the great Perpignan-Barcelona motorway snakes its way across the lowland plain less than ten kilometres (six miles) from the sea. But sandwiched between sea and speeding cars, in the heart of this piecemeal but ever-growing concrete conurbation, lies one of the last wetland refuges in Mediterranean Spain: Aiguamolls de l'Empordà.

The ruins of three great cities built on top of each other, remnants of Greek, Iberian and Roman civilizations, mark the southernmost limit of Aiguamolls de l'Empordà. It was known at various points in its history as Emporion, Empurias, Ampuñas, and today as Empúries (Ampurias); the name derives from the Greek for 'trading station'. All that remains today is a maze of partially excavated foundations.

As recently as the early 18th century, most of the coastal lowlands of Empordà were a wilderness of vast freshwater and salt-water lakes, interspersed with marshlands and riverine forests. At this time Castelló d'Empúries, lying on the Río Muga, in the north of the bay, was surrounded by low-lying swamps and lagoons. As this town declined in importance, so the marshes have gradually disappeared, being used originally for rice cultivation and limited cattle-rearing, but more recently for intensive farming of arable crops, such as maize, sunflowers and barley. Now only fragmentary lagoons persist, and the remaining wilderness areas are increasingly threatened by tourism.

The Golfo de Roses is separated from France by the ancient granite and slate spit of the Cadaqués peninsula to the north. The coastal depression curves upwards to the south and west in a series of dissected hills of Tertiary age, before rearing up to meet the nether regions of the Pyrenees beyond; the southerly promontory, on which the village of L'Estartit stands, is composed of limestone and has spectacular underwater caves at its tip.

In response to the obvious threats from agricultural intensification and tourist development, and as a result of a certain amount of environmental lobbying, the Catalan parliament declared a large area of the remaining wetlands a *parc natural* in 1983. There are three 'integral' reserves within the park: one is a salt marsh area — a large pentagonal block lying inland from the beach between the Muga and Fluvià rivers, where the existing lagoon system is to be extended to attract more breeding and migrating birds. There are eight such *llaunes*, or lagoons, which are connected with both rivers when the water levels are high, but are also very close to the sea, and thus are inundated several times a year when storms cause the Mediterranean to break over the dunes.

The second reserve lies further north, on the site of the former lake of Castelló d'Empúries. It consists of a number of *estanys* and *closes* — water meadows and grazing marshes — which receive freshwater from Alberes and the St Pere de Rodes mountains to the north all year round. L'Aigua Clara is the only remaining part of the great lake, and is now covered with reeds and reed-mace. Surrounding this central reserve is a large area of similar countryside, including La Rovina, which comprises tiny strips of land or *peces*, bordered by irrigation channels and tamarisk hedges. This wetland would seem more at home in central France or southern England, with its small fields, bounded by elm and ash hedgerows or by narrow ditches flanked with all manner of water-loving plants. The freshwater marsh overflows with sedges and club-rushes, stands of yellow flag and purple loosestrife, and the huge purple-pink blooms of the marsh mallow.

By far the smallest of the reserves is the Illa de Caramany, on the Río Fluvià, which was isolated in 1979 by dredging work on the river-bed and consequently has great value as untouched riverine woodland that serves as a refuge for wildlife. As recently as the spring of 1987 a species of iris new to Empordà was discovered here for the first time.

The salt-marsh 'steppes' form a complex mosaic of halophytic vegetation, interspersed with the irregular brackish lagoons. Pure mats of a succulent sea plantain, level enough for a football field, are dotted here and there with golden samphire and sea wormwood. Wetter areas support sea rush, sea purslane, several species of glasswort and sea lavender, while to the seaward side, in the summer, the continually shifting dunes are a blaze of pinks and mauves — flowering sea rocket and sea stock, sea holly and sea bindweed. The lagoons are filled with the delicate fronds of horned pondweed, tasselweeds, water milfoils and hornworts, attracting myriad wildfowl during the winter. One of the most memorable sights is of the white-studded sheets of brackish water crowfoot that bloom on the lake at Vilaüt in spring.

More than 20 mammal species frequent the park, although some, such as the otter, are now so uncommon that they are feared extinct, despite breeding further upstream in both rivers. Of the smaller creatures, oak dormice, European white-toothed shrews, Etruscan shrews, water voles, long-tailed field mice, short-tailed voles, moles and hedgehogs have all been recorded here, as have rabbits, hares, weasels and foxes. Beech martens are sighted occasionally and polecats are quite common in the marshes. The 11 bat species help to control the thriving mosquito population; they include three species of horseshoe bat, as well as bent-winged and Daubenton's bats. In the winter, families of wild boar sometimes leave the neighbouring hills to feed in the *closes*.

Amphibians and reptiles are no less diverse. The marshes ring with the calls of

The sun sets dramatically over the sand dunes, essential to the preservation of the unique salt-marsh habitat of Aiguamolls

painted frogs, and you can observe natterjack and common toads, western and common spadefoots, marbled and palmate newts and stripeless tree frogs; the latter is only about the length of your little finger with disc-shaped climbing pads on its feet. I was lucky enough to see a stripe-necked terrapin slipping silently into a pool; the European pond terrapin has been recorded here, too. The drier, rocky places are the haunt of the spiny-footed and Iberian wall lizards, as well as both species of psammodromus and Moorish geckos, or you may catch a glimpse

of the much larger green-and-yellow ocellated lizard. Montpellier and ladder snakes, the former mildly poisonous, occur here, as do grass snakes, viperine snakes, slow-worms and three-toed skinks.

But the wealth of birds in Aiguamolls de l'Empordà is the main attraction of these important wetlands: it is an ornithological paradise, particularly during the spring and autumn migratory seasons. The presence of the garganey so far south of its normal breeding quarters is one of the fascinating mysteries of this park. Notable breeding birds include stone-curlews, black-winged stilts and marsh harriers. In the more Mediterranean vegetation of the granite outcrops in the northern part of the reserve,

it is not unusual to see rollers, bee-eaters and great spotted cuckoos hunting among the nettle trees and fragrant, narrow-leaved cistus. The beach, although part of the salt-marsh integral reserve, is much visited by sun-seekers, and consequently only a few pairs of Kentish plovers manage to nest here successfully. There are hopes that, if access can be restricted during the breeding season, little ringed plovers and little terns will return to rear their young here.

During the winter, black-throated divers are a frequent sight in the bay, and red-throated divers and great northern divers can be seen occasionally. Winter is also the season when cormorants, razor-bills, eider-ducks and common and velvet scoters use the sheltered waters of the Golfo de Roses as a resting point, as do goosanders and red-breasted mergansers. If you are lucky, you may see a small flock of greater flamingoes, which drops in on the salt-marsh during migration time; lone individuals have been known to stay for the whole winter.

It is during spring and autumn migrations, however, that these marshlands come into their own. Some of the more exotic species that have been known to frequent Aiguamolls de l'Empordà are spoon-bills and glossy ibis, red-crested pochard, black-necked and Slavonian grebes, short-eared owls and common cranes. Almost all European members of the heron family have been recorded here, as well as some rare visitors from Africa: great white egret, bittern, squacco heron, little egret and cattle egret. Purple and night herons, little bitterns and grey herons all breed here and there are

hopes that some of the wild egrets will be attracted to an enclosure which contains several breeding pairs, so that these species return to nest here once again.

Small birds are no less exciting than these giants of the marshes; at any time you can hear the reed and Cetti's warblers that frequent the denser stands of vegetation. Both penduline and bearded tits are attracted to the relatively pollution-free Fluvià and Muga rivers to breed. Other breeding passerines include moustached, Savi's and great reed warblers, as well as nightingales and yellow wagtails. The three or four pairs of lesser grey shrikes that breed in the freshwater marsh represent the only regular pairs in the Iberian peninsula, apart from those in the steppes of Lleida. In all, some 300 species of bird have been recorded within the boundaries of the park, of which approximately 90 are known to breed here.

BEFORE YOU GO
Maps: IGN 1:25,000 and 1:50,000 Nos. 258 and 259; and IGN 1:200,000 Mapa Provincial of Girona.
Guide-book: Rose Macaulay, *Fabled Shore* (Oxford University Press, 1986).

GETTING THERE
By air: there is a wide variety of flights, both international and internal, to Barcelona.
By car: approaching from Girona or from France, leave the Autopista del Mediterráneo at Figueres, then take the C260 due east to Roses.
By rail: there are many fast trains every day between Barcelona and Figueres, from where local services take you to nearby stations such as Vilajuïga, close to the park.
By bus: 'Barcelona Bus', T: (93) 232 04 59, operates buses from the Estació del Nord in Barcelona to Girona, T: (972) 20 24 32, or Figueres, T: (972) 50 50 29. SARFA, T: (93) 265 65 08, operates services from the Estació del Nord to Figueres, T: (972) 67 42 98, and

Castelló d'Empúries, T: (972) 25 05 93. Alternatively, from Figueres, SARFA runs 10 buses daily to Castelló d'Empúries and 4 daily to Sant Pere Pescador. In July-Aug SARFA runs 2 buses daily to the *parc natural*, which is about 4 km (2.5 miles) from Castelló or Sant Pere.

WHEN TO GO
The best times to visit Aiguamolls de l'Empordà to see birds are Mar-May, and Aug, when large numbers of waders and wildfowl use the park as a migration-route 'stepping stone'. Morning and early evening are the times when you are most likely to be rewarded by sightings from the bird hides. Botanically, the park is at its best in May. Empordà is subject to a battering from the Mistral for up to a week in spring.

WHERE TO STAY
The nearest town is Castelló d'Empúries, where you can find the 4-star HA Briaxis, T: (972) 45 15 45, F: 67 27 71, and

several others. Sant Pere Pescador also has several places, including the 3-star Can Ceret, T/F: 55 04 33, and Roses, to the north, has plenty.
Outdoor living: in Castelló d'Empúries you will find Camping Nautic Almata, T: (972) 45 44 77, open 30 May-24 Sept; Camping La Laguna, T: (972) 45 05 53, open 23 Mar-24 Oct; Camping Castell Mar, T: (972) 45 08 22, open 9 May-27 Sept; and Camping Empúries, T: (972) 25 01 01, open all year. Several more camp-sites can be found in Sant Pere Pescador, and there are many others in the region.

ACCESS
When walking in the reserve, take heed of any signposts indicating the route or forbidding entry: these are there to protect the most sensitive breeding areas.

FURTHER INFORMATION
Tourist office: Pl. del Sol, s/n, 17600 Figueres, T: (972) 50 31 55, F: 67 31 86; Puigmal, 1, Empuriabrava, 17486 Castelló

d'Empúries, T: (972) 45 08 02,
F: 45 06 00, web-site:
www.empuriabrava.com.
Park information: the park
information centre is at El
Cortalet, at the entrance near
Castelló d'Empúries (on the
road to Sant Pere Pescador), T:
(972) 45 42 22.

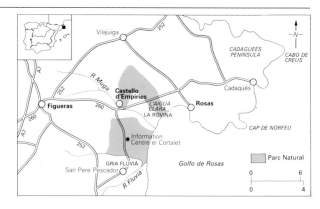

Illes Medes

*Small archipelago of
uninhabited islands, 2 km
(1¼ miles) off village of
L'Estartit
Reserva natural submarina
418 ha (1,032 acres)*

There are two islands (*illes*),
Meda Gran and Meda Xica,
and three islets (*illots*):
Magallot, Cavall Bernat and
Tascons. Collectively they
represent a far-flung spur of the
Montgrí massif whose
limestone has been deeply
eroded by the action of the sea.
Important colonies of gulls
have existed here for many
years, as well as breeding pairs
of cormorants and falcons. A

Cormorants are the most
conspicuous beneficiaries of the
ban on fishing in the waters
around the Illes Medes

project for turning the Illes
(Islas) Medes into a *parc
natural* is still under
consideration: meanwhile the
Generalitat de Catalunya has
declared the islands and the
surrounding seabed a *reserva
natural submarina*, prohibiting
fishing in the archipelago and
restricting access.

Beneath the waterline some
of the islands are honeycombed
with caves and tunnels. There is
a wide variety of marine life,
coral beds and a small amount
of surface vegetation — including sea fennel, or samphire.

The only island that can be
visited is Meda Gran, which
has a small quay known as the
Cos de Guardia since the island's former military garrison
once used it as a landing stage.

It was also once popular with
pirates but the present government intends to keep human
presence to a minimum.
Before you go *Maps:* IGN
1:25,000 and 1:50,000 No. 335;
IGN 1:200,000 Mapa
Provincial of Girona.
Getting there *By sea:* during
the summer months there is a
regular boat service which runs
from L'Estartit to the Meda
Gran.
Where to stay: L'Estartit is a
beach resort; there are many
standards of accommodation
from which to choose, ranging
from the 3-star Hotel Bell Aire,
T: (972) 75 13 02, F: 75 19 58,
to the 1-star Medas II, T: (972)
75 84 80, F: 75 81 49.
Further information *Tourist
office:* Girona, p112.

Montseny

*A parc natural of representative European
woodland growing on the hinterland of the
Costa Brava
Biosphere Reserve
17,370 ha (42,920 acres)*

The massif of Montseny resembles nothing so much as a geological castle bordered by a moat that acts as a watershed. The castle's four towers are the Turó de l'Home ('the man's peak', 1,714 metres/5,622 feet); Les Agudes ('the sharp ones', 1,707 metres/5,600 feet); Matagalls ('the cock-killer', 1,694 metres/5,556 feet); and Puigdrau (1,350 metres/4,430 feet). Together with the tableland known as El Pla de la Calma ('the plain of tranquillity'), they form a clearly defined ecological zone that lies a short distance inland from the Mediterranean coast, roughly midway between Girona and Barcelona. Montseny — which means 'the mountain of good sense' — was made a *parc natural* in 1978 and declared a Biosphere Reserve by UNESCO shortly afterwards.

The mountain landscape is gentle rather than dramatic, with rounded hilltops and

---

Trees of many kinds grow on the well-watered slopes of Montseny, just inland from Barcelona

wooded slopes occasionally interspersed with steep ravines. Just as Catalan culture combines both Spanish and northern European influences, the ecosystem of this region unites virtually every tree that grows in Western Europe: the Mediterranean pines and holm oak at the base of the mountains and the northern beech and fir higher up on the slopes, together with Scots pines, the maple of the Bohemian forests and the chestnut trees of Italy.

One of the higher passes of Montseny, Col Pregón (1,600 metres/5,250 feet), is reached by travelling through some of the most extensive beech woods in this part of Spain. On reaching the summit, the flora changes abruptly to dwarfed high-altitude species, the variety limited somewhat by the acidic granite and gneiss bed-rock. One plant worth a mention is the endemic *Saxifraga vayredana*, an aromatic species with resinous leaves and, like most saxifrages, small white flowers. It grows together with mountain cornflower (*Centaurea montana*), which usually favours a more calcareous environment. An orchid species typical of southern Spain and the Mediterranean region, the violet bird's-nest orchid (*Limodorum abortivum*) grows in the pine woods that flank the lower slopes of Montseny, its large upright spikes studded with curved, purple-flushed blooms at regular intervals.

Probably the most interesting species at Montseny — and in the immediately adjacent mountain areas — is an endemic race of the spring ringlet butterfly (*Erebia epistygne ribasi*). This rather ordinary-looking brown creature prefers open areas in the mountains, between 1,000-2,400 metres (3,300-7,900 feet), and flies between May and June.

The mountains are full of Romanesque ruins, but among the churches still standing is the thousand-year-old monastery of Sant Marçal near the centre of the massif: from here it takes about two hours to walk to the summit of Matagalls. Because amethysts have been found in this region, the poets have called Montseny 'the mountain of amethysts'. This is something of an exaggeration — but it may be worth your while to walk with downcast eyes while rambling through the park.

BEFORE YOU GO
Maps: IGN 1:25,000 and
1:50,000 Nos. 332 and 365;
IGN 1:200,000 Mapas
Provinciales of Barcelona and
Girona.
Guide-books: A. Jonch,
Montseny and *El Montseny,
parc natural* (Editorial Alpina,
Barcelona).

GETTING THERE
By car: take the Sant Celoni
exit off the A7 (E15)
Barcelona-Perpignan *autopista*,
then take your choice of the
villages of the massif, which
itself lies just north of the
highway.
By rail: there is a regular

service from Barcelona to Sant
Celoni, on the line to Girona;
and from Barcelona to Vic, on
the Puigcerdà line.
By bus: buses run from Sant
Celoni to most of the villages
of the massif, T: (93) 867 10 38.

WHERE TO STAY
At Montseny there is the 3-star
Hotel San Bernat, T/F: (93) 847
30 11, and a couple of other
places. Viladrau, a lovely
village to the north, has several
options, including the 2-star
Hotel de la Gloria, T: (93) 884
90 34, F: 884 94 65.

TOURIST INFORMATION
Tourist offices: C/ Campins, 24,
08470 Sant Celoni, T: (93) 867
47 80, F: 867 39 14, and Pl.
Mayor, 1, 08500 Vic, T: (93)
886 20 91, F: 889 26 37.

Montserrat

*A parc natural of unusual
landscape and rare
vegetation 50 km (30 miles)
from Barcelona
3,992 ha (9,864 acres)*

Famous for its religious
connotations and its serrated
silhouette, Montserrat has
drawn millions of visitors to its
9th-century monastery and
shrine of the Black Madonna.
The highest point of the
mountain is Sant Jeroni (San
Jerónimo — 1,238 m/4,060 ft),
but the towering pillars, eroded
into fantastic, smooth-walled
pinnacles, suggest a greater
altitude.

The Oligocene conglomer-
ates that make up much of this

Montserrat's fantastic
crenellations overlook orderly
bands of woodland

surreal landscape are responsible also for the acidity of the soil, and the relatively low botanical diversity. The middle slopes are clothed in forests of pine and evergreen oaks, with a dense understorey of junipers, snow mespilus (*Amelanchier ovalis*), strawberry tree, tree heath, box, shrubby hare's-ear (*Bupleurum fruticosum*) and laurustinus. Among this largely evergreen display stand out the bright yellow flowers of scorpion senna (*Coronilla emerus*).

On the south-facing slopes there is a more Mediterranean vegetation, characterized by fewer trees and more aromatic shrubs, such as cistus and rosemary, as well as Kermes oaks (*Quercus coccifera*). This latter, also known as the grain tree, is the host plant of the scale insect *Coccus ilicis*, the female of which produces a red dye when dried.

More open patches within this *matorral* are colonized by such herbs as grass-leaved buttercup (*Ranunculus gramineus*), easily distinguished by its linear, glaucous leaves and large golden flowers, and thyme and snapdragons, with trailing stems of the woolly white-leaved *Convolvulus lanuginosus*, studded at intervals with pink, candy-striped, bell-shaped flowers. Broomrapes and grape hyacinths shelter beneath the tall stems of *Thalictrum tuberosum*, which is topped by spectacular, shaggy cream-coloured flowers.

Other parts of Montserrat harbour an assemblage of species more typical of north-eastern Spain and the Pyrenees. On the rocky, exposed summit, for instance, bloom Spanish broom (*Genista hispanica*) and the gromwell (*Lithodora fruticosa*).

Before you go *Maps:* IGN 1:25,000 and 1:50,000 Nos. 420 and 421; IGN 1:200,000 Mapa Provincial of Barcelona.

Getting there *By car:* Montserrat is about 50 km (30 miles) from Barcelona on the NII Barcelona-Lleida (Lérida) road. Turn right off this road on to either the C1411 to Monistrol or, a little further north, on to a small road towards Guardiola.

By rail: a regular train service from Barcelona to Montserrat, the 'Ferrocarriles Catalanes', leaves from below the Plaza d'Espanya. The train connects with a cable-car that takes you up the mountain – a popular and splendidly scenic trip.

By bus: not the best option.

Where to stay: since Montserrat can easily be explored in a day, most people will stay in nearby Barcelona: try the 2-star Mesón Castilla, T: (93) 318 21 82, F: 412 40 20. At Montserrat, the 3-star Abat Cisneros, T: (93) 835 02 01, F: 835 06 59, is the best choice.

Outdoor living: there is a campsite near the monastery of Montserrat.

Further information *Tourist office:* Barcelona, p112.

Delta del Ebro

A parc natural at the mouth of the Ebro near Tortosa; tens of thousands of birds are attracted to these vast wetlands
Ramsar, ZEPA
7,736 ha (19,107 acres)

The Ebro — the ancient River Iberus that gave its name to the entire peninsula — is the only one of the five great rivers of Spain that flows into the Mediterranean. Draining a vast watershed, it reaches the sea near the southern boundary of Catalunya, where its delta forms a conspicuous projection in an otherwise regular coastline: from the air it resembles a giant green-and-brown arrowhead jutting 30 kilometres (19 miles) out to sea.

It is an area of rice fields and wetlands that attracts birds by the tens of thousands. An ornithological census conducted in 1980-81 determined that the autumn population included some 53,000 ducks and 13,000 coots, with, in each case, a little less than half that number wintering in the region. Among the delta's most closely watched and carefully protected species is the red-crested pochard, which is on the endangered list. The drakes are truly spectacular: large birds with bright crimson bill, eyes and legs, contrasting strongly with the vermilion-orange head and black breast. The flamingo gatherings in the Salinas (Salines) and the Punta de la Banya are one of the major attractions of the Parc Natural del Delta de l'Ebre, as the park is locally known.

Waders such as sandpipers, plovers, snipe, curlew and lapwing also find this a congenial habitat. Thousands of them migrate here from the Baltic and other northern regions, while others remain throughout the year. At any given time the number of birds in residence varies from 50,000 to 100,000, drawn from about 250 species — which is all the more remarkable considering that the delta has an area of only 32,000 hectares (79,000 acres).

The Delta del Ebro reminds me of Holland, not only on account of its wind-swept expanses of flat fields but by virtue of its tidy houses and villages, its canals and river boats. Everything here seems to move as slowly as the water in the ditches and canals. Along the narrow tracks leading past canals and rice fields you still see carts pulled by marsh ponies, bells jingling on their harnesses. The whole landscape has a handmade look, and indeed, although tractors have taken over much of the heavy work, many farmers still perform stoop labour of the kind more often seen in Asia than in Europe. Often there are patches of cane between the fields and shallow ponds in which stilt-legged birds are busy looking for a midday snack.

The rice paddies change dramatically with the seasons. In winter the fields are dry and covered with stubble and weeds; in spring they plough up the fields and the whole delta smells of newly turned earth. Once the rice is sown, the fields are flooded and transformed into shallow lagoons. When the rice shoots up, they turn bright green and finally to reddish gold.

Whatever it might lack as a wilderness, the birds certainly find the delta a good environment in which to nest and raise their young. And although only a few areas of the delta have been set aside as a *parc natural*, all of it strikes me as an exceedingly restful place to visit if you want to get away from it

all. Except during the hunting season, when an average of 34,000 ducks are shot.

The hunting season aside, among the memorable delta experiences, though only for early risers, are the huge flights of duck that pass noisily overhead just after the sun comes up; often, thousands spend the night in the large lagoons on the right bank of the Ebro — L'Encanyissada and La Tancada. But some of the most interesting birds are difficult to find: the squacco, purple and night herons, the marsh harrier, bittern, pratincole and short-eared owl, as well as the oystercatcher, avocet, slender-billed and Audouin's gull. Several species of tern find a suitable summer home here. Among the rice fields whiskered terns hawk for insects and build their nests. Gull-billed terns, regarded as 'sea' terns, mainly nest on drying islands in the lagoons, and plunge into the sea in search of fish. Sandwich terns have a major Mediterranean colony here.

The *salinas* are the preferred breeding ground of terns, avocets and black-winged stilts. Some 500 pairs of little terns have been observed at Punta del Fangar, where there is also a colony of gull-billed terns; at Punta de la Banya there are colonies of little terns, common terns and black-headed gulls. Whiskered terns are particularly common on the Canal Vell lagoon, and purple herons breed in the reeds on Buda Island (which is privately owned but within the park boundaries) at the easternmost point of the delta.

Otters are to be found in the park too, along with several other protected species: the Valencian and Iberian toothcarp, the stripeless tree frog and the stripe-necked and European pond terrapins.

BEFORE YOU GO
Maps: IGN 1:25,000 and 1:50,000 Nos. 522, 523 and 547; and IGN 1:200,000 Mapa Provincial of Tarragona.
Guide-books: Rafael Balada, *Guide to the Ebro Delta* (Ketres Editora, 1985); Enric Balasch & Yolanda Ruiz, *El Parque Natural del Delta del Ebro* (Planeta, 1998); Paul Jenner & Christine Smith, *Landscapes of Cataluña* (Sunflower, 1993).

GETTING THERE
By car: on the A7 (*autopista* Barcelona-València) take the exit for L'Aldea and Amposta. The N340 runs parallel to the A7, but through the villages on the western boundary of the delta. Near Amposta you have to decide whether to drive along the right or the left bank of the Ebro — there are no bridges further downstream, just flat-boat ferries that

operate between Deltebre and Sant Jaume d'Enveja, at the centre of the delta, but only during daylight hours. The 2 roads on either bank run parallel to the river and both continue to the mouth of the Ebro, about 25 km (15 miles) to the east of Amposta, where you may well want to begin your explorations. The name Deltebre, incidentally, was created when two adjoining

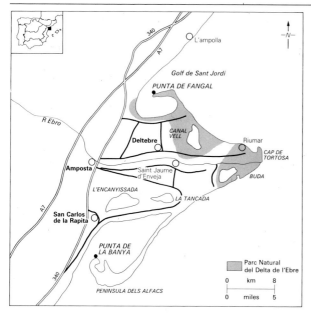

The stripe-necked terrapin starts life with vivid orange stripes which fade to creamy yellow in the adult

T: (977) 26 76 80, open all year and with room for 185, are in Deltebre; and Camping Mediterrani Blau, T: (977) 46 81 46, open 1 Apr-30 Sept and holds 240, in Amposta.

villages were amalgamated.
By rail: the delta can be reached from any of 3 stations — L'Aldea-Amposta, Camarles and L'Ampolla — on the line between Barcelona and València. However, beware: only *Regional* services stop at these stations, not the long-distance trains.
By bus: the long-distance Barcelona-València buses stop at Amposta, from where there is a local bus service to all the villages within the delta. For information, call T: (93) 322 78 14 in Barcelona or T: (977) 44 03 00 in Tortosa.

WHERE TO STAY
Accommodation is not difficult to find in and around the delta. The resort of Sant Carles de la Ràpita has a host of places, including the 2-star Hotel Plaça Vella, T: (977) 74 24 96, F: 74 43 97; in Deltebre there is the 3-star Hotel Delta, T: (977) 48 00 46, F: 48 06 63, and several smaller places; and in Amposta the 2-star Hotel Montsia, T: (977) 70 19 67, F: 70 10 27. The

Casa Can Gilabert, T: (977) 74 42 34, at El Poblenou del Delta, is a typical regional house. Ask at the tourist offices for a full list of hotels and of the *casas rurales* operating under the umbrella of *turismo verde*.
Outdoor living: Camping L'Aube, T: (977) 44 57 06, open all year with capacity for 963 people, and Camping Riomar,

Astralagus monspessulanus is a form of vetch adapted to dry, stony soils

FURTHER INFORMATION
Tourist offices: Avda. Sant Jaume, 1, 43870 Amposta, T: (977) 70 34 53, F: 70 41 32; and C/ Martín Buera, 22, 43580 Deltebre, T: (977) 48 96 79, F: 48 95 15.
Park information: Information Centre, C/ Ulldecona, 22, 43580, Deltebre, T: (977) 48 96 79. Open Mon-Fri, 10 am-2 pm and 3 pm-6 pm, Sat, Sun and holidays, 10 am-1 pm. The Casa de Fusta Refuge and Museum, opposite the Encanyissada Lagoon, open Tues-Fri, 10 am-2 pm and 4 pm-6 pm, Sat, 10 am-1 pm and 3:30 pm-6 pm and Sun and holidays, 10 am-1 pm.
Delta cruises: operated by Transbordador Olmos, T: (977) 48 05 48, F: 48 13 69, sailings every day.
Delta guides: Activats i Serveis Turísticas, Sant Jaume d'Enveja, Mon-Sun, 10 am-1:30 pm and 4 pm-9 pm.

As it nears its mouth, the Ebro flows slowly through reed-fringed channels between a succession of small islands

'Between Tortosa and the sea spreads the marshy, lagoon-strewn delta of the Ebro, and the strange encircling hook, like a parrot's beak, of the Punta del Calacho curls protectingly round the almost enclosed harbour basin that for centuries was fought for by Romans, Carthaginians, Saracens, French and Spaniards. It is indeed a harbour, as Tortosa is a city, and the Ebro a river, worth fighting for.'

Rose Macaulay, *Fabled Shore*

Puertos de Beseit

Region of forested mountains and cultivated valleys, spanning three Spanish provinces and encompassing nearly 30,000 ha (74,000 acres) of reserva nacional

This is another of the half-forgotten corners of Spain, notable for the striking contrasts of its rugged mountain terrain and the neatly tended fields and orchards of its unspoiled valleys. The massif forming the Puertos de Beseit constitutes a kind of bridge between the Sistema Ibérico and the Prelitoral mountains of Catalunya. The range starts south-west of the Ebro and continues inland in a chain of calcareous peaks that rise from the Tossal d'En Grilló (1,076 m/3,530 ft) to Encanadé (1,396 m/4,579 ft). Nearly 30,000 ha (74,000 acres) of the Puertos have been designated a *reserva nacional* which abounds in vast numbers of ibex, wild boar and red partridges.

Beseit includes portions of three provinces — Tarragona, Castelló and Teruel — and takes its name from the little fruit-growing village of Beceite, the last in the Teruel province. The Tossal dels Tres Reis (1,356 m/4,450 ft) rises at the meeting point of the three regions, near Fredes on the road to Los Puer-

tos. According to legend, the three kings of Catalunya, Aragón and València used to arrange meetings here in days of old, each standing on a slice of his own domain.

A range of mountains called Rafelgarí forms a wedge between the provinces of Castellón and Teruel. The mountains were named after a now-vanished village founded by a monk named Rafael Garí: the village became a famous hideout for bandits after the peasants had wisely moved down to the plain. The bandits have long since disappeared, however, and nowadays the only disreputable characters you are likely to meet there are your fellow hikers. There is a refuge for hikers in the Rafelgarí, about 12 km (7 miles) from Fredes and separat-

Some of the finest beech trees in Europe grow in the Puertos de Beseit

ed by a steep ravine from a historic chapel, the Ermita de San Miguel. The bare bones that are always dropping into this ravine are crumbs from the table of the many vultures which have their natural feeding trough high above the gorge, at the edge of an almost sheer cliff.

Fredes is lost among the mountains at 1,090 m (3,575 ft). It has only a handful of residents in the winter but numerous inhabitants in the summer, when it still manages to live up to its name: *fred* means cold in Catalan. The Barranco del Retaule, in the southern part of the Puertos, near La Sénia, is noted for its remarkable forest of beech trees, pines and box trees (whence its name, for Catalan altar pieces, or *retaules*, used to be made of box wood). Some of these beeches, growing at 1,200 m (4,000 ft), are not only among the most southerly in Europe but among the largest: 'El faig pare' ('the father of trees') is enormous as beeches go. The same forest also contains the biggest pine tree in Catalunya, El Pi de la Vall Canera, which measures a massive 5 m (16½ ft) in circumference. It would take four good-sized people standing finger-tip to finger-tip to span its trunk.

Before you go *Maps:* IGN 1:25,000 and 1:50,000 Nos. 496, 520, 521, 545 and 546; and IGN 1:200,000 Mapas Provinciales de Castelló, Tarragona and Teruel.
Guide-books: Antonio Calero Pico, *Los Montes de Tarragona* (Alcoy, 1982); Paul Jenner & Christine Smith, *Landscapes of Cataluña: Delta del Ebro and Puertos de Beceite* (Sunflower, 1993).
Getting there *By car:* the Puertos de Beseit can be approached from north or south from the N232 Vinaròs-Zaragoza road. At Monroyo, turn on to the TE302 side road

to Valderrobres; from there a dramatic 7-km (4½-mile) mountain road (TE304) takes you to Beceite. Starting from Tortosa, take the N230 toward Gandesa and after some 40 km (25 miles) turn west towards Prat de Comte on to the T330, which again leads to Valderrobres. From Tarragona, the most direct route is via the N420 in the direction of Gandesa. *By bus:* Autos Mediterraneo, Pl. Fadrell, 2 y 3, Castelló, T: (964) 22 05 36, F: 22 15 07, operates services between Vinaròs, Morella and Alcañiz, the route that comes closest to

the Puertos. **Where to stay:** the place to stay in this region is, undoubtedly, La Torre del Visco, T: (978) 76 90 15, F: 76 90 16 — magnificent architecture, service, food and mountain views. Alternatives are the Casa Más del Pi, T: (978) 76 90 33, in Valderrobres and the 3-star Hotel Cardenal Ram, T: (964) 17 30 85, F: 17 32 18, in the impressively walled city of Morella. *Refuges:* there are 2 refuges in the Rafelgarí mountain range. Les Clotes is in the north about 12 km (7 miles) from Fredes, while Caseta del Frare is

located more in the centre. **Activities** *Walking:* a particularly enjoyable excursion is that following the track from Embalse de Ulldecona up to the village of Fredes. The trail skirts impressive ravines such as El Mangraners and La Tenalla, and crosses the dramatic Portell del'Infern ('the Gate of Hell') to reach Fredes in about 5 hrs of walking. **Further information** *Tourist offices:* Oficina Comarcal de Turismo del Bajo Aragón, C/ Mayor, 1, 44600 Alcañiz, T/F: (978) 83 12 13, and Pl. de San Miguel, 3, 12300 Morella, T: (964) 17 30 32, F: 17 07 62.

L'Albufera de València

A parc natural, one of the largest bodies of freshwater in Spain, located just south of València and attracting birds of passage Ramsar, ZEPA

This famous *laguna* south of València is an important wetland, and birds of passage love to feed in its surrounding rice fields. People like to eat here, too: the village of El Palmar, more or less surrounded by L'Albufera, has been transformed from a collection of reed-thatched fishermen's huts into an agglomeration of restaurants, each trying to outdo the others with the magnificence of its *paella valenciana*. You come here, therefore, to watch birds through binoculars and then, when the sun has set, to study menus with equal intensity. It is sometimes very difficult to move after one of these gargantuan feasts of rice, game birds and seafood. Fortunately for the co-matose (although not for resident birds), there is a surfeit of nearby beach hotels along the strip of land between the *laguna* and the sea; in any of these you can sleep off the effects of a too-rich *paella* and be none the worse for it the next day.

The hydrographics of L'Albufera are

complex. In the winter it fills up with fresh-water from the Río Túria and the Acequia de Rey, but although it is one of the largest bodies of freshwater in Spain — 2,837 ha (7,010 acres), of which about a tenth is taken up by reed beds and interior islands called *matas* — it is very shallow, varying from 1 to 2.5 metres (3 to 8 feet) in depth. At the southern end of the *laguna* there is a canal, the Perelló, which can be opened and closed at will to allow water to flow into the Mediterranean. It is estimated that the *laguna* receives eight times more water, on average, than it can accommodate without flooding the surrounding area, notably the sandbank separating it from the sea, the Platjas (Playas) del Saler and de la Devesa.

The shoveler uses its broad bill to sieve the muddy water of L'Albufera

125

The rise and fall in the level of the *laguna* is thus closely watched. Equally importantly, experts have detected a growing contamination of its waters by industrial effluvia, domestic sewage and agricultural residues that are washed into the *laguna* every year and are threatening its ecological balance. L'Albufera is a wetland under 'stress'; it is not only threatened by chemical poisoning but also by a gradual silting process that adds heavy layers of sediment to the bottom with each annual flooding.

L'Albufera has already shrunk enormously. In the Middle Ages it was over ten times its present size, but as farmers took over the western marshlands and turned them into rice paddies the *laguna* was gradually reduced. In recent years the conflicting interests of local duck hunters and conservation groups have led to heated controversies concerning the legislation and management of what has become, at the eleventh hour, a *parc natural* with stringent protective measures imposed by the autonomy of València.

The birds, unaware of the battles that have been fought for and against their interests, have continued to flock to L'Albufera by the tens of thousands. About 250 species of birds — 90 of which breed here regularly — have been recorded at the ornithological station of L'Albufera, near Mata del Fang; cattle egrets, little egrets, red-crested pochards, mallards, shovelers and wigeon, all counted in their thousands.

The census of passage birds includes between 1,000-2,000 lapwing, 2,000-14,000 red-crested pochard, more than 6,000 black-tailed godwit and somewhat fewer little ringed plover, as well as snipe, dunlin, sanderling, golden plover and redshank.

Among the species that breed in the reed beds of L'Albufera are great crested grebe (about 100 pairs) and black-necked grebe, egrets, night, purple and squacco herons, bittern and little bittern (about 30 or 40 pairs), little ringed plover, Kentish plover, redshank and avocet. Noted for the large number of breeding pairs are black-winged stilt, pratincole, common and gull-billed tern, fan-tailed, reed and great reed warblers, and the penduline tit.

The recent increase in breeding numbers indicates that L'Albufera, although threatened on all sides by pesticide pollution and the proximity of urban developments, is all the more important to Europe's bird life now that so many other natural marshes have been destroyed or are under threat and the number of alternative wetlands is steadily decreasing.

The river which carved this deep ravine in the Puertos de Beseit (opposite) has dried to a trickle, while a little bittern (below) enjoys the plentiful water of L'Albufera

'As ever in this deep clear water over rock, the sea was a polished inter-weave of sombre but refulgent colours that contained no blue. Past every headland the view opened on a new adventure of riven cliffs and pinnacles, of caves sucking at the water, of rock strata twisted and kneaded like old-fashioned toffee. Boulders of colossal proportions had fallen everywhere from the cliffs and we threaded through a maze of them over water possessed of a surging, muscled vivacity to reach an inlet where the fishing would take place, and where the shallows were of such transparency that the weeds under us showed through, like the fronds, the fanned-out petals and the plumes of a William Morris design...

I left him, to explore the deeper water... Everything in this sunny scene, every form and colour, was fresh. The panorama was one of the sea-gouged and polished bed-rock, splashed all over with scarlet and ochreous algae, with its sierras, its jungles of weed and its teeming population of fish. Apart from the birds, the visible life of our world is largely restricted to surfaces. Here limitless stratification encouraged a dense marine populace with fish of all sizes from darting coloured particles to enormous bull-headed meros stacked at varying depths to feed, to circulate in a slow ruminative way, to rise or sink with a gentle ripple of fin or a flicker of tail...

I turned back, making for shallow water through bead curtains and chain mail of fish; fish sable and silver, fish glistening like Lorca's small, stabbing knives, fish that sparkled in their shoal in unison, off and on, like an advertising sign, as with common impulse they changed the angles of their bodies to the light.'

Norman Lewis, *Voices of the Old Sea*

BEFORE YOU GO

Maps: IGN 1:25,000 and 1:50,000 Nos. 722 and 747; IGN 1:200,000 Mapa Provincial of València.

GETTING THERE

By car: either the N333 or *autovía* to El Saler, and on to El Palmar.
By bus: a regular half-hourly service runs from València, Pl. El Parterre, to L'Albufera.

WHERE TO STAY

The 5-star Hotel Sidi Saler, T: (96) 161 04 11, F: 161 08 38, in El Saler, is not only right on the beach, but has marvellous spa amenities. València has numerous hotels. Try the stylish 4-star Astoria Palace, T: (96) 352 67 27, F: 352 80 78.
Outdoor living: Camping El Palmar, T: (96) 161 08 53, open July-Aug, and Camping El Saler, T: (96) 183 00 23, open all year.

ACTIVITIES

Boating: boats can be hired, or boat trips taken, throughout L'Albufera.

Diving: contact the Federación Actividades Subacuáticas Levantina, Pl. San Nicolas, 2, València, T: (96) 386 50 23, F: 386 50 06.
Fishing: information/permits from the tourist office.

FURTHER INFORMATION

Tourist office: València, p112.
Park information: Centre d'Informació "Raco del'Olla", El Palmar, T: (96) 162 73 45, web-site: www.gva.es. Open Mon, Wed and Fri, 9 am-2 pm; Tues, Thurs, weekends and holidays, 9 am-2 pm and 3:30 pm-5:30 pm.

Sierra Espuña

A parque regional, the largest reserve in Murcia province
17,804 ha (43,993 acres)

The sierra occupies part of the eastern end of the Cordillera Bética, just at the point where the mountains meet the coastal plain. The cliffs and crags of the two highest peaks — Espuña (1,585 m/5,200 ft) and Morrón (1,446 m/4,750 ft) — are used by mountain climbers for training exercises. Lessons learned in the Sierra Espuña can then be applied, with far more spectacular results, in the Sierra Nevada at the western end of the same *cordillera*.

The sierra is home to at least two species of rare and endemic butterflies. It is the type locality for the small brown Spanish argus (*Aricia morronensis*). The species is confined to Spain, and occurs in very small colonies, each of which varies slightly, the northern ones, for example, being larger. It flies at middle altitudes in open mountain areas during July and early August. The other rare butterfly is the Nevada grayling (*Pseudochazara hippolyte*), known in just four localities in south-east Spain, but also in southern Russia and parts of Asia. It is a handsome brown and gold butterfly that flies in

June and July between 2,100-2,700 m (6,900-8,900 ft) on stony slopes, often over crystalline bed-rock. The larvae eat various mountain grasses.

The park is based on the old *reserva nacional*, which was originally established in the 1970s as part of a comprehensive programme that introduced herds of Sardinian *mouflon* and African *aoudad* (Barbary sheep) into the game reserves of southern Spain. Since the *aoudad* was accustomed to a very similar habitat in the Atlas mountains, it has done very well in the Sierra Espuña. Wild boar, foxes and wild cats are also on the list of residents, along with eagles, owls and partridges. But for most visitors the park's main attractions are neither its wildlife nor its rock-faces, but rather its vast tracts of untouched Mediterranean pine forest where hiking and camping are an unmitigated pleasure.

The summers are hot and dry — Murcia is one of the driest provinces of Spain — but in

The wild sheep, or *mouflon*, has been introduced to the Sierra Espuña from Sardinia

winter the sierra normally receives about 15 cm (6 inches) of snow. In former days the snow-cutters of the mountains had storage 'wells' of packed snow or *neveros*, which they would haul down to Murcia during the summer, where it was used for making ice cream. You can still come across some of the *nevero* wells, and also the abandoned coal mines, on the southern slope of the Perona (1,185 m/3,900 ft). Nowadays the only modern intrusion in this archetypal forest is a Spanish air force station on top of the highest mountain, which prevents hikers from actually ascending to the summit of Espuña. Still, the views from lower down are sufficiently panoramic, and the summit of the neighbouring Morrón affords absolutely breathtaking views to both the south and east.

Before you go *Maps:* IGN 1:25,000 and 1:50,000 Nos. 932, 933, 953 and 954; and IGN 1:200,000 Mapa Provincial of Murcia.

Getting there *By car:* take the N340 Murcia-Almería road to the village of Alhama de Murcia, about 23 km (14 miles) south of Murcia, then turn north on the well marked side road, Alhama-Mula, turning west after 5 km (3 miles) up a steep hill that leads into the park.

By bus: there is no service to the Sierra Espuña. The nearest bus stop is at Alhama de Murcia, about 10 km (6 miles) from the centre of the park as the crow flies.

Where to stay: plenty of accommodation options to choose from. You could try either the 2-star Hotel Los Bartolos, T: (968) 63 16 71, or the Casa El Aljibe, T: (968) 63 21 98, both in Alhama de Murcia. In Murcia try the 4-star Arco de San Juan, T: (968) 21 04 55, F: 22 08 09, or one of

The maritime pine can reach heights of more than 30m (100ft)

the many lower-category hotels. *Outdoor living:* within the park, no permit is needed for camping only 1 night. If you intend a longer stay, you should apply for a permit from the Servicio de Montes, Caza y Pesca, C/ Juan XXIII, s/n, Murcia. The park wardens will help you find one or another of the many *fuentes* which will provide you with plentiful spring water.

Activities *Walking:* no marked paths, but plenty of scope for hiking.

Further information *Tourist office:* Murcia, p112.

129

CHAPTER 6

Andalucía

Many of the things that the rest of the world considers quintessentially Spanish are native to Andalucía, the glorious south of Spain. This is the home of flamenco music and of such electrifying dances as the *sevillana.* Here you'll find the remarkable mosque of Córdoba and the marble fountains and audience chambers of the Alhambra of Granada; the rolling countryside of Jaén, dotted with olive tree patterns as far as the eye can see; the perpetual snows of the Sierra Nevada; the processions of *penitentes* who move through the streets of Seville at Easter time; the horse and sherry fairs at Jerez de la Frontera; the gypsy cafés of Triana; the bullfights in Cádiz or Arcos de la Frontera. The excitements and pleasures of Andalucía are as varied as the region itself, for no other part of Spain enjoys greater contrast and variety. Even the snob capital of Spain, Marbella, and the crowded beaches of the Costa del Sol contribute to this extraordinary kaleidoscope of Andalucian images.

I'll never forget my first introduction to Andalucía, years ago, when a friend and I rode there on horse-back from La Mancha. In one remote valley that consisted entirely of olive groves and was still untouched by electricity pylons, we came upon a young farmer who was working by himself and singing a nonchalant flamenco melody that floated out over the empty landscape like smoke carried by the breeze. There was not a cloud in the sky and the air was crystal clear; the yellow-ochre earth looked as though it could not possibly be fertile (although, in fact, it produces

Generations of Andalucian people have toiled to maintain their neatly terraced olive groves in the shadow of the badlands of Almería

some of the world's finest olives) and off to one side loomed the dark blue mountains of the Sierra Morena. It was an incredibly secluded spot, made all the more haunting by the endless *melismas* of that ancient peasant song, half Arabic, half European.

Although Andalucía is now one of the most important of the autonomous communities of modern Spain, it still has innumerable out-of-the-way corners in which you can feel a very un-European sense of loneliness. It is a vast and often underpopulated land. The forest-covered Sierra Morena forms its northern rampart; in the south it is bounded by the Mediterranean and in the west by the Atlantic — a very different kind of sea — while its tip faces the African continent across the blue waters of the Straits of Gibraltar.

Andalucía covers nearly 9 million hectares (22 million acres), an area almost as large as Portugal, although with a population density that is only about 80 per cent of that country's. Essentially it consists of a great plain, the valley of the Río Guadalquivir, hemmed in by mountains on every side except the south-west, where it descends to the Atlantic. But before reaching the Gulf of Cádiz the river forms a blocked-up delta, the marshes of Doñana, which were once one of the great hunting preserves of Spain and are now its foremost national park.

The lowlands, known as Andalucía *baja*, contain a number of brackish lakes — often important bird habitats — and salt-impregnated wastelands (*despoblados*) which are partly attributable to the fact that the whole area was covered by the sea in the not very distant geological past. The Guadalquivir rises in the mountains of Jaén and is joined by a large number of tributaries on its way to the sea. To the south, its valley is

flanked by mountains, notably the immense massif of the Sierra Nevada, which includes the highest peaks of the Iberian peninsula. These highlands, together with the mountains of Almería and Jaén, constitute Andalucía *alta*.

As a result of these dramatic topographical variations, Andalucía possesses a series of ecosystems that have fascinated generations of naturalists. Indeed, vegetation in the most 'typically Spanish' of regions runs the whole gamut from bougainvillea to gentians. The lowest belt, from sea level to about 500 metres (1,650 feet), is characteristically Mediterranean, dominated by olive and mastic trees, holly oak and so on, along with the caper bush, the aloe, the cactus, orange and lemon trees, palms and other semi-tropical plants that thrive in the warm climate of the coast. Above this there are the forests of holm oak, up to 1,600 metres (5,250 feet), succeeded by a 300-metre (1,000-foot) zone of thick marescent forests with sporadic stands of Corsican pine and, more rarely, Scots pine.

From 1,900-2,600 metres (6,200-8,500 feet) there is a belt of juniper and savin brushwood, although much deteriorated and fighting to hold its own against a massive invasion by members of the broom family. In the Sierra Nevada are two high-altitude belts that have both received a great deal of botanical attention in recent years. Up to 2,900 metres (9,500 feet) the 'Sierra Nevada tundra' produces peat bogs with mosses and montane pasture plants (such as *Carex fusca* of the sedge family and the grass *Festuca frigida*); deep-soil areas, or *borreguiles*, where the pastures are always green; and patches known as *cascarajes*, with cushion-shaped vegetation. The highest belt has been called 'the cold desert' because it contains few plants and only lichens are plentiful, although in some sheltered areas there are pastures of *Festuca clementei* and the bent-grass *Agrostis nevadensis*. The vegetation of these two highest belts includes 40 plants found only in the Sierra Nevada, another 12 species that grow in nearby mountains of Andalucía, about 20 that are also found in the high mountains of Morocco and a further 70 that are shared with the Alps. One rarity that has been saved from extinction by conservation measures is *Artemisia granatensis*, a type of wormwood, which was endangered because of excessive collection by the local people for use in herbal teas.

Another notable native of Andalucía is the rare Spanish fir, *Abies pinsapo*, whose last major forest lies within the boundaries of the Parque Natural de Grazalema, west of Ronda. Elsewhere in the region this remarkable 20- to 30-metre (65- to 100-foot) tree was threatened by the voracious grazing habits of the local goats, whose appetite for seedlings prevented the *pinsapo* from reproducing naturally. To encourage the regeneration of these forests, the Sierra de las Nieves — part of the Serranía de Ronda — was also declared a *parque natural*, from which hungry goats are rigorously excluded.

The cork oak, *Quercus suber*, also thrives in Andalucía, where sherry bottlers regard it as an essential national resource. Unlike the *pinsapo* it holds its own very well in many areas as long as there is sufficient rainfall; in the *reserva nacional* at Cortes de la Frontera, for example, cork oaks cover some 93 per cent of the total area. Cork forests are usually carefully managed so that layers of the bark that grows around the trunks can be removed every eight to ten years; meanwhile black Iberian hogs are left to shift for themselves among the acorns that fall from the trees, and

in due course develop into a *jamón ibérico* that is highly prized for its nutty flavour.

Andalucía is also home to some 4,000 distinct species of vascular plant — approximately half the total ever recorded in peninsular Spain and the Balearic Islands — more than 150 of which are found nowhere else in the world. Perhaps the main reason for this extraordinary botanical diversity is that Andalucía lies at the crossroads of Europe and Africa: a meeting point for species from both continents. Particular centres of endemism include the Sierras de Cazorla, Segura y Las Villas, the Serranía de Ronda and the Sierra Nevada, the latter weighing in with no less than 65 endemics: one of the main reasons for its declaration as a national park in 1998, Spain's largest and the most recent addition to this category. The fact that many of these endemics are unique to a single locality makes them very vulnerable to changes in land use, forest fires and the attentions of over-zealous horticulturalists; of the 300 species listed in the Spanish Plant Red Data Book, no less than 212 can be found in Andalucía, 123 exclusively so.

The wealth and variety of Andalucía's flora is paralleled by an abundance of birds and beasts. Doñana National Park is a paradise for birds of both Europe and Africa. There are golden eagles and eagle owls in the sierras of Tejeda and Almijara, and other highlands are inhabited by Bonelli's eagle, the goshawk, the peregrine falcon and Egyptian and griffon vultures. Roe deer thrive in the mountains of Cádiz and western Málaga, and the red deer reintroduced by state ecologists has done well in Doñana and Cortes de la Frontera. Wild boar flourish in the national and regional parks, though they are hunted regularly in the game re-

133

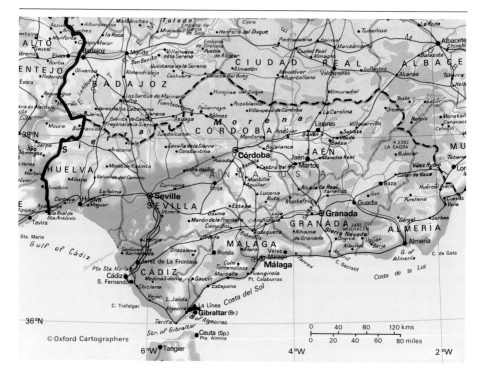

serves and so numbers there are less.

Unlike some of the other autonomous regions of Spain, Andalucía was never a single, independent kingdom. Historically it either formed part of other empires, such as those of Rome or Damascus, or was divided into petty kingdoms that were often at loggerheads. Since 1833, Andalucía has consisted of eight provinces: Almería, Cádiz, Córdoba, Granada, Jaén, Huelva, Málaga and Seville. Although now governed by a central body, the Junta de Andalucía, the individual provinces are still fiercely protective of their local traditions and prerogatives — and at the same time concerned about expanding their nature reserves as a way of safeguarding their ecological patrimony. Hence the provinces are doing more than ever before in the realm of conservation, placing lakes, forests, marshes and other animal habitats under the

protection of the local departments of the environment.

The Andalucían government has declared no less than 82 protected areas, covering around 17 per cent of its total surface area. There are 2 national parks (state-run) and 22 natural parks (Andalucían-run); while the rest are *reservas*, *parajes* and *sitios naturales*.

Not so long ago, travellers would shake their heads over the 'backward' condition of Andalucían agriculture. 'Almost half Andalucía is abandoned to a state of nature,' grumbled Richard Ford in the middle of the 19th century, wondering how they could go on using mule-powered irrigation wheels rather than centrifugal pumps. But today, many of us give grateful thanks to the happy circumstance that has preserved so much of the Andalucían landscape from 'progress' and kept so much of it in the once-lamentable state of nature.

These dunes at Punta Paloma on the Atlantic coast have been stabilized by the planting of pine trees

BEFORE YOU GO
Maps: Michelin 1:400,000 No. 446.

GETTING THERE
By air: Málaga is the most important airport in Andalucía, handling the most international flights; Seville has many fewer. Jerez de la Frontera and Almería have some international flights — with Almería's being mainly charter services — but all of them, as well as Córdoba and Granada, handle internal flights.
By sea: Andalucía's principal ports are Almería, Motril, Málaga, Algeciras, Cádiz and Huelva. Trasmediterránea operates ferry services between Algeciras, T: (956) 66 52 00, F: 66 52 16, and Tangier or Ceuta; and between Cádiz, T: (956) 28 43 11, F: 25 84 33, and the Canary Islands.
By car: the main north-south axis of Andalucía is the E5/NIV, Autovía de Andalucía, from Madrid to Seville, via Córdoba; the E902/N323 branches off at Bailén to Jaén, Granada and Málaga. The E803/N630, Ruta de la Plata (Silver Route), runs from the north coast at Gijón, south through León, Salamanca, Cáceres and Mérida, to Seville. The E26/N340, the longest road in Spain, runs from Cádiz all the way round the coast to Barcelona.
By rail: RENFE's principal connection to Andalucía is the AVE high-speed link between Madrid, Córdoba and Seville. Other express services use those tracks to Córdoba, and then branch off to Málaga or Algeciras, or continue to Córdoba, Seville, Jerez de la Frontera and Cádiz. There are also express (actually not too fast) and overnight services from Madrid to Granada, and a very slow day-time service from Madrid to Seville, via Cáceres Mérida and Zafra.

For information, call RENFE in Madrid, T: (91) 328 90 20, or consult the schedules on RENFE's web-site, www.renfe.es.
By bus: most services out of Madrid leave from the Estación Sur bus station, T: (91) 468 45 11. Two of the principal operators between Madrid and Andalucía are Grupo ENATCAR, T: (91) 467 35 77/527 99 27, and Sevibus/Secorbus, T: (91) 530 44 17.

Within Andalucía different operators run bus services, which are detailed in the fact-packs for individual exploration zones.

WHEN TO GO

Some mountain excursions are impossible in winter. On the other hand, skiing in the Sierra Nevada is particularly pleasant because there is so much sunshine at these latitudes and altitudes, even in January, when northern Europe has short days and cloudy skies. The summer may be too hot for strenuous activities in certain areas. Spring and autumn are the ideal times for exploring.

WHERE TO STAY

The cities, towns and countryside of Andalucía have large numbers of hotels and other accommodation in every price range, from the simplest *pensiones*, to *paradores* and extremely luxurious private hotels. For information on the best places to stay, see the individual fact-packs.

ACTIVITIES

Mountaineering clubs: Federación Andaluza de Montañismo, Camino de Ronda, 101, Edificio Atalaya 1°, 18003 Granada, T/F: (958) 29 13 40.
Skiing: the only ski resort of Andalucía is Solynieve in the Sierra Nevada, T: (958) 24 91 04.
Excursions: the so-called Ruta de los Pueblos Blancos (Route of the White Villages) is a well established circuit of some of the best preserved hill-towns and villages of western Andalucía. One suggested route begins at Arcos de la Frontera, taking in Prado del Rey, El Bosque, Benamahoma, Grazalema, Ubrique and Benaoján (all in Cádiz province) and terminates in Ronda, with its spectacular setting above the Tajo.
   Other circuits take in Ronda, Atajate and La Jimera de Líbar, in the province of Málaga and Arcos, Bornos,

Villamartín, Algodonales, Zahara, Olvera, Torre Alháquime, and Setenil de las Bodegas.
   There are daily bus connections between all the villages on the routes. Most of them have official camp-sites and offer fishing in season.

FURTHER INFORMATION

Algeciras (956): tourist office, Juan de la Cierva, s/n, 11207, T: 57 26 36, F: 57 04 75.
Almería (950): tourist office, Parque Nicolás Salmerón, s/n, 04002, T: 27 43 55, F: 27 43 60. Red Cross, T: 25 73 67, F: 25 53 25.
Cádiz (956): tourist office, Calderón de la Barca, 1, 11003, T: 57 26 36, F: 57 04 75. Red Cross, T: 27 76 70, F: 27 05 21.

Córdoba (957): tourist office, C/ Torrijos, 10, 14003, T/F: 20 05 22. Red Cross, T: 43 38 78, F: 43 64 04.
Granada (958): tourist office, Pl. de Mariana Pineda, 12 — bajo, 18009, T: 22 66 88, F: 22 89 16. Red Cross, T: 22 14 20, F: 22 87 40.
Huelva (959): tourist office, Avda. de Alemania, 12, 21001, T/F: 25 74 03. Red Cross, T: 26 12 11, F: 26 14 15.
Jaén (953): tourist office, Arquitecto Berges, 1, 23007, T/F: 22 27 37. Red Cross, T: 25 15 40, F: 26 26 14.
Málaga (95): tourist office, Pasaje de Chinitas, 4, 29015, T: 221 34 45, F: 222 94 21. Red Cross, T: 221 76 31, F: 222 01 88.
Seville (95): tourist office,

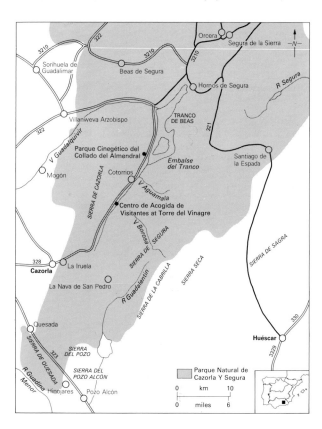

Avda. de la Constitución, 21 B, 41004, T: 422 14 04, F: 422 97 53. Red Cross, T: 437 66 13, F: 438 82 31.

FURTHER READING
Gerald Brenan, *South from Granada* (London, 1957); Robin Collomb, *Gredos*

Mountains and Sierra Nevada (Reading, 1987); Ernest García & Andrew Paterson, *Where to watch birds in Southern Spain* (Christopher Helm, 1994); Gabriel García Guardia, *Flores Silvestres de Andalucía* (Editorial Rueda, 1988);

Washington Irving, *Tales of the Alhambra* (Madrid, 1832); John & Christine Oldfield, *Landscapes of Andalucía and the Costa del Sol* (Sunflower, 1999); Andy Paterson, *Bird-watching in Southern Spain,* (Golf Area S.A., 1987).

Sierras de Cazorla, Segura & Las Villas

Limestone parque natural *birthplace of the Río Guadalquivir with several peaks over 2,000 m (6,600 ft)*
ZEPA, Biosphere Reserve
214,300 ha (529,545 acres)

The great Río Guadalquivir (literally, 'big river' in Arabic) rises in the Sierra de Cazorla, amid some of the wildest landscape in Spain, in the Cañada de las Fuentes. For a while the resulting stream flows confidently north and east, as if it were going to make its way to the Mediterranean. But the mountains will not let it pass; it meets the Sierra de Segura head on and is forced to make a dramatic change of course, curving suddenly westward to begin its long run down to the Atlantic and the marismas of the Doñana National Park.

At the start of its long march to the sea, the Guadalquivir gives its name to a valley bounded by the sierras of Cazorla, Segura, del Pozo and de la Cabrilla; it continues to widen toward the south-east, confined by a series of peaks over 2,000 metres (6,600 feet) high. The highest peak in this immense *parque natural* is Cerros de las Empanadas (2,107 metres/6,910 feet), and virtually everything within the boundaries of the park is higher than 700 metres (2,300 feet), except the land located on the shores of the artificial lake occupying its heartland, the Embalse del Tranco, which is fed by the infant Guadalquivir and its first tributaries.

Innumerable brooks and rivulets pour from the sides of this mountain enclave, and virtually all rush to join the Guadalquivir (except the waters of the nascent Río Guadalentín, which eventually flow into the Guadiana Menor). The area has more than 20 rivers and brooks important enough to have names of their own.

The park includes several valleys adjacent to the main valley of the Guadalquivir, such as that of Guadalentín and the canyons (*barrancos*) of Borosa and Aguamala: dramatic narrow cuts in the landscape, with steep slopes covered in bushes and pine trees, and high mountain meadows full of succulent grasses and wild flowers — rich pasture for flocks of sheep.

The sierra is composed of hard limestone, beneath which lies a softer layer of clays and red sands; they can be seen in section in some of the larger gorges. Its sheltered position between the Montes Universales and the Sierra Nevada meant that it was ideally situated to provide a refuge for high-altitude plants during the tremendous climatic changes in the Ice Ages. Consequently, these mountains contain a number of Tertiary relict species not found anywhere else in the world. *Viola cazorlensis*, a shrubby violet with unusual deep crimson or carmine flowers and very long slender spurs, is one of the most interesting. It flowers in May, from the depths of shady rock crevices; its nearest living relatives are found as far away as Mount Olympus in Greece, and Montenegro. Another example is the butterwort *Pinguicula vallisneriifolia*. This insectivorous plant is found in a highly specialized habitat under towering limestone cliffs drenched in continually dripping water, and totally out of reach of the rays of the sun.

Two endemic species of daffodil also thrive in these mountains: *Narcissus longis-*

137

pathus and *N. hedraeanthus*. The second is a tiny hoop-petticoat daffodil found in early May in snow-melt areas high in the mountains. A further endemic to this range is the columbine *Aquilegia cazorlensis*, which is known only on the shady limestone slopes around the summit of Pico de Cabañas (2,028 m/6,653 ft) and flowers in early June.

All told, the park contains over 1,100 species of plants, but you needn't be a specialist to enjoy the forests of tall pines that reach over 20 metres (65 feet) in height, and the sweet profusion of thyme, rosemary, sweet marjoram and lavender. Along the banks of the streams are 'tunnels' of flowers, grasses, ferns and shrubs; the minor rivers are lined with poplars, ash trees and willows. On the lower slopes the pine forests are made up of aleppo pine (*Pinus halepensis*), while above 1,300 metres (4,260 feet) mar-

itime pine (*P. pinaster*) dominates. Oaks are also common. The high valleys, called *navas*, are covered with grasses and wild flowers — ideal fodder for *mouflon*, red deer and ibex. Some of the mountain tops are treeless; occasionally this bareness is due to natural causes, but usually it is because overgrazing has tipped the ecological balance in favour of low-growing shrubs rather than trees.

Cazorla is a fine camping and hiking area. You can wake up in the middle of the night to the sound (and smell) of boars snuffling around outside your tent. This is the spot where you are most likely to happen upon a herd of red deer in the underbrush. They're not tame, and will turn tail at your approach, but encounters are frequent and help give Cazorla a sense of being part of the 'peaceable kingdom' where the camper can, as it were, lie down with the ibex.

The Spanish ibex, an almost mythical member of the goat family, once lived throughout the Iberian peninsula, but was

The Guadalquivir is already impressively wide as it leaves the Sierra de Cazorla

hunted for its splendid scimitar-shaped horns. Today only small isolated groups exist, often of distinct sub-species (ssp.), each with slightly different characteristics. Cazorla is home to a population of ssp. *hispanica*, which is also found in Grazalema and the Sierra Nevada. Further north, in the Gredos, there are larger numbers of ssp. *victoriae*, and a small herd of ssp. *pyrenaica pyrenaica* still survives in the Pyrenees, in Ordesa. Ibex are known in Spanish as *cabra montés* and are very much more difficult to observe than the fallow and red deer that inhabit the lower regions of the reserve.

By contrast, deer-watching is easy. If you happen to be on hand in September or the beginning of October you can observe the extraordinary spectacle of the *berrea*, when the stags stake out both their territorial claims and their harems. Tilting back their heads so that their antlers rest on their backs, they bay to the winds to attract any females within earshot. Sometimes their cry is answered by a challenge and there then follows fierce butting and crashing of antlers until the weaker male gives way.

The red deer and roe deer are not easily intimidated by the presence of human intruders. Their visibility varies, however, according to the season. During the summer, when the days get very hot, especially in the rocky and treeless areas, the animals come out only at night, so you may catch a glimpse of them in the evening or at dawn. In winter their habits change, however, and with a reasonable amount of discretion you can come close to them before they run off.

Water is often a rarity in Spanish wild places, especially in the south. Here, there is more than enough of it, thanks to a weather pattern that provides an abundance of rainfall, particularly during the summer thunderstorms that hurl banks of dark clouds against the perpendicular walls of the high sierras. The mountains catch the moisture from the Atlantic and the Mediterranean, and their effectiveness as a natural barrier is enforced by the thermal masses of warm air from the Levant which usually prevent the Atlantic clouds from moving further east: rain falls in sheets when warm air meets cold air above Cazorla. These periodic inundations are irregular and unpredictable. During the summer, the woods turn to tinder and the frequent dramatic electrical storms have often led to major forest fires.

Because of the high rainfall and despite the southerly location of these mountains several birds occur here which you would normally expect to see further north. There is an isolated population of alpine accentor (and another in the Sierra Nevada), and alpine choughs have also been recorded, although not normally found in the southern half of Spain. Other species include rock thrush, blue rock thrush and ortolan bunting. The Embalse del Tranco attracts mallard and teal; wood-pigeons and turtle-doves inhabit the pine forests in spring and summer, when quail (and to a lesser extent, red-legged partridge) abound in the high meadows. Birds of prey include Egyptian vultures, eagles, kites, sparrow-hawks and kestrels.

The wild, untamed parts of the Parque Natural represent only one facet of what is one of the great unspoiled regions of Spain. It is nearly a hundred kilometres long and 35 kilometres wide, from Hinojares to Villarrodrigo, which means that the protected zone encompasses some of the oldest and most beautiful villages in all Andalucía. These villages are ideally suited to serve as base camps for long hikes in the mountains.

The fortified hill village of Segura de la Sierra, near the northern end of the park, supplies a spectacular case in point. It looks out over one of the richest olive-growing valleys of the province of Jaen (the name derives from the Arabic 'passage of caravans'), and its cliff-hanging houses are topped with an immense medieval fortress. From here countless walks can be taken along unpaved roads and tracks leading through the olive groves; alternatively, one can set out for the high peaks of the range, to watch the ibex, eagles and Egyptian vultures. These villages afford a rare opportunity to feel part of the landscape, and to understand the tenacious people who cling to their ancient stone houses and go on cultivating the orchards that their ancestors carved out of these inhospitable mountains when they were still inhabited by wolves.

139

Viola cazorlensis is a cherished rarity of the Sierra de Cazorla

BEFORE YOU GO
Maps: IGN 1:25,000 and 1:50,000 Nos. 790, 816, 841, 842, 865, 866, 886, 887, 906 and 907; IGN 1:200,000 Mapas Provinciales of Albacete, Granada and Jaén.
Guide-book: Jordi Bastant, *Sierras de Cazorla, Segura y La Sagra* (Cúpula, 1996).

GETTING THERE
By car: from Granada or Jaén, the best access is through Jódar; an alternative route, though much longer, is the scenic drive through Guadix, Pozo Alcón and Quesada, which takes in the valley of the Guadiana Menor. From Madrid, take the E5/NIV to Bailén, then the N322 east towards Ubeda and the J314 to Cazorla — or you can turn off at La Carolina on the C3217 towards Beas de Segura, and the northern end of the range.
Entering the Sierra from the north is often the preferred route during the winter, since the southern approach is sometimes blocked by heavy

snowfalls.
By bus: Alsina Graells operates a service between Jaén, T: (953) 25 15 14, and Cazorla, where buses stop in the main plaza. Manuel Córcoles, T: (967) 21 22 40, operates one bus a day, each way, between Albacete and Orcera, at the northern end of the Sierra.

WHERE TO STAY
Along the Carretera del Tranco, one of the prettiest parts of the park, there are many interesting places to stay. These include the 3-star Hotel Noguera de La Sierpe, T: (953) 71˙30 21, F: 71 31 09; 2-star Hotel Montaña, T: (953) 72 70 11, F: 72 70 01; the Complejo Residencial Los Enebros, T: (953) 72 71 10, F: 72 71 34, comprising hotel, apartments, camping and attractive wooden cabins; and the charming, remote, 1-star Hospedería Las Cañadillas, T: (953) 12 81 42, in the Sierra close to the dam at El Tranco. At the southern end of the valley is the Parador of Cazorla, T: (953) 72 70 75, F:

The butterwort *Pinguicula vallisneriifolia*, endemic to the mountains of south-eastern Spain, traps insects on its strap-shaped leaves

72 70 77. Just outside the park the 2-star Hotel Las Villas, T: (953) 44 01 25, on the N322 at Villacarrillo, offers great value. Ubeda also has two interesting choices: the very modern 4-star Meliá Confort, T: (953) 79 10 11, F: 79 10 12, and the historic 2-star Hotel Palacio de la Rambla, T: (953) 75 01 96, F: 75 02 67.
Outdoor living: an ideal area for camping; many spots are marked *zona de acampada* and are under the supervision of forest wardens. For stays of more than one night a permit is necessary. Some of the many camp-sites in the area are: Camping Chopera de Coto Ríos, T: (953) 71 30 05, open all year and with a capacity of 450 people, and Fuente de La Pascuala, T: (953) 71 30 28, open 1 Feb-30 Nov and holding 500 people, both at Coto Ríos; Complejo Los Enebros, T: (953) 72 71 10, open all year and with a capacity of 360, at La Iruela; Camping Garrote Gordo, T: (953) 12 61 59, open 15 Mar-30 Sept and with capacity for 300 people, at Segura de la Sierra.

ACTIVITIES
Walking: there are innumerable possibilities for walks and excursions, including well marked hiking trails. Details at the information centre (see below).
Swimming: the village of Coto Ríos has a small artificial lake that is open to swimmers.
Deer-watching: Cabeza de la Viña, an island in the Embalse de Tranco, for which deer have a special penchant.
Gardens/collections: the Parque Cinegético del Collado del Almendral (open 8 am-9 pm in summer and until 6 pm in winter) on the shores of the Tranco contains representatives of the Sierra's main animal species. The botanical gardens

(*jardín botánico*) at Torre del Vinagre are open mornings 11 am-2 pm and afternoons in the summer 5 pm-8 pm and in the winter 4 pm-7 pm. The Freshwater Fish Centre (*Centro acuopiscícola*), displaying the ecology of the park's rivers, is 2 km (1¼ miles) from the Torre del Vinagre.

FURTHER INFORMATION
Tourist office: Jaén, p136.
Park information: Centro de Interpretación Torre del Vinagre, Carretera del Tranco, Km 17, 23470 Cazorla, T: (953) 72 01 15, F: 71 00 68. Open Tues-Sun 11 am-2 pm and 5 pm-8 pm in the summer, and 4 pm-7 pm in winter.

Park tours: Excursiones Quercus, Guías de la Naturaleza, Centro de Interpretación Torre del Vinagre, offers trekking and horse-back excursions, four-wheel-drive tours of the restricted areas, wildlife photography trips and professional guides.

Sierra Nevada & Las Alpujarras

Recently created parque nacional, *encompassing the highest mountains in mainland Spain, reaching 3,482 m (11,424 ft); great diversity of flora, guaranteed by proximity of the Mediterranean Biosphere Reserve*

The highest road in Europe is the highway 'de la Sierra' which leads from Granada to the ski resort known as Solynieve (literally, 'sun-and-snow') in the Sierra Nevada. It is a pleasant, scenic route that gently wafts you up 2,500 metres (8,000 feet) or so, and almost before you realize it you will have arrived at altitudes more familiar to pilots than car-drivers.

Most of the year the highest part of the road is snowed in, so that the only way to proceed to the famous look-out point on the Pico Veleta ('the weathercock') at 3,398 metres (11,148 feet) is on foot, on skis or by means of the *telecabina* installed there for the convenience of skiers. The road and the *telecabina* have made it almost too easy to ascend to the top of what are the highest, and were once the remotest mountains in mainland Spain. The modern conveniences of La Veleta are close to the untrodden wilderness of its even higher neighbour, Mulhacén (3,482 metres/11,420 feet) and the rest of the Sierra Nevada — literally the 'snowy mountains', since the higher peaks are snow-covered the year round.

This is the main mountain chain of the Cordillera Penibética, a mighty barrier some 70 kilometres (45 miles) long which runs parallel to the Mediterranean coast about 48 kilometres (30 miles) inland. Altogether the range has 14 major peaks over 3,000 metres (9,800 feet), where the perpetual snow contrasts with black schists. Until recently one of the highest valleys contained a small glacier, Corral de Veleta, the southernmost such formation in Europe, but it is no longer permanently covered with ice. In general, however, the deep *barrancos* show little evidence of past glacial activity — except the well formed cirques high up at their heads.

Structurally, the Sierra Nevada resembles the alpine system, composed of nappes (rock-sheets) which have been thrust from the south northwards. These folded strata are rich in zinc, copper, lead, mercury and iron. The central dome of the range (the mica schists) has weathered to form rounded, smooth contours at high altitudes, but the Triassic limestones and sandstones of the flanks have been deeply dissected by powerful rivers to form gorges.

Just to the south of the Sierra Nevada lies the range of Las Alpujarras, which consists mainly of valleys descending at right angles

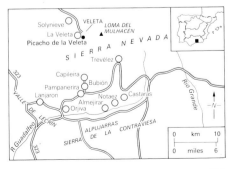

FLORA AND FAUNA OF THE SIERRA NEVADA

Rising to an extreme altitude, yet standing close to the Mediterranean, the Sierra Nevada harbours an incredible diversity of life-forms. Most of the endemic species are concentrated in the alpine zone, above 2,600 m (8,500 ft). The unique community here boasts some 200 snow-tolerant herbs, of which approximately 40 are endemic to these mountains. Many of the plants have dense hairs, usually whitish, covering their leaves. This feature is characteristic of high-altitude species, functioning as a means of coping with high levels of ultra-violet radiation. And many of the typical species here carry spines as a defence against the large number of herbivores, both wild and domestic, that inhabit these middle-mountain zones.

The endemic daffodil (*Narcissus nevadensis*) is one of the first flowers to appear in the spring, growing in boggy areas, especially around melting snow patches. Alongside its golden-yellow trumpets you can often see the slender-stemmed pink flowers of the crocus *Colchicum triphyllum*, a mountain species of southern and central Spain. On the stony slopes above, thousands of blue, white and mauve Nevada crocuses (*Crocus nevadensis*) spring from apparently barren ground; though exclusive in name, this species can also be found in various other sierras of southern Spain.

Another feature of the vegetation of the Sierra Nevada is the band of dome-shaped, spiny, xeromorphic shrubs that lies between 1,700-2,000 m (5,575-6,500 ft), appropriately known as the 'hedgehog' zone. A major component of the flora here is the hedgehog broom (*Erinacea anthyllis*) with blue-violet flowers which form in clusters at the ends of stems bearing vicious spines. It grows with a number of other leguminous shrubs such as *A. granatensis, Echinospartum boissieri* and the Nevada race of the mountain tragacanth, *Astragalus sempervirens* ssp. *nevadensis*.

The Sierra Nevada shares several of its butterfly species with the Pyrenees, though often the colonies differ slightly. The Glandon blue, *Agriades glandon* is an example. In the Sierra Nevada this lycaenid, more brown than blue in colour, is of the sub-species *zullichi*; in the Pyrenees it is much more blue-flushed, especially the male, and of the type race *glandon*. Within the Sierra Nevada, it is restricted solely to altitudes above 3,000 metres (9,800 feet) and to peaks in the east of the range in the province of Granada. The larvae are thought to feed off various plants of the primrose family, but as with many of these highly restricted butterflies, study of its ecology has been very limited and little is really known, except that it flies in July and August.

A species with an almost identical range within the Sierra, but this time found nowhere else in the world, is the Nevada blue, *Plebicula golgus*.

Another Pyrenean/Sierra Nevada butterfly is the Spanish brassy ringlet (*Erebia hispania*), again flying in the Granadan part of the Nevada mountains. It is a species with a world distribution confined to Spain and the French Pyrenees, feeding on mountain grasses such as poas and fescues growing at altitudes in excess of 1,800 metres (5,900 feet). The Sierra Nevada contains the type race of the Spanish brassy ringlet; the Pyrenean subspecies is *rondoui*, found in the central part of the range.

Although the valleys and lowlands surrounding the Sierra Nevada offer a fine cross-section of birds typical of Andalucía and the Mediterranean coast, it is sheer altitude that gives the range its special character. Birds typical of more northerly latitudes find a southern-most European outpost here — it is strange for a visitor from England, France or Germany to be confronted suddenly with greenfinch, crossbill, great tit or blackbird whose compatriots have been left behind hundreds of kilometres to the north. Here too are those typically montane birds, alpine accentors, which gather around the ski resorts like sparrows. Choughs wheel in great flocks over the gorges and golden eagles soar effortlessly across their huge territories. Searching for birds is always more productive in the lusher valleys rather than the bare mountain tops . Rock buntings feed among the rocky walls and where a scree runs down to some isolated farmstead the black wheatear may be found.

The Sierra Nevada owes its name to the perpetual snows of its highest peaks

from the crest of the Sierra Nevada; midway down the slope white villages cling precariously to the terraced mountainside. The name Alpujarras derives from the Moorish Al-Busherat, 'the grassland', and it was the Moors who terraced and irrigated these valleys, cultivating semi-tropical fruits on the slopes of the white-capped mountains. 'Ever faithful to the precepts of the Koran,' writes Pedro Antonio de Alarcón, they 'introduced every such species of exotic fruit or herb as was calculated to flourish and enrich the land.' As a result, these are some of the most fertile valleys in Spain, noted for their grapes, oranges, lemons and figs. About 80 villages, 40 hamlets and countless *cortijos* (farmsteads) make up the nucleus of Las Alpujarras. They form two parallel strips that are quite different in altitude and climate: La Alpujarra Alta lies just south of the great peaks, and La Alpujarra Baja is in the Sierra de la Contraviesa, which borders the Mediterranean.

Between these two mountain ranges lies the Valle de Lecrín, at whose entrance the last Moorish ruler of Granada, Boabdil, is said to have paused in his flight to cast a final glance at his lost kingdom; the spot is known as El Ultimo Suspiro del Moro ('the Moor's last sigh'), a name used by Salman Rushdie as the title of a recent novel. Between Orgiva and Trevélez the vegetation changes dramatically as the altitude increases: pines, chestnuts, almonds, olives, palmettos, poplars, holm and cork oaks grow in the carefully tended woods and orchards. At the far eastern end of the Sierra Nevada, to the north of Almería, lie the deserts of Tabernas. Best known as the scene of several 'paellawesterns', this is also the only European habitat of the African trumpeter finch.

The way to the heart of Las Alpujarras leads up the Valle de Poqueira, a Cyclopean incision in the landscape that provides space for three perfect villages — Pampaneira, Bubión and Capileira with their houses jutting out over the cliff. The flat roofs are covered with heavy stones known as *launas*, and often serve as terraces for the houses situated above them. It was understandable that the Tibetan monks sent out by the exiled Dalai Lama should have chosen this valley for one of their European centres. A boy from Bubión has recently been identified as the reincarnation of a Tibetan lama who died two years before. 'In Las Alpujarras every legend is possible,' as Alarcón wrote.

The massive Mulhacén, the very roof of the Iberian peninsula, was named for the penultimate Caliph of Granada, Mujley-Hacen, who is said to be buried in some glacial niche of this great peak. There is a road up the mountain but as it approaches the summit, at the 3,000-metre (9,850-foot) level, drifts of snow up to 2 metres (6½ feet) deep impede progress. Climbers trying to reach the summit from the road have often been forced to turn back by winds that threaten to hurl them off the ridge. Where the snow has melted there is a riotous assembly of tiny wild flowers attended by swarms of brilliant butterflies that somehow manage to continue their dance without being blown away.

This is a landscape that reveals its greatest beauties only to the traveller on foot or on cross-country skis. In the 1920s the writer Gerald Brenan used to cover the distances between his home in Yegen and the other villages of Las Alpujarras on foot; he would even walk to Málaga. 'The path from Yegen to Orgiva was always an adventure,' he told a reporter in the 1970s. 'There were always many ravines, and the extremely cold weather in the winter carried with it the added risk of dangerous storms finding you away from the shelter of an inn or a cave. But the feeling of pleasure and well-being provided by this way of travelling cannot be matched by modern methods of travel.' It would be doing the Sierra an injustice — and showing the white feather — to drive through it by car without getting out to walk.

BEFORE YOU GO
Maps: IGN 1:25,000 and 1:50,000 Nos. 1,011, 1,026, 1,027, 1,028, 1,041 and 1,042; IGN 1:200,000 Mapas Provinciales of Granada and Almería; IGN 1:100,000 Parque Natural de Sierra Nevada.
Guide-books: Jordi Bastant, *Sierra Nevada y La Alpujarra* (Cúpula, 1996); Gerald Brenan, *South from Granada* (London, 1957); Pablo Bueno Porcel, *Sierra Nevada, Guía Montañera* (Editorial Mont Blanc, 1963); José Martín, *Aivar, Sierra Nevada y Alpujarra Alta* (Editorial Everest, 1985).

GETTING THERE
By car: access to the Sierra

Nevada ski resort, Solynieve, is via the winding 35-km (21-mile) GR420 from Granada. The road that leads from La Veleta across Mulhacén and down into Las Alpujarras is open to traffic only in Aug. At other times it is necessary to retrace the route to Granada and then head south on the E103/N323 to Lanjarón, and east into Las Alpujarras.
By bus: Autocares Bonal, T: (958) 27 31 00, Avda. Calvo Sotelo, 19, operates one bus daily — departing at 9 am, returning 5:30 pm — from Granada to the Solynieve resort.
Alsina Graells (Granada, T: (958) 18 50 10; Lanjarón, T: (958) 77 00 03; and Motril, T:

(958) 60 00 64) operates frequent services from the new bus station on the Avda. de Jaén to every major destination in the area.
However, bus connections amongst the various villages of Las Alpujarras are sporadic; walking is still considered a standard means of local travel.

WHERE TO STAY
The Solynieve resort, open only during the ski season, usually Dec-late May, has numerous hotels, including the 4-star Hotel Meliá Sierra Nevada, T: (958) 48 04 00, F: 48 04 58, and 3-star Nevasur, T: (958) 48 03 50, F: 48 03 65. The Alpujarras have many *casas rurales* and small country hotels, and the

following can be recommended: 2-star Hotel Los Berchules, T/F: (958) 85 25 30, in Berchules; the Villa Turística de Bubión, T: (958) 76 31 11, F: 76 31 36, in Bubión; the 3-star Hotel Taray, T: (958) 76 31 11, F: 76 31 36, just south of Orgiva, and the 1-star Hotel La Fragua, T: (958) 85 86 26, F: 85 86 14, in Trevélez – the highest village in Spain; the attractive 2-star Hotel Alquería de Morayama, T/F: (958) 34 32 21, in Cádiar and Hotel La Casa del Viento, T: (958) 34 70

The buttercup *Ranunculus acetosellifolius* is unique to the Sierra Nevada

09, in Lanjarón.
Between Granada and before turning east to Lanjarón, the road runs alongside the beautiful Lecrín valley; in Dúrcal there is the Hotel Mariami, T/F: (958) 78 04 09. Granada itself has a huge array of accommodation: try the central 4-star Hotel Saray, T: (958) 13 00 09, F: 12 91 61, and 3-star Hotel Victoria, T: (958) 25 77 04, F: 26 31 08; or the huge 4-star Hotel Alhambra Palace, T: (958) 22 14 68, F: 22 64 04, up in the Alhambra park and overlooking the city.
Outdoor living: the Sierra Nevada camp-site in Granada is open 1 Mar-30 Oct, T: (958) 15 00 62.
Refuges: there are several refuges in the Sierra Nevada: Postero Alto, T: (958) 34 51 54 at Jeres del Marquesado; El

Poqueira, La Carihuela and la Caldera at Capileira and Cortijo Rosales at Dílar.

ACTIVITIES
Walking/climbing: the road across the mountains from Las Alpujarras to La Veleta affords an uncomplicated route for high-mountain hiking and for back-packers.
The walk from Capileira to the ski resort below the Veleta is possible in late spring and during the summer and early autumn. It requires sturdy boots, sleeping bag and a 2-day supply of food. As a mountain adventure it is not quite the same as scaling the north face of the Eiger, but for the average, fit person it offers an exciting way to become acquainted with Las Alpujarras and the Sierra Nevada. The road leaves the village of Capileira as a fairly wide stony track that winds uphill through an afforestation zone of neatly planted pines. El Chorillo is the midway point, and a favourite overnight stopping place. The road continues toward the massive bulk of Mulhacén, skirting it and curving westward past the Puntal and Lagunas de La Caldera below: the lakes are partly iced over and there is snow on all surrounding faces. The track sweeps southward along the Loma Pela and then turns northward again toward the Veleta, where it crosses yet another ridge and finally descends to Solynieve.
Cross-country skiing: the area offers good opportunities for cross-country skiing.

FURTHER INFORMATION
Tourist office: Granada, p136.
Mountain club: Federación Andaluza de Montañismo, Camino de Ronda, 101, Edificio Atalaya 1°, 18003 Granada, T/F: (958) 29 13 40.
Park information: Parque

Natural de Sierra Nevada, Centro de Visitantes, El Dornajo, Carretera de Sierra Nevada, Km 23, Güéjar Sierra, T: (958) 34 06 25.

El Torcal de Antequera

A paraje natural 15 km (9 miles) south of Antequera, a limestone landscape renowned for its orchids and spring bulbs
ZEPA
1,171 ha (2,894 acres)

The bare, tortured rocks of El Torcal de Antequera are one of the most famous geological formations in Spain. Geologists call it the most important karstic phenomenon in southern Europe; lay people tend to think of it as a fantastic city in stone.
The landscape is characterized by vast limestone blocks and outcrops, sinks and ravines that have been gradually eroded into an endless series of Henry Moore sculptures to which whimsical imaginations have given such titles as La Muela ('the molar'), El Aguilucho ('the eaglet'), La Copa ('the wine glass'), El Lagarto ('the lizard'), La Loba ('the she-wolf') and Los Dos Iguales ('two of the same'). From the rock called Peña de las Siete Mesas, the whole of the madly inventive surface of El Torcal can be contemplated at leisure: the high walls, towers, spires, alleys and temples, with their air of ruined grandeur, suggest a petrified city that once had sacrificial altars at every street corner.
Fortunately, there is rarely anyone else to share the ruminations engendered by

145

these bizarre effects of rain, wind and geological eons. The whole thing is what the psychologists call a projective technique, akin to a giant Rorschach test in stone, and one woman's molar may well be another's butterfly. Quite apart from its scientific and sculptural interest, however, El Torcal is a wonderfully wind-swept spot, overgrown with ivy, hawthorn and wild roses. The only animals are small reptiles, common birds and occasional vultures. The highest point, about 1,600 m (5,200 ft), is the rock Camorro de las Villas.

Although vegetation is sparse, there is considerable botanical diversity, due to the absence of highly competitive dominant species. Most of those that grow well in these mountains are low, cushion-forming species, or ones that sprout from crevices. You'll find the tiny, violet-flowered spring rock-cress (*Arabis verna*), *Viola demetria,* an annual with bright yellow blooms, and the endemic *Saxifraga biternata,* whose delicate ferny foliage and white, bell-shaped flowers grace no other locality in the world. Other species typical of these dry limestone rocks are the Spanish bluebell (*Hyacinthoides hispanica*) and shining cranesbill (*Geranium lucidum*). The most spectacular feature of this flora is the colour combination in May of carmine peonies and the tall elegant stems of *Iris lutescens* ssp. *subbiflora* bearing velvety blooms of deep purple; this iris is found nowhere else in Spain, but occurs in parts of Portugal.

El Torcal de Antequera is especially renowned for its orchids. Some 30 species have been recorded, including the evocatively named brown bee orchid (*Ophrys fusca* ssp. *atlantica*) and mirror orchid (*O. speculum*), both of which have flowers of an iridescent blue with borders of chocolate-coloured fur, as well as woodcock and sawfly orchids (*O. scolopax* and *O. tenthredinifera*). Green-winged, bog and Jersey orchids (*Orchis morio, O. palustris and O. laxiflora*) flower in wetter seasons in the damp shady valleys beneath the towering pillars and peaks, while the lovely pink butterfly orchid (*O. papilionacea*) blooms on the sun-baked rock surfaces above. Three species of tongue orchid have been recorded here, as has the unhealthy looking and unpleasantly scented bug orchid (*Orchis coriophora*).

The cooler grassland habitats and woodland glades are decorated with the summer spikes of the dark red and broad-leaved helleborines (*Epipactis atrorubens* and *E. helleborine*). The intricate, trailing flowers of the lizard orchid (*Himantoglossum hircinum*) grow along the sides of the road in summer, where earlier in the year are found the huge, robust spikes of the closely related giant orchid (*Barlia robertiana*). Other notable examples are the dense-flowered orchid (*Neotinea maculata*), a characteristic plant of limestone soils, and the rose-pink, frilly *Orchis italica,* a plant more typical of acid environments. Both summer and autumn lady's tresses (*Spiranthes aestivalis* and *S. spiralis*) can be seen here, too.

Whether or not you join in the El Torcal game of name-that-rock or spot-the-orchid, this particularly rugged bit of scenery should not be missed.

Before you go *Maps:* IGN 1:25,000 and 1:50,000 Nos. 1,023, 1,024, 1,037 and 1,038; IGN 1:200,000 Mapa Provincial de Málaga. *Guide-book:* R. Cadanás, *Sierra del Torcal* (Editorial Alpina,

1968). **Getting there** *By car:* El Torcal is situated 15 km (9 miles) south of Antequera. Follow the C3310 road on the way to Villanueva de la Concepción, taking the first main turning on the right to El Torcal. *By rail:* Bobadilla — the important junction for all trains between Algeciras, Córdoba, Granada, Málaga and Seville — is one stop to the west of Antequera's station, on the Bobadilla to Granada line. *By bus:* Antequera, T: (95) 284 19 57, is well served by buses from Málaga, T: (95) 231 59 08, and Seville, T: (95) 441 88 11. From Antequera take the bus to Villanueva de la Concepción, and alight at the entrance to El Torcal — leaving a walk of several miles to the famous rock formations. **When to go:** spring and autumn are the best seasons for undertaking the journey; in winter El Torcal is blasted by icy winds and in summer the rocks radiate heat like a Bessemer furnace. **Where to stay:** La Posada del Torcal, T: (95) 203 11 77, F: 203 10 06, almost directly underneath El Torcal and with views to the coast, just outside Villanueva de la Concepción, is an excellent choice. The *casa rural* Casa de Elrond, T: (95) 275 40 91, in Villanueva de la Concepción, and the Parador at Antequera, T: (95) 284 09 01, F: 284 13 12, offer contrasting options. Restaurants are not normally recommended, but there is one in Antequera that shouldn't be missed: La Espuela, T/F: (95) 270 34 24, is the only restaurant in the world located inside a *Plaza de Toros*, and it serves excellent food. *Refuges:* the one mountain refuge for El Torcal can be found at Llanes de los Polvillares, at the end of the metalled road.

Few landscapes in the world can boast formations as bizarre as the limestone 'sculptures' of El Torcal

Activities

Walking: from the refuge at Llanos de los Polvillares follow the trail marked on the rocks with yellow arrows through the Vereda de la Losa ('path of the flagstone') to La Maceta ('the flowerpot'). Then, via 3 *callejones*, or alleys, the Oscuro, Tabaco and Ancho, the trail arrives at Los Arregladeros, whereupon it ascends to the Mirador de las Ventanillas and returns to the refuge; takes about 2 hours to complete.

A more ambitious itinerary is the one marked on the rocks with red arrows. It starts at the refuge, passes Sima del Chaparro and takes in the Camorro de las Siete Mesas, with its panoramic view of El Torcal. The path skirts past the Peñón de Pizarro, then leads you through the Callejón de la Maceta, Callejón Oscuro and the Vereda de los Topaderos to a spot called El Asa ('the handle') before turning back towards the refuge. Hiking time about 6 hrs.

Caves: 3 dolmen caves, *Las Cuevas de Menga y Viera*, just outside Antequera, beside the road heading toward Granada; open Sat-Mon and Wed 10 am-1 pm and 4 pm-7 pm.

Further information *Tourist office:* Pl. de San Sebastián, 7, 29200, Antequera, T: (95) 270 25 05, F: 270 39 32.

147

'What had really brought me here were the famous dolmens, the prehistoric burial caves which form a curious, ancient link between Spain and Britain. The people we call Picts ("painted ones") appear to have been Iberians who had populated Britain and Ireland by the beginning of the Bronze Age. So it is not surprising that the British Isles (and Brittany) are the main places outside Spain where anything really comparable with the megalithic tombs of Antequera is to be found.

The Cueva de Menga, the finest of the An-tequera dolmens, is only a few minutes' walk across the fields. As I stood outside the tumulus, gazing at the giant rock that formed the roof, the guardian brought me the visitors' book... someone had written: "Stonehenge underground". And indeed, the same question poses itself here as it does at Stonehenge. How did these primitive people, whose main tools were deers' antlers, shift such enormous stones?'

Alban Allee,
Andalusia — Two steps to Paradise

Fuente de Piedra

This reserva natural *is Andalucía's largest natural lake with a major flamingo population and 75 other species of birds*
Ramsar, ZEPA
1,384 ha (3,420 acres)

Flamingoes have long made the Laguna de Fuente de Piedra their favourite stop in southern Spain. Every spring thousands of the big birds swoop in for a landing in this shallow lake, which is nearly 15 kilometres (9 miles) in circumference and contains an islet known as La Colonia which, in spring, is one of the most densely populated bird habitats in the world.

This elliptical lake is the only place in Europe where the greater flamingo breeds inland, as it does in the African lakes. (There are three other regular breeding sites in the whole of Europe: the Doñana National Park, Las Marismas del Odiel and France's Camargue; a few other sites have recently been established elsewhere in Spain.) They come here to breed almost every year; in 1996, for example, ornithologists counted more than 16,000 breeding pairs. They are very easy to observe from the path that circles the lake, which is just beyond the village, on the road to the Sierra de Yeguas. At a spot called the Cerro del Palo, with the aid of a pair of binoculars, you can undertake your own bird census.

The stars of the show stalk through the water, grunting and trumpeting their incessant comments while rummaging the lake bottom for microscopic bits of food. On the crowded islet they build their conical nests with mud dredged up from the bottom. These are built so close together the effect is that of a flamingo tenement, with scarcely enough room for them to spread their wings on take-off: it's an astonishing sight to see their glides, dives and splash-downs.

Throughout the spring, water is continually evaporating and by mid-summer the lake is often bone dry. For the flamingoes, breeding is a race against time — the young must leave their nests before the island can be reached by predators: dogs, cats and foxes. The adults will eventually desert these nests, leaving any young birds to survive on their own. Some years they make it and others they do not. Fortunately, the birds do not need to breed each year to maintain their numbers.

They have to share the premises with a lot of smaller birds, notably mallards, red-crested pochards, marsh harriers, water rails, moorhens, black-winged stilts, avocets, black-headed gulls, the rare slender-billed gulls and gull-billed terns. Sometimes the *laguna* is visited by storks, who seem to be walking on water, and frequently there are large delegations of Kentish plover looking for their place in the sun.

Seventy-six species of birds directly connected with this *laguna* have been identified and a further 77 take advantage of the surrounding environment for feeding, breeding and refuelling during north-south migrations. In winter it is evident that coots are particularly happy in this habitat: the greatest concentration of the species ever observed in Spain occurred here in January 1972, when 51,300 coots were counted.

The *laguna* is surrounded by the remains of a canal designed to control the inflow of freshwater and so prevent the flooding lake from inundating adjoining fields with its salty water. But the streams that once fed the lake have since been absorbed by agricultural irrigation projects, and nowadays it is fed only by rain-water — a seasonal and highly undependable source in this part of Andalucía. The Andalucían government has improved this situation by putting in pumps to bring water in times of drought.

The flora bordering the *laguna* consists mainly of *Arthrocnemum glaucum*, *Halopeplis amplexicaulis*, *Suaeda vera*, *Salicornia fruticosa* and the grass *Parapholis incurva* — a typical salt-marsh community. The erstwhile canal is overgrown with tamarisk and reeds, and areas of scrubland abound in *Genista umbellata*, French lavender, *Micromeria graeca* and *Ulex parviflorus*. Amphibians and reptiles enjoy the opportunities of Fuente de Piedra, too, especially in the remnants of the freshwater canal. Look for marsh frogs, parsley frogs, western spadefoots and common toads as well as stripe-necked terrapins, viperine snakes, grass snakes, Montpellier snakes, ladder snakes and the horse-shoe whip snake. The ocellated lizard, the large psammodromus and the Iberian wall lizard are the most common reptiles around the lake.

BEFORE YOU GO
Maps: IGN 1:25,000 and 1:50,000 Nos. 1,005 and 1,006; IGN 1:200,000 Mapa Provincial of Málaga.

GETTING THERE
By car: take the N334 north from Antequera, then the A92 *autovía* to the Fuente de Piedra exit. Fuente de Piedra is situated approximately 24 km (15 miles) north-west of Antequera.
By rail: only *Regional* services on the Granada to Córdoba

and Seville, and Córdoba to Málaga lines stop at Fuente de Piedra.
By bus: Automóviles Casado (Málaga, T: (95) 231 59 08, and Antequera, T: (95) 284 19 57) operates a service between Málaga and Antequera stopping at Fuente de Piedra.

WHERE TO STAY
In Fuente de Piedra itself there is the small 2-star Pensión La Laguna, T: (95) 273 52 92. However, the Hotel Molino de Saydo, T: (95) 274 04 75, F: 274

04 66, at Mollina, just a few kilometres from Fuente near the A92 and N334 junction, is larger and more comfortable. Camping Saydo is a part of the hotel, and is open all year with space for 600 people. You could also try the Parador, T: (95) 284 09 01, F: 284 13 12, in Antequera.

FURTHER INFORMATION
Park information: Centro de Interpretación, T: (95) 211 10 50, open every day 9 am-2 pm and 5 pm-8 pm.

Lagunas de Córdoba

Six inland salt lakes, all reservas naturales

A long the southern flank of the province of Córdoba there are six little-known inland salt lakes that play more or less the same ecological role as the Laguna de Fuente de Piedra: these are the Lagunas de Zóñar, Rincón, Amarga, Tíscar, Los Jarales and El Conde. In winter they are visited by large numbers of migrating waterfowl: a recent census recorded 13 different species. At the head of the list of breeding birds is the

white-headed duck, which was on the brink of disappearing altogether but has made a remarkable come-back, thanks largely to the efforts of the society known as the Asociación de Amigos de la Malvasía ('friends of the white-headed duck').

This handsome, short-necked duck, with a bright blue bill, is the only representative of the 'stiff-tail' family in the whole of the Palaearctic region. It is highly aquatic and avoids flying even when threatened, preferring to hide in the reeds. The white-headed duck is scarce and decreasing in Western Europe, the only known breeding sites being located here in southern Spain; the closest

149

to these lie in North Africa and Turkey. The Laguna de Zóñar near Aguilar is the largest lake with permanent water: it occupies 38 hectares (94 acres) and has a maximum depth of 16 metres (52 feet). The lake is surrounded by vineyards, olive groves and wheat fields; reeds and marsh grasses along the edge provide the birds with a measure of concealment. This is a favourite winter resort for the white-headed duck, and in some years almost the entire Spanish population can be found here; there were 100 pairs at the last count. Other species found here include red-crested pochard, mallard, great-crested grebe, tufted duck, shoveler, coot and marsh harrier.

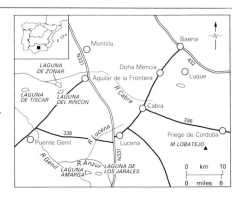

The small kidney-shaped Laguna Amarga ('bitter lake') derives its name from the fact that its water contains both salt and magnesium sulphate. It occupies 4.5 hectares (11 acres) near the village of Jauja. The water is about 4 metres (13 feet) deep and is protected by a wide belt of vegetation in which white-headed ducks and purple gallinules breed every year.

Surrounded by vineyards and measuring less than four hectares (ten acres), the Laguna del Rincón ('corner'), near Aguilar, is the smallest of the three permanent lakes. The lake shrinks in the summer months, and was once on the brink of drying up, but is now regarded as the optimum breeding ground for the white-headed duck.

The seasonal lakes disappear during the summer, leaving behind a layer of salt, but once the rains have come and flooded them, they abound with birds. Laguna del Conde, alias Laguna del Salobral, near Luque, is the largest of all the six lakes, covering an area of 47.5 hectares (117 acres) but has a depth of only 70 centimetres (27 inches). Here you will see greater flamingo and shelduck. The salty waters of the Laguna de Tíscar, near Puente Genil, are only 50 centimetres (20 inches) deep, but enough to make it a breeding ground for plovers, black-winged stilts, avocets and mallards; sometimes young flamingoes fly in from Fuente de Piedra on reconnaissance missions. The sixth lake, the Laguna de Los Jarales, with 2.6 hectares (6½ acres) and only 40 centimetres (15 inches) of water after the rains, is a favoured spot for many ducks and plovers. It is a stone's throw from the Laguna Amarga, near Lucena.

BEFORE YOU GO
Maps: IGN 1:25,000 and 1:50,000 Nos. 966, 967, 988 and 989; IGN 1:200,000 Mapa Provincial of Córdoba.

GETTING THERE
By car: the towns of Aguilar and Lucena, both on the N331 between Córdoba and Antequera, make ideal bases for seeing the *lagunas*. Puente Genil, a much less attractive town, is joined to Aguilar by the CO329 and to Lucena by the CO338.
By rail: Puente Genil is on the Córdoba to Granada and

Córdoba to Málaga lines. *Regional* trains run on both lines, but other classes of train run only on the Córdoba to Málaga line.
By bus: Linesur, T: (95) 498 82 22, operates services from Seville to Baena, via Puente Genil, Lucena and Cabra. Lucena and Aguilar are on the route running between Antequera, T: (95) 284 19 57, and Córdoba.

WHERE TO STAY
All of the towns mentioned above have their own, rather limited, range of

accommodation. Nearby Rute, however, home of the drink *anís*, has the exceptional 2-star Hotel María Luisa, T: (957) 53 80 96, F: 53 90 37. The Apartamentos Cortijo de Frías, T: (957) 33 40 05, just outside Cabra, is also an interesting option. If you choose to stay in Córdoba, a very good choice indeed is the 4-star Hotel N. H. Amistad Córdoba, T: (957) 42 03 35, F: 42 03 65, a modern hotel in the heart of the old town.

FURTHER INFORMATION
Tourist office: Córdoba, p136.

Grazalema

A parque natural consisting largely of
mountain wilderness, with 3 species of
eagle and many other birds
ZEPA, Biosphere Reserve
51,695 ha (127,740 acres)

When you get to Grazalema, whatever
the time of year, it will probably be
raining. The Grazalema weather observato-
ry registers the largest annual rainfall in all
of Spain — for the local mountains have a
knack of catching all the clouds drifting in
from the Atlantic. As a result this vast, stony
area furnishes an ideal environment for a
very full complement of birds, mammals
and reptiles.

The main feature for which Grazalema is

From its source in the Sierra del Pinar the young Río
Guadalete loops round north of the Parque Natural
de Grazalema

renowned is the Spanish fir forest on the
north-eastern slopes of Torreón (1,654 me-
tres/5,425 feet), the second-highest peak in
the Serranía de Ronda. This tree species
(*Abies pinsapo*) is restricted to just four localities in these mountains around Ronda,
all occurring between altitudes of 1,000 and
1,700 metres (3,300 and 5,600 feet).

The *pinsapo* (as it is known in Spanish) is
thought to have arrived in Andalucía during
the Quaternary, pushed south by the ice-
sheets and becoming isolated in a few montane areas when the glaciers retreated. It
owes its continued existence to the fact that
it has a microclimate all of its own: 210 centimetres (82 inches) of rainfall during the average year, plus northern exposure, which
means that the forest is wet and cool all sum-

151

mer long. To keep this arboreal jewel intact, the Andalucían environmental agency requires visitors to obtain a permit (see below) and keeps guard over the trees, to make certain they are not exposed to avoidable fire risks.

The greater part of the *parque natural* consists of mountain wilderness lands belonging to 13 villages in Cádiz province and five in Málaga. The grey limestone of these slopes is so friable that hiking is often a chore. One day, as I bent over to take a close-up photo of some wild flowers near the pass, I slid down a scree slope for about 15 metres (50 feet) before my frantic braking efforts — with heels and elbows — finally brought me to a stop. It was my longest-ever impromptu descent of a mountain.

The high rainfall in the park has produced a rich flora noted for ferns and other plants that thrive in wet climates. Birds do well here, and the park is famed for the large number of griffon vultures that nest among the high stone cliffs (both parents share the chore of sitting on the eggs, during an incubation period lasting 59 days). The tiny chicks grow into very large birds indeed, with a wing-span of about 2.5 metres (8 feet). They share their carrion meals with a number of other resident scavengers, including the Egyptian vulture.

Other members of the park's bird population include golden, booted and short-toed eagles, tawny, barn and Scops owls, kestrel, peregrine, hoopoe, bee-eater, short-toed tree-creeper, redstart, Sardinian warblers, white-throat, cuckoo, jackdaw, spotted flycatcher, golden oriole, green and great spotted woodpeckers, nightingale, wryneck, wood lark, alpine swift, serin and red-legged partridge.

A good deal of farming goes on within the confines of the park, but human activity is largely confined to sheep raising and the collecting of carob beans. Grazalema, from which the park takes its name, is an ancient peasant village that has carefully preserved its traditional architecture and has won several important prizes for conservation. Situated at an altitude of 890 metres, it makes an ideal jumping-off point for bird-watching or botanical tours of the park.

BEFORE YOU GO
Maps: IGN 1:25,000 and 1:50,000 Nos. 1,049, 1,050 and 1,051; IGN 1:200,000 Mapas Provinciales of Cádiz and Málaga; IGN 1:50,000 Sierra de Grazalema.

GETTING THERE
By car: the road from El Bosque to Grazalema leads you directly through the park to the Puerto del Boyar. Coming south from Seville, follow the road from Zahara de la Sierra to Grazalema which leads over the imposing Puerto de las Palomas.
By bus: El Bosque, T: (956) 71 60 31, has connections to Jerez de la Frontera, Cádiz, Seville, Ubrique, T: (956) 46 10 70, and Grazalema. All buses leave from Plaza de la Constitución.

WHERE TO STAY
Try the Villa Turística, T: (956)

13 21 36, F: 13 22 13, and 2-star Pensión Casa de las Piedras, T: (956) 13 20 14, F: 13 22 38, both in Grazalema; 2-star Hotel Las Truchas, T: (956) 71 60 61, F: 71 60 86, in El Bosque; 2-star Hostal Marqués de Zahara, T/F: (956) 12 30 61, in the stunning village of Zahara de la Sierra; the intriguing complex of the 2-star Hotel Apartamentos Los Chozos, T: (956) 23 41 63, just outside Benaocaz; and the 2-star Hotel Molino del Santo, T/F: (95) 216 71 51, in Benaoján.
Outdoor living: Camping La Torrecilla, T: (956) 71 60 95, open 1 Feb-15 Dec, in El Bosque; and Camping Tajo Rodillo, T: (956) 23 40 15, open 1 Mar-31 Oct and 1 Dec-31 Jan, in Grazalema.

ACCESS
Permits are needed for all three

walks listed below, and you will generally have to pay to be accompanied by a guide.

ACTIVITIES
Walking: a series of basic itineraries for hikers has been laid out by the park authorities. The most popular route starts on the road between Grazalema and Puerto de las Palomas and ascends the ridge to overlook the *pinsapar* — a forest of Spanish fir — which it then traverses before dropping back into the village of Benamahoma. It offers the best opportunities for studying the *pinsapo* and other endemic plants of the region. A secondary itinerary begins at the Puerto de los Acebuches ('the pass of the wild olives') on the road between Grazalema and Zahara de la Sierra; it leads to the Puerto del Sabinarejo via la Cañada de

Cornicabra. This is undoubtedly the best route for studying varied vegetation of a typical area of *maquis* and scrub forest. A third hiking route also departs from the Puerto de los Acebuches and goes to the Ermita de la Garganta (872 m/2,861 ft), and the steep slope of the Garganta Verde ('green gorge').
Driving: if you haven't the time or inclination to study the park on foot or horse-back, there remains the far less exciting alternative of driving. The recommended route starts at Zahara de la Sierra, goes to Puerto de los Acebuches, from

where you can look across to the *pinsapar*, and takes in the Puerto de las Palomas, which affords a superb view of the Sierra del Endrinal. You can continue via the Puerto del Boyar to Benamahoma and then through El Bosque to Ubrique, another of the beautiful *pueblos blancos* ('white villages') of the Sierra; the road leads past stands of wild olive and large tracts of evergreen forest and *dehesa*.
Riding: for horse-back tours of the park, contact Ecuestre Bosque Sierra, El Bosque, T: (956) 71 62 23; or Cuadra El Tinte, Bar Alameda,

Grazalema, T: (956) 13 20 12, F: 13 22 71.
Park adventures: Horizon, Naturaleza y Aventura, T/F: (956) 13 23 63, web-site www.ubrinet.net/asoc.turismor-ural/horizon, offers hiking, four-wheel-drive tours, star observation, pot-holing, canyoning and others.

FURTHER INFORMATION
Tourist office: Cádiz, p136.
Park information: Avda. Diputación, s/n, T: (956) 72 70 29, El Bosque; Las Piedras, 11, T: (956) 13 22 25, Grazalema; and T: (956) 12 31 14, Zahara de la Sierra.

THE FLORA OF GRAZALEMA

The sierras of Grazalema are geologi-cally very similar to those of El Torcal de Antequera, but Grazalema is by far the more famous for its botanical rari-ties. Two spectacular species growing in the rocks above the village were de-scribed by Dwight Ripley in his paper 'A Journey through Spain' (1944): the crucifer *Biscutella frutescens*, 'with its showers of gold and thick rosettes of scalloped velvet', and the endemic 'deli-cate brick[-red]' poppy *Papaver rupifragum*, which is confined to the mountains of the Serranía de Ronda. Another interesting species which he mentions, albeit in less emotive terms, is the handsome, white-woolly *Centaurea clementei*, a yellow-flowered knapweed that is known only from Grazalema and the Sierra de Yunquera in southern Spain.
If you look in rock crevices, you can find three saxifrage species that are con-fined to the southern Spanish sierras: *Saxifraga haenseleri*, *S. globulifera* and *S. boissieri*. All have small, whitish flowers and the latter two are particu-larly frequent in the Serranía de Ronda.

On the high ridge of the Serranía de Grazalema grows an almost alpine fis-sure and scree community, including species such as Spanish whitlow-grass (*Draba hispanica*), large-flowered trea-cle-mustard (*Erysium grandiflorum*) and another crucifer species with lilac flow-ers, *Ionopsidium prolongoi*.
In the fir forest of El Pinar, the trees cast a good deal of shade and a special-ized shrub flora has evolved beneath the canopy, including evergreen species such as spurge laurel, small-flowered gorse (*Ulex parviflorus* ssp. *funkii*) and lau-rustinus (*Viburnum tinus*), whose berries are highly poisonous. More colourful species, such as Spanish barberry (*Berberis hispanica*) and the hedgehog broom, can be found in clearings. Stony areas support the dwarf woody crucifer *Ptilotrichum spinosum*. At lower alti-tudes, the resinous smell of the firs is en-hanced by the presence of two aromatic cistus species — grey-leaved and poplar-leaved (*Cistus albidus* and *C. populifolius*) — which also attract myri-ads of flying insects when they are in full bloom.

Laguna de Medina

Small lake, stopping place for migratory birds going to and from Africa; a reserva natural Ramsar, ZEPA
121 ha (299 acres)

This small saline lake in the wheat-growing, horse-rearing country around Jerez de la Frontera takes its name from the ducal house of Medina Sidonia, one of the great noble families of Spain, whose ancestral seat — the hilltop town of the same name — lies some distance to the south. In recent years the lake has often been dry, but at other times it makes an ideal refuge, ringed with reeds and marsh grasses, for waders, terns and birds of prey. It is important at times for birds of passage, situated as it is close to the point where Europe

and Africa almost meet. From the end of August, birds migrating from central and northern Europe make it their last stopover before flying on to Africa.

In times of drought, the lake also attracts birds from the Doñana National Park just across the Río Guadalquivir. If the *marismas* are drier than usual at the end of the summer, some of the Doñana birds come looking for food and water east of the river. In November 1973 ornithologists counted 22,626 birds on this one lake. Altogether about 47 species have been recorded here, including spoonbills, the white-headed duck, crested coot and the greater flamingo.
Before you go *Maps:* IGN 1:25,000 and 1:50,000 Nos. 1,048 and 1,062; IGN 1:200,000 Mapa Provincial de Cádiz.
Getting there *By car:* the *laguna* is in the open country on the

Jerez de la Frontera to Medina Sidonia, CA440 road.
By rail: Jerez, 10 km (6 miles) to the west, has train connections to Seville.
By bus: there are daily services from Jerez, Estación Municipal, T: (956) 34 10 63, to Medina Sidonia. Linesur, Estación del Prado, T: (95) 498 82 22, in Seville, operates services between Seville and Jerez.
Where to stay: the cities nearest the *laguna* are Jerez de la Frontera and El Puerto de Santa María, on the outskirts of Cádiz, both with plentiful accommodation. Try the very charming 4-star Hotel La Cueva Park, T: (956) 18 91 20, F: 18 91 21, just outside Jerez, and the very modern Puerto Sherry Hotel & Yacht Club, T: (956) 87 30 00, F: 85 33 00, in El Puerto de Santa María.
Further information *Tourist office:* Cádiz, p136.

Doñana

Wetlands, sand-dunes and pine forests, in lowland parque nacional at the delta of the Río Guadalquivir
Ramsar, ZEPA, Biosphere Reserve, European Diploma, World Heritage Site
86,208 ha (213,020 acres)

The first time I visited the Doñana National Park I was impressed mainly by the landscape — the vast dunes engulfing the forests that lay just behind them, the sandy woodlands inhabited by red and fallow deer and the teeming marshes adjoining the estuary of the Guadalquivir, where there seemed to be no end to the ducks and herons feeding noisily among the reeds and bullrushes. What stayed with me was a sense of almost limitless space, a wilderness of wetland, sand-dune and pine forest that was bounded

on one side by a river as blue as the sky and on the other by as lonely a beach as it is still possible to find.

But it was not until my second visit that I began to grasp the real significance of the last great lowland wilderness sanctuary in southern Europe. This time I made the trip in a Land Rover filled with professional bird-watchers — mostly editors and writers of nature magazines. The leader of the group was one of the grand old men of British ornithology, who had an uncanny way of raising his binoculars to the sky and announcing, about some pin-point in the far distance: 'There's a marsh harrier just rising to the left of that oak.' Or he would deliver short impromptu lectures such as, 'Here's a short-toed eagle, a snake hunter and nature's killing machine. It's armoured with a helmet of feathers against snake bites and with short, powerful talons to grasp its prey. The feathers on its wing tips splay out aerodynamically to prevent drag and turbulence...'

In the marshlands known as the *marismas*

These spoonbills return from Africa to breed in the same colony in Doñana year after year

we watched a group of excited shrikes mob a booted eagle that had made the mistake of invading their territory — our mentor spotted the eagle even before the shrikes did. Not long afterwards he had the satisfaction of telling us, in his matter-of-fact voice: 'Here's the rarest bird we're going to see today, the imperial eagle.'

Doñana's proximity to Africa is one of the principal reasons for the wealth and variety of its bird life. Birds with large wingspans, such as the eagles and kites that abound here, cannot fly across water for long distances because they require thermal updrafts for the long glides that allow them to rest their wings during migrations. Hence they cross the Mediterranean at its narrowest points — the Dardanelles, Gibraltar and Tarifa. For those making the journey from West Africa, the *marismas* of the Doñana are a logical, indeed essential, resting place and hunting ground. Here, if all goes well, the flamingoes will find the shrimps that play such an important part in their life

cycle; if they find no shrimp to eat they will not turn a contented pink, and if they do not turn pink, they will be less successful in attracting mates and going on to breed (in locations such as Fuente de Piedra and, more recently, Las Marismas del Odiel), but may simply wait out the season and return home without having reproduced.

The Parque Nacional de Doñana — or, as it used to be known, the Coto ('hunting estate') Doñana — thus plays a critical role in the reproductive cycle of several species, the more so since other Andalucían wetlands have dried up or been 'reclaimed'. In years when not enough rain falls to flood the *marismas* to a sufficient depth, these natural cycles can be badly affected.

Doñana's ecosystems are more seriously threatened by man-made hazards, in particular mining and agriculture. North of El Rocío, which lies less than a mile outside the park's boundaries, new rice fields have been planted and other agricultural projects started. The irrigation of crops has lowered the regional water-table, drying out the marshes. Strawberries are the worst offenders; they are grown through winter for sale in UK su-

155

permarkets from March onwards. Further damage is caused by pesticides in the run-off water. In 1986, an estimated 30,000 birds died in the area from pesticide infiltration.

The mining industry poses further threats to the marshes. For years the sulphur mines at Aznalcóllar have been dumping effluvium into the Río Guadiamar and waste reservoirs. Mine-workers warned repeatedly that these deposit lakes were shoddily built and liable to rupture at any time, but no action was taken. In April 1998, one of the reservoirs burst its dykes, contaminating vital aquifers, polluting much of the surrounding land and causing the death of great numbers of fish and birds. The Spanish Ministry of the Environment claims that the park itself has largely been saved by the diversion of the contaminated water in the Río Guadiamar, but the full extent of the damage is not yet known.

The topography and history of Doñana have made it a difficult place to protect. It is, essentially, the delta of the Guadalquivir, the 'Great River', or Wada-l-Kebir, of the Moors. But unlike most deltas, the river has only one outlet to the sea, just below Sanlúcar de Barrameda. Its other outlets have gradually been blocked off by a huge sandbar that stretches from the mouth of the Río Tinto, near Palos, to the river bank opposite Sanlúcar, and which the sea winds have gradually formed into high dunes. Behind this natural barrier stretch the *marismas*.

The effect of this extraordinary *mélange* of land and water was to create an environment shunned by people but ideal for wildlife. As early as the 13th century, the kings of Castile set aside a portion of what is now Doñana as a royal hunting estate; later the dukes of Medina Sidonia made it their private *coto*. One of the duchesses of Medina Sidonia, Doña Ana de Silva y Mendoza, indulged her antisocial instincts by building a residence there that was more hermitage than palace. As a result the entire region came to be known as the 'forest of Doña Ana', or Doñana. In the 18th century, Goya is known to have visited the Duchess of Alba at the Palacio de Doñana when she was its proprietress. Subsequently, the land passed through many hands before the official cre-

ation of the *parque nacional* in 1969.

Meanwhile, adjoining areas of wetland were being dramatically reduced. Across the Guadalquivir vast marshes were drained and converted to farm land, until only the protected lands of the Doñana remained intact. For centuries there had been only a vacant space on the map between Lebrija in the east and Almonte in the north-west, but in recent years whole towns and villages have sprung up west of the Guadalquivir, and the resort town of Matalascañas has brought urban sprawl to the south-western edge of the Doñana, a place once occupied by reed-thatched fishermen's huts.

The proximity of these settlements has further complicated the work of the park's wildlife guardians. Far too many of the Doñana's precious lynxes, for example, are run over by cars on the road to Matalascañas; cats and dogs straying out of the nearby towns kill animals in the park, particularly ground-nesting birds; and birds that overfly the park's fences run the risk of being gunned down by trigger-happy hunters, despite stringent conservation laws.

What you see here depends on the time of the year and the luck of the draw. November, December and January are an ideal time to see waterfowl, since the autumn rains have brought life back to the *marismas* and filled the *lagunas*. Gradually the water attains a uniform depth of 30-60 centimetres (12-24 inches) over vast areas, and the resulting marshes attract huge flocks of wildfowl, ducks, geese and other water birds of the most varied kind. These are freshwater marshes, incidentally, although there are traces of sea salt in the underlying clay. Here and there small islands known as *vetas* rise above the water; these remain dry throughout the year, creating an ideal breeding ground for waders and terns.

Towards the end of February the geese which have migrated here from northern Europe commence their return journey, but at the same time the spoonbills arrive from North Africa to nest in the cork oaks. In March the waters begin to recede and spring begins in earnest. This is also the time when the Spanish imperial eagle hatches its eggs; 15 breeding pairs of these formidable hunters were counted recently in the park — about a third of the entire Spanish population. Each pair requires nearly 2,600 hectares (6,425 acres) of land to hunt over in summer, and even more in winter. This is a far from perfect environment for these great birds and Doñana pairs seldom raise as many young as those elsewhere in Spain.

In spring the *marismas* are alive with birds — some settling down to breed, others *en route* for more northern climes. Huge numbers of kites hang in the air, harriers send the duck scurrying skyward in fear of their lives. There are black-tailed godwit and ruff on their way to Holland and beyond, greenshank and wood sandpiper bound for Scandinavia, little stint and curlew sandpiper heading for northern Siberia and usually a marsh sandpiper that should be a thousand kilometres or more further east. Overhead vast flocks of whiskered terns wheel and circle along with a few gull-billed terns and racy collared pratincoles. There are swallows galore, some of them red-rumped, and bee-eaters and rollers perch on post and wire. All of these and more can be seen from the bridge at El Rocío — perhaps the best free bird-watching in Europe.

From bird hides at the reserve centre just south of the bridge you will hear Cetti's and

The purple gallinule, an exotic tropical relative of the coot, leads a retiring life among the reeds

Savi's warblers and watch egrets, herons and little bitterns come and go. Marsh harriers and kites are continually on view and sometimes a majestic Spanish imperial eagle will soar from the woods of Doñana over El Rocío to the Coto del Rey.

In midsummer the temperature in the parched *marismas* easily exceeds 40°C (100°F). Aquatic birds that remain in the stagnant pools often die of botulism, and each year thousands more die during the advancing drought. In August there is almost nothing left of the marsh's aquatic fauna, but it is a good time for observing dozens of summer residents, which include griffon vulture, booted eagle, red and black kites, and short-toed eagle. There is, in fact, no end to the life cycle of this wilderness, where 125 species of bird are known to breed, as well as 28 mammal species, 17 reptiles, 9 amphibians and 8 species of fish.

The park contains three distinct kinds of ecosystem: the *marismas*, the *matorral* and the dunes. A typical motorized visit to Doñana will take in a sample of all three, but the amount of exposure to each environment varies with the seasons. The last time I toured the park was during the month of May. Although no two visits will be alike, my notes will give potential visitors a rough idea of what to expect from Doñana.

'It is a bright, sunny morning with unseasonably high temperatures as we enter the park just south of El Rocío, a village that resembles a set for a Hollywood western. We are driven along a rutted dirt track that leads through a forest of eucalyptus trees, giving way after a time to a landscape of native scrubland: *halimium* thickets with scattered cork oaks. This is the favourite abode of the park's pardel lynxes, which currently number about 25 pairs and represent some of the last survivors of their species in southern Europe. Of course they stay out of sight, but the movements of about a quarter of their number are monitored by means of electronic collars. Kites seem to fill the sky, and a herd of red deer peer out from behind the bushes; nearby we see some marsh cattle grazing in a densely overgrown meadow.

A small permanent stream flows to our left: it is the Caño de la Madre de las Maris-

Flamingoes congregate in the shallows of the saline lagoons of Las Marismas del Odiel

mas del Rocío, one of the two main arteries through which the upland waters reach the marshes. Beyond it stretches an endless plain, part water, part mud, and everywhere clogged with marsh grasses. It seems incredible that during Roman times this bog was a broad gulf, and ships could bring their cargoes into Lebrija, a town now seven kilometres (4½ miles) from the nearest stream, on the other side of the Guadalquivir.

The Land Rover makes another stop to enable us to observe some of the *pajareras*. These venerable cork oaks are located within the park's special biological reserve, the Reserva Científica, which is off limits. On this occasion the area seems occupied by an Afro-European parliament of birds, and the tree-tops are alive with some of the greatest herons in Europe: little egret, cattle egret, night heron, spoonbill and grey heron.

A man on horseback comes riding past. He is one of the park wardens, for at this time of the year a horse is the only satisfactory means of transport through the *maris-*

mas. Soon our Land Rover is taking us over trails of loose beach sand where even a horse might have found the going difficult. We look in on the Palacio de Doñana, where there are storks and peacocks as well as a stable full of horses. Beyond it lie rolling sand dunes and open places overgrown with brambles, with an occasional stone pine holding down the sand. We bounce along the ruts until we reach a more humid environment — a brilliantly coloured quagmire.

Further on are the dunes, which the Land Rover negotiates only with the greatest of difficulty. There are flamingoes in a small *laguna* to our left, obviously in the very pink of condition.

Flamingoes hatch their eggs sitting astride high conical mounds of mud, which safeguards their nests when the water-level rises. In 1883, Abel Chapman found a colony of greater flamingoes sitting on a mass of nests raised above the muddy water, deep in the *marismas*: 'We approached within some seventy yards [65 metres] before

In Andalucía and Extremadura the cork oaks of the *dehesa* provide an invaluable commodity

their sentries showed signs of alarm, and at that distance, with the glass, observed the sitting birds as distinctly as one need wish. The long red legs doubled under their bodies, the knees projecting as far as, or beyond the tail, and their graceful necks neatly curled among their back-feathers like a sitting swan, with the heads resting on their breasts — all these points are unmistakable.'

The dune barrier responsible for creating this paradise is still on the move, creeping inland at the rate of three to six metres (10-20 feet) a year. Wandering among the dunes we see that some of them have half swallowed the stone pines growing in the hollows behind them. This strip of coastal territory is a breeding ground for the stone curlew and the thekla lark, and a favourite hunting zone for short-toed and Spanish imperial eagles.

Eventually we reach the seashore, where the long Atlantic rollers beat against the coast. The beach is covered with terns; in fact I have never seen so many black terns in my life. At the edge of the dunes stand old coastal watch-towers, now deserted except for breeding peregrines. Kentish plovers also rear their young in this environment.

A little further on we see Audouin's gull, one of the world's rarest gulls: it is so specialized that it only knows how to fish from the surface of the sea. While other gulls have become inland scavengers, taking advantage of rubbish tips and ripe olives, Audouin's gulls are more discerning and feed themselves the hard way, by dipping in after fish in a similar manner to terns. We also see a flock of flamingoes on the beach, presumably just arrived from Africa and waiting for the sundown to show them the direction of the marshes; not surprisingly, they seem very tired after their long journey.

And so are we, after a day of watching, learning and being astonished and delighted by the immensity of this wilderness.'

BEFORE YOU GO

Maps: IGN 1:25,000 and 1:50,000 Nos. 1,001, 1,018, 1,033 and 1,047; IGN 1:200,000 Mapa Provincial de Huelva; IGN 1:50,000 Parque Nacional de Doñana.

Guide-books: Carlos Carrasco-Muñoz de Vera, *El Parque Nacional de Doñana* (Editorial Everest); Guy Mountfort, *Portrait of a Wilderness* (Hutchinson, 1958); J. Vozzmediano, *Doñana, manual práctico* (Pentathlon, 1983).

GETTING THERE

By air: the usual way to reach Doñana is via Seville, which has excellent train and internal aeroplane connections. Cheap charter flights to Málaga also offer a convenient means of flying to within striking distance of the park.

By car: from Seville take the E1/A49 westwards, then turn south at Bollullos del Condado on to the H612 and follow it through Almonte and El Rocío to Matalascañas, the modern

and crowded beach resort which is the customary jumping-off point for visits to the *parque nacional*.

The red-crested pochard commonly breeds and winters in southern Spain and along the Mediterranean coast

Alternatively, from Huelva follow the coastal road, the N442 (which becomes the C442), to Matalascañas through the little-known dune country.

By bus: Empresa Damas, T: (95) 490 80 40, operates a

frequent service to Matalascañas from the Plaza de Armas bus station in Seville.

WHERE TO STAY

The bright, modern, 2-star Hotel Toruño, T: (959) 44 23 23, F: 44 23 38, in the unusual village of El Rocío, has an observation room overlooking the marshes. El Cortijo de Los Mimbrales, T: (959) 50 61 66, F: 44 23 85, close to El Rocío, is a particularly attractive option. The Grand Hotel del Coto, T: (959) 44 00 17, F: 44 02 02, and 3-star Hotel Carabela, T: (959) 44 80 01, F: 44 81 25, are good choices for Matalascañas. Those choosing to splash out in Seville can't go wrong if they choose the 5-star Hotel Casa Imperial, (95) 450 03 00, F: 450 03 30, or alternatively try the 3-star Patio de la Alameda, T: (95) 490 49 99, F: 490 02 26, both in Seville's monumental centre. **Outdoor living:** there are 3 official camping areas, all vast: Rocío Playa, T: (959) 43 02 40, Doñana Playa, T: (959) 53 62 81, and Playa de Mazagón, T: (959) 37 62 08, all on the road between Matalascañas and Huelva.

ACTIVITIES

You cannot visit the park on your own. The park's five visitor centres have a

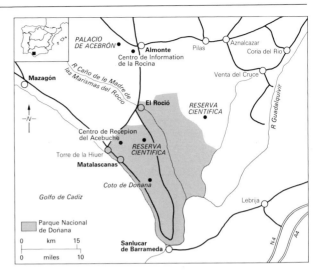

combination of exhibitions, audio-visual displays, observation points and footpaths with observatories. Doñana Ecuestre, S. L., Avda. La Canariega, 1, El Rocío-Almonte, T: (959) 44 24 74, offers 4-hr four-wheel-drive tours of the park showing its vast array of flora, fauna and wildlife. The same company also offers horse-back tours.

FURTHER INFORMATION
Tourist office: Huelva, p136.
Park information: visitor centres: El Acebuche, at Km 26 on the Almonte-Matalascañas road, T: (959) 44 87 11; La

Rocina, at Km 16 on the Almonte-Matalascañas road, T: (959) 44 23 40; the Palacio del Acebrón, with access from the La Rocina centre; the José Antonio Valverde/Cerrado Garrido, access from nearby villages, route map from the head office, (see below); the Ice Factory in Sanlúcar de Barrameda, across the Guadalquivir river south of the park, T: (956) 38 16 35.
Park office: Parque Nacional de Doñana, Centro Administrativo El Acebuche, 21760 Matalascañas, Huelva, T: (959) 44 87 39, F: 44 85 76, e-mail: donana@mma.es.

Las Marismas del Odiel

Paraje natural within Huelva's city boundaries. Breeding ground of flamingoes Ramsar, ZEPA, Biosphere Reserve 7,185 ha (17,754 acres)

The first time I visited the Marismas del Odiel I happened to be present at an historic moment. Accompanied by Juan Carlos Rubio, the young naturalist who had just been appointed director of the recently created *paraje natural* of the Odiel marshes, we made a jeep journey into the very centre of these wetlands, to the *lagunas* and salt pans of the Salinas de Bacuta. It was a clear, sunny spring day, and there was a large flock of flamingoes in the middle of the principal *laguna*. They were not at all disturbed by our arrival at the embankment that formed its eastern edge, but went on holding what seemed to be a rather noisy family reunion of about 400 birds. Some of them were walking up and down in their restless, peripatetic way, and they were making the goose-like sounds that have been compared to the grumblings of a discontented crowd at a football match. Others were holding their heads under water and sifting mud through their bills to screen out molluscs, crayfish and salt-water algae.

My guide, who had spent many hours of his life watching these gregarious birds through his binoculars, suddenly grew very excited; he had just realized that the flamingoes were building nests and getting ready to raise their young here in the Laguna de Aljaraque. It was the first time flamingoes had been known to breed in the Marismas del Odiel, and their settling-in represented a triumphant vindication of a conservation programme to which Señor Rubio had devoted several years of intensive effort.

Sometimes as many as 2,000 flamingoes migrate from Africa to the wetlands of the Odiel. The fact that some of them now stay here to breed, rather than go to the Fuente de Piedra, or the *marismas* of Doñana, 120 kilometres (75 miles) to the east, may be due to the fact that these *lagunas* do not dry up during the summer months, like most of those at Doñana; they may also prefer the greater salinity of the Laguna de Aljaraque. For the Marismas del Odiel differ from the freshwater wetlands of Doñana in that they consist of tidal marshes and the large salt pans of the local *salinas*, which have long been a feature of the Huelva region. The Atlantic tides that irrigate these salt marshes sometimes run as high as 4 metres (13 feet). But the reserve itself is also far smaller — 6,791 hectares (16,780 acres) — and much closer to civilization than the Coto Doñana. The *paraje natural*, indeed, is just across the water from the port facilities and industrial installations that line the navigable main channel of the Río Odiel for its last 15 kilometres (9 miles) to the sea.

The Río Tinto, of course, is the industrial artery from which the greatest copper and manganese mines in Europe derive their name (at its confluence with the Odiel stands the Monasterio de La Rábida, where Columbus planned his voyage to the Indies in 1492 — a circumstance which permits the residents of Huelva to regard their city as the 'cradle of the New World'). Las Marismas del Odiel have thus had to vie for space, air and government funds with a modern port authority, agricultural reclamation projects and the commercial requirements of the *salinas*. Even so the *paraje natural* has managed to hold its own as a wildlife reserve of international importance, giving sanctuary to its colonies of flamingoes, spoonbills, purple herons and other wintering and breeding visitors.

BEFORE YOU GO
Maps: IGN 1:25,000 and 1:50,000 No. 999; IGN 1:200,000 Mapa Provincial of Huelva and IGN 1:25,000 Paraje Natural Marismas del Odiel.

GETTING THERE
By car: take the H414 from Huelva to Punta Umbría.
By bus: Empresa Damas, T: (959) 25 69 00, operates a frequent service between the new bus station in Huelva and Punta Umbría.

WHERE TO STAY
There is plenty of choice in the area. In Punta Umbría, a summer resort placed between the river and the sea, try the 3-star Hotel Pato Amarillo, T: (959) 31 12 50, F: 31 12 58, or Hotel Pato Rojo, T: (959) 31 16 00, F: 31 12 58. In Huelva the modern, 3-star Monte Conquero, T: (959) 28 55 00, F: 28 39 12, can be recommended.
Outdoor living: try the Playa La Bota, T: (959) 31 45 37, in Punta Umbría; the Catapum, T: (959) 39 91 65, in El Rompido; the Playa de Mazagón, T: (959) 37 62 08, or Fontanilla Playa, T: (959) 53 62 37, in Mazagón.

ACCESS
If you wish to go bird-watching the best areas are within the confines of the Salinas de Bacuta, the gates of which are kept firmly locked against uninvited human visitors. Make prior arrangements with the management of the *paraje*, by contacting the tourist office (see below).

FURTHER INFORMATION
Tourist office: Huelva, p136.

A patchwork of gold and green fields, a flourishing olive grove, bare-ribbed mountains: this is the elemental landscape characteristic of Andalucía

Sierra de Aracena

Low range of mountains rising to not more than 1,000 m (3,300 ft) where Spanish lynx, black vulture and imperial eagle are found; Parque Natural de Aracena y Picos de Aroche ZEPA 184,000 ha (455,000 acres)

Huelva, home of Spain's best known national park, the marshes of Doñana, also has an immense upland region that is virtually unknown to the outside world. The Sierra de Aracena forms the western edge of the Sierra Morena that separates Castille from Andalucía. This is an isolated region that contains some of the oldest working mines in the world, but its economy is basically agricultural, with whitewashed farming villages surrounded by imposing forests of oaks and chestnuts. Although 40 per cent of all the villages in Huelva are located in the Sierra, this is also the province's most thinly populated *comarca* — which is just as well for the region's wolves, lynxes, imperial eagles and black vultures.

As mountains go, the Sierra de Aracena is hardly more than a range of rugged hills, with median altitudes between 500 and 600 metres (1,650 to 2,000 feet) and the highest peaks not over 1,000 metres (3,300 feet). The *comarca* as a whole encompasses nearly 300,000 ha (741,315 acres), of which two-thirds is protected as a *parque natural*. What is fascinating about hiking through these mountains is the contrast between half-forgotten villages with orange and lemon groves and the superb oak forests — silent woods in which you can, at your peril, find the

164

hallucinogenic mushroom *Amanita muscaria*, the fly agaric, whose juice gave the shaman-priests of ancient Europe their second sight.

The oak forests of the Sierra are the happy rooting-ground of a breed of half-wild pigs, who are put out to pasture among the acorns for a season and are then made into the famous air-cured *Jamón de Jabugo*, regarded by gourmets as the greatest *jamón serrano* of them all. Jabugo is one of the villages of the Sierra, though the same fine-quality ham is produced by other villages as well: it is the all-acorn diet made possible by these prodigious oak forests that gives this *jamón* its peculiar nutty flavour.

From the summit of the Peña Arias Montano — named in honour of Benito Arias Montano, the Spanish polymath and advisor to Felipe II, who retired to this region to live out the last decade of his life — you can look down on the

---

Dense stands of the sea club-rush grow in the salt-marshes and ditches of the Doñana wetlands

whole of the *serranía*. This was a sacred peak in pagan times; the Christians built a shrine to the Madonna de los Angeles on the spot — perhaps because the view from here is nothing short of angelic.

Approaching Aracena from either Seville or Huelva, you pass through a very different region, the Andévalo, once famous for its pyrite fields and now the summer retreat of *sevillanos*. Having arrived in Aracena you will hardly be able to escape the local attraction known as the Gruta de las Maravillas ('grotto of the wonders'), which was discovered by chance by one of the thousands of black pigs rooting hereabouts, while snuffling for a stray acorn. They should have given the pig a medal, but I suppose its only reward was to be turned into *Jamón de Jabugo*.

Before you go *Maps:* IGN 1:25,000 and 1:50,000 Nos. 918, 938 and 939; IGN 1:50,000 No. 917; IGN 1:200,000 Mapas Provinciales of Huelva, Seville, Córdoba and Jaén.

Getting there *By car:* from Huelva, take the N435 north to Jabugo, then east on the E52/N433 to Aracena. From Seville, drive north on the E803/N630, and turn west on the E52/N433 to Aracena. *By bus:* Empresa Damas, T: (95) 490 80 40, operates a limited daily service between Seville, Plaza de Armas bus station, and Aracena. The same company also offers a limited service between Huelva, T: (959) 25 69 00, and Aracena. Between the villages, though, the service is sporadic.

Where to stay: the Finca Valbono, T: (959) 12 77 11, F: 12 76 79, in a wonderful location just outside Aracena, is a delight; the family that runs it also owns the charming 2-star Hotel Sierra de Aracena, T: (959) 12 61 75, F: 12 62 18, in the centre of Aracena. Farther west, near the junction of the E52/N433 and N435, try the attractive 2-star Hotel Galaroza Sierra, T: (959) 12 32 37, F: 12 32 36.

Activities: the Gruta de las Maravillas in Aracena is Spain's largest cave and is well supplied with stalactites, *lagunas* and underground waterways. A fascinating spot (though definitely not for the claustrophobic); open daily 10 am-1:30 pm and 3:30 pm-6 pm.

Further information *Tourist office:* Pl. de San Pedro, s/n, 21200 Aracena, T: (959) 12 83 55; and Huelva, p136.

Sierra Morena

Seven parques naturales spanning a 300-mile-long mountain chain
ZEPA
524,000 ha (1,290,000 acres)

The Sierra Morena, formerly known as the Cordillera Mariánica or Montes Mariani, extends over some 500 kilometres (300 miles) from the mountains of southern Portugal and the Sierra de Aracena, eastwards to the Sierras de Cazorla, Segura y Las Villas and the steppe region of Albacete. This mountain chain represents the eroded edge of the Meseta. While its maximum height is only 1,323 m (4,340 ft), its breadth (more than 65 km/40 miles) is responsible for the historic and continuing economic and cultural separation of Andalucía from the rest of Spain.

The main ridge of the Sierra Morena is composed of slates and greywacke, largely covered with an evergreen mantle of

Cistus scrub; if you stand on the ridge summit and look southward you see an extensive area of *matorral*, with its full complement of holm, cork and Lusitanian oaks. The only important break in this formidable wall is the pass of Despeñaperros.

These convoluted and irregular mountains are rich in metals and minerals, including the famous copper mines of Tharsis and the Río Tinto. Seven natural parks form an almost unbroken chain of protected areas along the Sierra Morena mountain range: from west to east, these are the Sierra de Aracena y Picos de Aroche, Sierra Norte de Sevilla, Sierra de Hornachuelos, Sierra Cardeña y Montoro, Sierra de Andújar, Despeñaperros and Sierras de Cazorla, Segura y Las Villas. Due in great part to this protection, the Sierra Morena has become the stronghold of the Spanish lynx population. Also known as the pardel lynx, it is nowadays considered to be a separate species from the bulk of the European population, being

The deadly fly agaric was used by ancient Iberians as a hallucinogen

smaller and having more distinct spots than its northern counterparts. Primeval forest cover is essential to its survival: with the cutting down of much of this forest its numbers had declined drastically, but are now more or less stable. Recent censuses indicate a Spanish population of between 1,000 and 1,200, nearly half of which are to be found in the Sierra Morena and Montes de Toledo.

Before you go *Maps:* IGN 1:200,000 Mapas Provinciales of Huelva, Badajoz, Córdoba, Jaén and Albacete; there are at least fifty large-scale (1:25,000) IGN maps covering this area, numbered in the range 879-941. Obtain the IGN catalogue to identify which map you need. Addresses, p212.

Getting there *By car:* the main road south from Madrid, the N-IV, crosses the Sierra Morena at the pass of Despeñaperos and continues westward, to Bailén, Córdoba, Seville and Huelva. This road skirts the southern edge of the Sierra Morena from where numerous roads lead northward up into the mountains.

Further information *Tourist office:* enquire at the provincial offices, p136/7.

CHAPTER 7

The Balearic Islands

The Balearic Islands — Mallorca, Menorca, Ibiza, Formentera and Cabrera — are neatly positioned in the navel of the western Mediterranean, a little closer to Europe than to Africa. They were pushed up from the sea bed when the African continent squeezed against Europe in one of those great shifts known as plate tectonics, which explains why there are marine fossils on top of the highest mountains.

Robert Bourrouilh, the French geologist, has demonstrated that the Balearics were not, as it might appear on the map, simply a continuation of the mountains of Andalucía. Indeed, there is this significant difference: that while Ibiza, Formentera and Mallorca are an extension of the Cordillera Penibética of southern Spain, Menorca is a 'displaced' piece of central Mediterranean geology.

People and nature have worked together in harmony for many centuries in these beautiful islands, producing such extraordinary landscapes as the terraced mountainsides of northern Mallorca and the rolling hills of Menorca, neatly outlined with fieldstone walls whose tops are regularly whitewashed — as though a titanic Mondrian had decided to carve up the meadows. I know of few more striking views in all Europe than the one from Las Salinas of Formentera across the intervening strait to Ibiza with its shining white citadel.

Unfortunately, during the last 40 years or so, the tourist trade has made tremendous inroads on the natural

The sun rises over Cap de Formentor, the long, narrow promontory that forms the rugged northernmost tip of Mallorca

beauty of the Balearics. In a sense, the islands have become the Miami Beach of Europe. Yet roads, hotels and apartment blocks have affected the three main islands very differently, and travellers should disregard hearsay and judge each on its particular merits.

After many years of agitation by conservationists there is now a *parque nacional* in the Balearics: Cabrera, established in 1991. There are 85 other protected areas, most classified as *Area Natural de Especial Interés*, covering a total area of more than 187,000 ha (462,000 acres), or over 37 per cent of the islands' total surface area.

There are important climatic differences among the islands. On the two northern ones, Menorca and Mallorca, the prevailing winds are from the north, and they have what amounts to 'Catalan' weather. Statistically, Maó (Mahón) and Ciutadella (Ciudadela), on Menorca, have approximately 35 very windy days per year, and Pollença, in north-eastern Mallorca, has 75; but Palma, sheltered by Mallorca's mountain range, has only 19 and Campos only four such days a year. The islands all average around 2,500 annual hours of sunlight. The wettest place is Lluc, high in the Mallorcan mountains, with 115 centimetres (47 inches) of rain per year, almost three times more than Palma, Maó and Eivissa (Ibiza's principal town). This means, in broad terms, that Ibiza is without rain fully half the year, Menorca and the plains of Mallorca have a dry season that lasts for four months, while mountainous Mallorca has only a three-month dry season. Yet it is the wettest, wildest part of Mallorca that holds the greatest attraction for hikers, bird-watchers and botanists.

Time of year is important in the Balearics, whose seasons differ from those of northern Europe. January usu-

ally brings some wet and windy days but is also famous for the *calmos de enero* — the calm, sunny fortnight known to the ancient Greeks as halcyon days — when many people are found sunning on the beaches. February, the month when the vulture and peregrine falcon lay their eggs, usually brings cold weather and sometimes snow on the highest peaks; people from the north are often surprised that there is a real winter here when the *tramuntana*, the north wind, howls and the local residents huddle around their stoves and fireplaces.

But late in February the first signs of the Mediterranean spring appear, along with the first asphodels: hiking in the mountains on cold days but under clear blue skies is an unmitigated pleasure. At the same time the islands' almond trees burst into bloom, frosting the landscape with a layer of white or pink blossoms until one day a strong wind puffs them all to the ground in a flurry of floating petals. (Something like three-quarters of all the almonds consumed in Europe are produced in these islands.)

In March and April the Balearic spring begins in earnest. Migrating birds arrive on the islands and begin to breed. The hoot of Scops owl and hoopoe and the shriek of the stone-curlew are heard. March is the best month for seeing wild orchids in bloom; from now until the end of May the myrtle, spurge, lentisk, strawberry tree and a lot of other plants with magical and mythological associations put out their strongest scents to encourage the bees to do their thing. There is something about this springtime effusion that arouses your senses without drowning them in odours, as the tropics do.

May is virtually a summer month. Nightingales sing by moonlight near open springs. Occasional migrants still arrive, and this is the breeding season for summer visitors such as the black-winged stilt and the bee-eater. In June the dry season starts: the ants take flight and swarm in the mountains. The summer's dryness turns green fields a dusty beige and brings much of nature to a standstill. When the *sirocco* — known locally as the *xeloc* — blows up from the Sahara for more than two or three days at a time, the whole of creation seems prostrated by the heat. This is definitely not the moment to go hiking over the bare, broiling rock of the high sierra.

In September the weather cools; shore birds begin their autumn migration. Lentisk and other wild berries ripen, providing the basic diet for some wintering birds. The rains begin in October and revive the greenery of Mallorca and Menorca — in Ibiza it takes a little longer — and the two-tailed pasha butterfly (*Charaxes jasius*) makes its appearance amid the ripe fruit of the strawberry tree. When the olives ripen in November vast flocks of starlings and gulls wheel out of the sky to rob the farmers of their crop, and the migratory painted lady butterfly (*Cynthia cardai*) arrives in the islands. December brings more rain, even to Ibiza; in Mallorca the black vulture's mating season is in full swing. In spite of what you may have thought, there is indeed wildlife in the Balearics.

BEFORE YOU GO
Maps: Michelin 1:400,000 No. 443.

GETTING THERE
By air: the islands are well served by international and internal flights to Son San Joán airport, Palma de Mallorca; Es Codola airport, Ibiza; and Maó airport, Menorca.
By sea: Trasmediterránea has regular ferry services from the mainland — Barcelona, T: (93) 443 25 32, F: 443 27 81, and València, T: (96) 367 65 12, F: 367 33 45 — to Palma de Mallorca, T: (971) 40 50 14, F: 70 06 11; to Eivissa (Ibiza), T: (971) 31 50 50, F: 31 66 74; and to Maó, T: (971) 36 60 50, F: 36 99 28. For comprehensive coverage of the routes, timetables and offices see www.transmediterranea.es.
Flebasa Lines operates ferries from Denia, T: (96) 578 40 11, F: 578 76 06, to Palma de Mallorca, Eivissa, Sant Antoni (San Antonio, Ibiza) and between Palma de Mallorca and Eivissa. Call T: (971) 40 53 60 on the islands for information. The web-site, www.bdr.es, gives full details of Flebasa Lines' services.
A new and much faster way to cross between Barcelona and Palma de Mallorca is to take the huge catamaran-like vessel known as the *Buquebus*. Carrying 900 passengers and 240 cars, it cuts the journey to just three hours. Call T: (93) 481 73 60, in Barcelona, and T: (971) 40 58 84, F: 70 32 69, in Palma. Before deciding to travel to the Balearics by sea, it is wise to check the cost of inter-island flights; some are much cheaper than the sea crossings.

WHERE TO STAY
From mid-June to mid-Sept accommodation can be in short supply and therefore advance booking is advisable. The whole range of accommodation is available, from 5-star hotels to small *pensiones*, *hostales* and *casas rurales*. However, prices tend to be considerably higher than those you will encounter on mainland Spain.

ACTIVITIES
Mountaineering club: for detailed information about walks, climbing and cave exploration in both Mallorca and Menorca, contact the Federación Balear de Muntanyisme, C/ Pedro Alcántara Penya, 13, 07013 Palma de Mallorca, T/F: (971) 46 88 07.

FURTHER INFORMATION
Tourist offices: Pl. Reina, 2, 07071 Palma de Mallorca, T: (971) 71 22 16, F: 72 02 40; Red Cross, T: 29 50 00, F: 75 26 89; Vara del Rey, 13, bajo, 07800, Eivissa, T: (971) 30 19 00, F: 30 15 62; Pl. de la Explanada, 40, 07703 Maó, T: (971) 36 37 90, F: 36 74 15; and Edificio Obras del Puerto, 07013 La Savina (Puerto de la Sabina), Formentera, T: (971) 32 20 57, F: 32 28 25.
Languages: outside the main towns, and since the devolution of power to the regions, you are more likely to hear, and see, a local dialect rather than Castilian Spanish. *Mallorquín*, *Menorquín* and *Ibizenc* are all closely related to the Catalan language.

FURTHER READING
Anthony Bonner, *Plants of the Balearic Islands* (Editorial Moll, 1985).

A lone pine stands sentinel among rocks overlooking the peaceful Mediterranean

Mallorca

An island rich in plant and bird life, with good trekking routes and a bird sanctuary at S'Albufera
111,400 ha (275,000 acres)

For more than 20 years I have lived at the edge of one of the last great wilderness regions of Europe, the Sierra (in Mal-

lorquín, *Serra*) de Tramuntana that runs the full length of the north-west coast of Mallorca. The olive farm where I live turns its back on a range of mountains that rises by giant steps to the Puig Major (Mayor), which is a kilometre and a half (one mile) high but plunges abruptly into the sea; you could almost toss a stone into the Mediterranean from its summit.

In times past the lower slopes of the Sierra were tilled by olive farmers while the

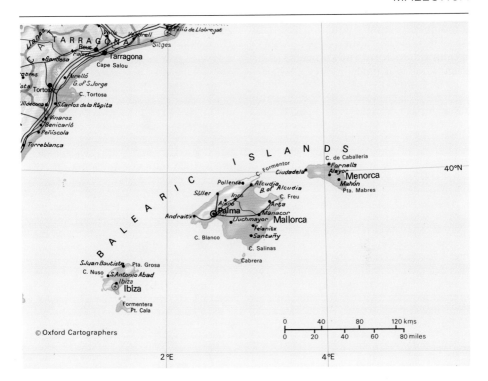

holm oak forests higher up were tended by charcoal burners. The former built the countless fieldstone terraces that enabled olive trees to take root on these precipitous mountainsides. They terraced the coast wherever the lay of the land permitted, from sea level to altitudes of one thousand metres (3,300 feet) or more, and the result is a feat of landscape engineering comparable to the Cyclopean walls of the Peruvian Andes.

Nowadays there is no money to be made from olives in the Sierra and the orchards are virtually deserted; you can walk for hours through the terraced groves at whatever level you choose. Follow some of the old footpaths that lead from village to village, which skirt the sheer rock faces of the high Sierra but afford magnificent views of the rocky shore that lies beneath your feet. If you climb higher you are, literally, on the roof of the island — the wind-swept peaks and high plateaux that scarcely any tourist has ever seen. Here, the limestone surface has been scarred and pot-holed by wind and

weather, but wherever there is soil the ground is covered with wild flowers such as orchids, foxgloves and hellebore. In some areas, between 60 and 70 per cent of the ground cover consists of endemics — species unique to the island. In the 1960s the Belgian botanist Jacques Duvigneaud stretched out for a summer *siesta* on a mossy cliff-top overlooking the sea and found himself gazing at a small plant he had never seen before and was unable to identify. It turned out to be not just a new species but a hitherto unknown genus, which received the name *Naufraga balearica*. This created an enormous shift in the botanical world; to find a new genus anywhere in the world is spectacular but to find one in Europe was almost incredible.

If you hike through the mountains of the Sierra you will have the world to yourself, for there is nothing for 50 kilometres (30 miles) or more, except the ruins of erstwhile charcoal-burners' huts and a few half-wild sheep. A single road meanders along the corniche, but except for the small port of Sóller there are no tourist resorts, only a few villages perched precariously on the lower slopes of the mountains — a sort of Switzerland set down in the middle of the Mediterranean. Holidaymakers do occasionally come through on sightseeing buses to look at the views, but they tend to stay on the other side of the island, where they can stretch out on sandy beaches and wade into the water. Along most of the north-west coast you have to be a mountaineer to get down to the sea.

This sense of solitude is what makes Mallorca — and the other Balearics as well — a kind of Jekyll and Hyde among Mediterranean islands. On the one hand it is everybody's package holiday destination: every summer about four million tourists arrive in Palma, which means that there are seven tourists to every resident. The island is not large — about 111,400 ha (275,275 acres) — and yet it has found ways of absorbing this annual influx of sun-seekers, most of whom head for concrete-block hotels on or near the sandy beaches and proceed to acquire sun-tans.

The topography of Mallorca resembles a clenched fist laid on a table: the Sierra peaks are the knuckles and the rest of the island slopes toward the south like the back of a giant hand, though here and there isolated hilltops provide a better view. Many of them are the sites of ancient sanctuaries, chapels or shrines to the Virgin. One favourite hike through the southern half of the island, the Mitjorn (Midjorn), takes in the Monasterio de Nuestra Señora de Cura on Randa (the mountain where the mystic poet Ramon Llull is said to have meditated during the 13th century), the Santuario de Montesión ('Mount Zion') and the hilltop castle of Santueri, a Roman and medieval fortress used by both Moorish and Aragonese kings as a base for defending the south-east corner of Mallorca.

But the wildest parts of the island all lie in the north, where there are great trekking routes that begin and end in one or another part of the Sierra de Tramuntana. The Sierra was recently declared an *Area Natural de Especial Interés* covering 69,947 ha (172,840 acres), which should help to protect the region against further commercial exploitation. Along the north-eastern coast of the island lies the most important bird sanctuary of the Balearics, the *parque natural* of S'Albufera, which was opened in 1991 and comprises 1,709 ha (4,223 acres) of marshland.

Among the special glories of this landscape are the ancient olive trees, which time and the north wind — the *tramuntana* — have twisted into an astounding variety of shapes. Some trunks fan out like a prehistoric theatre curtain; others spiral upwards, leaving a hollow core that has been worn away by centuries of weathering; still others resemble giant gargoyles. 'When walking in their shade at dusk,' George Sand noted, 'you have to remind yourself that they are trees, because if you accept the evidence of your eyes and imagination, you will be terror-stricken by these fairytale monsters, looming over you like enormous dragons.' Some of the more corpulent veterans are up to an astounding six metres (20 feet) in circumference.

Few farmers now keep up the practice of pruning their trees every year, and many have ceased ploughing up the earth between them. As a result, oleaster shoots are taking over from the sweet olive, and pine seedlings are moving in among the olive groves, undo-

---

THE FLORA OF MALLORCA

Large areas of the island are covered in *matorral*. Herbs are restricted to the edges or sunny glades where there is sufficient light for them to flourish. White asphodels, both *Asphodelus albus* and *A. aestivus*, produce their towering spikes in summer.

The greatest number of endemics occur in the mist-swept heights of the north-western mountain range, especially in the vicinity of Puig Major. A few of the more attractive or unusual species are the birthwort *Aristolochia bianiorri*, occurring especially at Faro de Puerto Pollença; a huge species of parsnip with unpleasant smelling leaves (*Pastinaca lucida*); a Balearic species of shrubby hare's ear, *Bupleurum barceloi*; and *Hippocrepis balearica*.

ing the work of centuries. Eventually the pines crowd out the olives and destroy the terraces; torrential downpours wash away the earth no longer held in check by the terrace walls, and sooner or later the whole hillside crumbles away. Hence the paradox that the Sierra's last remaining farmers have a vital role to play in preserving Mallorca's wilderness.

Ornithologically, Mallorca is one of the most interesting islands in the Mediterranean. A local bird-watchers' guide lists 270 species, including the rare Eleonora's falcon. This gregarious bird migrates to Madagascar in the winter, but returns to the Mediterranean each summer to rear its young. The population of this dark, long-tailed falcon is always very small, and the birds are thus vulnerable to any adverse outside influences. They nest on rocky cliffs along the northern coast as far as Cap de Formentor (Cabo Formentor), and have the remarkable habit of breeding in late summer when the flood of south-bound migrant birds provides a plentiful food supply with which to raise their young. The bird is named after a 14th-century Sardinian princess who introduced probably the first law protecting nesting hawks and falcons.

The Sierra is also one of the last haunts of the black vulture, the largest bird in Europe, whose wingspan has been known to reach three metres (almost ten feet). It likes these mountains because it needs updrafts for its long glides, and it feeds on the carcasses of dead sheep.

At Ses Salines, an area of salt pans on the south-west tip of the island, you can see little egrets and black-winged stilts, as well as black, white-winged black and whiskered terns. Mediterranean and Audouin's gulls also use this area, the latter species being endemic to the Mediterranean and easily identified by its green legs and red bill with a black-and-yellow tip. It is closely related to the herring gull, but unlike this ubiquitous bird, it is the rarest breeding gull in Europe.

Other interesting elements of the bird fauna of Mallorca include the Balearic race of the Manx shearwater and the yellow-billed Cory's shearwater, both of which breed on the offshore islets and marine cliffs

The attractive bee-eater has chestnut, blue-green and yellow plumage and a flute-like call

of the island. The shearwater is the largest of the tube-nose family (*Procellariidae*) breeding in Europe. Marsh harriers and booted eagles also breed here, the former wintering in the islands, as well. Birds on migration which drop in from time to time include flamingoes, whiskered terns, pratincoles and the spectacular glossy ibis.

S'Albufera (also known as La Albufera), the *parque natural* and bird sanctuary just south of Alcudia, derives its name from the Arabic *Al-Buhayra*, a lake or lagoon. The large lake at one end of it has now been taken over by a housing project, unfortunately, but the rest of S'Albufera remains an untouched basin of reed-covered marshes fed by the waters that descend from the eastern Sierra de Tramuntana and the low hills of the central plain.

With its whispering reeds and croaking frogs as a sort of *continuo* accompaniment, S'Albufera is alive with bird song, for this is a garden of Eden for the birds whose flyways cross the Mediterranean, as well as a year-round residence for many other species. The purple gallinules and night

173

herons that were sent from Mallorca to Rome for gastronomic purposes in the days of the Empire were probably caught in S'Albufera. During their periods of migration it harbours red-footed falcons, whiskered tern, collared pratincole, ringed plover, nightjar, sand martin and many other species. Winter visitors who stay for the season include shelduck and the greylag goose, red-crested pochard, teal and pintail, wigeon, Montagu's harrier, golden plover, kingfisher, little stint, bluethroat, black redstart and others. The summer census is headed by Eleonora's falcon, little bittern, purple heron, woodchat shrike, little ringed plover, tawny pipit, turtle dove, cuckoo, bee-eater, yellow wagtail, nightingale, Sardinian and reed warblers and black-winged stilt. There are large numbers of other species

Spring arrives at the end of February, as Mallorca's almond trees burst into blossom

that live here the year round, among them the marsh harrier, peregrine falcon, barn and long-eared owls, to say nothing of the stonechat, crag martin, fan-tailed, Cetti's and moustached warblers, corn bunting and many more; altogether more than 200 species have been recorded here. The authorities have made things easy for bird-watchers by building a hide not far from the reception centre; the way to it leads over a rickety pontoon bridge and a path of stepping stones made of second-hand building blocks.

Aficionados return from the hide with tales of superb views of moustached and great reed warblers, of osprey fishing before their eyes and Eleonora's falcons deftly catching and devouring birds in flight.

Most bird-watchers base themselves at Port de Pollença (Puerto Pollença) and in May they are sufficiently numerous to hold weekly meetings at one of the local hotels in order to exchange news.

Even at extreme heights snow is rare in the mountains of Mallorca

BEFORE YOU GO
Maps: IGN 1:25,000 and 1:50,000 Nos. 643, 644, 645, 670, 671, 672, 697, 698, 699, 700, 723, 724, 725, 748, 749 and 774; IGN 1:200,000 Mapa Provincial of Baleares and 1:150,000 Mapa Guía Isla de Mallorca.
Guide-books: Valerie Crespi-Green, *Landscapes of Mallorca* (Sunflower, 1998); Herbert Heinrich, *Classic Hikes through Mallorca* (Editorial Moll, 1987); K. J. Stoba, *Birdwatching in Mallorca*

(Cicerone); Eddie Watkinson, *A Guide to Birdwatching in Mallorca* (J.G Sanders, 1982).

GETTING THERE
By air: Mallorca's airport, Son San Joán, is one of the busiest in Europe during the summer months, with flights arriving from all over northern Europe and mainland Spain.
By sea: Trasmediterránea runs regular car-ferry services from Barcelona and València to Palma, and between Palma and Ibiza, and Palma and Maó. Flebasa runs a daily service between Denia and Palma. *Buquebus* operates very high-speed vessels between

Barcelona and Palma de Mallorca. See p169 for further details.
ON THE ISLAND
By car: the most convenient way to see the island and to approach its wilder areas is by car. To see the whole island, drive along the corniche road on the north-west coast from Andratx to Sóller and then to Lluc and Cap de Formentor, completing the circuit by way of Alcúdia, Artà and the south coast. Rental cars are reasonably inexpensive, and a full listing of companies supplying them can be obtained from the tourist office.
By rail: a regular service runs

175

between Palma and Inca. The Palma-Sóller train, which runs 5 times a day, provides a lovely ride with spectacular views from the heights of the Sóller Pass; built by Swiss engineers, it behaves just like a Swiss narrow-gauge mountain train, running through tunnels and dizzying switchbacks before finally descending into the valley of Sóller.

By bus: the island is covered by an excellent network of buses, which take you to the best starting points for hikes and excursions. Current schedules available from the tourist office.

WHERE TO STAY

Mallorca has many hundreds of hotels, of every category; however, during the summer most of them are crowded with tourists. Look, though, for small, wonderful country-house hotels, which are recommended here. Good bases include Port d'Andratx near Mallorca's northern Cordillera; Estellencs, which clings to the mountainside beneath the 1,025-m (3,363-ft) Puig de Galatzó; and Valldemossa, where Chopin and George Sand spent 2 rainy months during the winter of 1838, and where some of the most

enjoyable mountain routes start. Try the Mofarés, T: (971) 72 15 08, F: 71 73 17, in Calvià; Son Ferrà, T: (971) 61 04 05, in Esporles; and the Son Brondo, T: (971) 61 22 58, in Valldemossa. Heading north along the coast there are the S'Hotel d'es Puig, T: (971) 63 94 09, F: 63 92 10, at Deià (Deya); the Hotel Ca N'ai, T: (971) 63 24 94, F: 63 18 99, and Can Coll, T: (971) 72 15 08, F: 71 73 17, e-mail: can-coll@todoesp.es, and www.todoesp.es/can-coll, both in Sóller; and the Ca'n Faveta, T: (971) 72 15 08, F: 71 73 17, at Alcúdia, not far from the S'Albufera bird marshes.

Other options are 5-star Hotel Son Vida, T: (971) 79 00 00, F: 79 00 17; and 4-star Hotel Playa Cala Mayor, T: (971) 40 32 13, F: 70 05 23, both in Palma de Mallorca.

Outdoor living: Camping Club San Pedro, T: (971) 58 90 23, open 1 June-15 Sept, with space for 500 people, at Artà; and the Sun Club Picafort, T: (971) 86 00 02, open all year with capacity for 500 people, in Platja de Muro.

Monasteries: most of the mountain monasteries will accommodate visitors for short stays. Facilities are simple, and

prices correspondingly low. To make reservations at Nuestra Señora de Lluc, T: (971) 51 70 25; San Salvador, near Felanitz, T: (971) 82 72 82; and Nuestra Señora del Cura, between Algaida and Llucmajor in the centre of the island, T: (971) 66 09 34, F: 66 20 52.

ACCESS

A permit is required for entry to S'Albufera. It is a short walk or drive from the main road to the reception centre, Sa Roca, where park wardens issue the necessary permit – gratis to visitors, who must leave their cars at the centre and proceed through the marshes on foot.

ACTIVITIES

Walking: there are innumerable footpaths through the wilder parts of Mallorca. It is easy to get lost in these mountains because the resident sheep have made their own paths which look exactly like footpaths – but often turn out to end suddenly at the edge of some precipitous drop.

One of my favourite walks is the all-day hike along what used to be the bridle path of the Austrian archduke Ludwig Salvator (1847-1915), from Valldemossa to the Teix (1,062 m/3,484 ft). The archduke must have been utterly fearless, for part of the path skirts a really breathtaking bluff: clearly this is not a route for people suffering from vertigo. You can enjoy some of the same views from a less spectacular altitude by taking the old footpath that led from Deià and Sóller before a road was laid. The track is narrow, paved with fieldstones, and winds high above the coast, through abandoned olive groves and stands of pine.

Some other notable treks in this area are the descent from Son Marroig to the rocky peninsula known as Sa Foradada ('the perforated

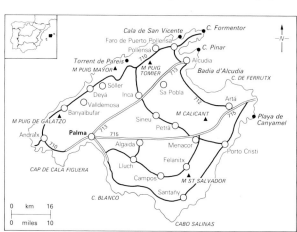

Eleonora's falcon breeds on coastal cliffs in late summer, preying on small birds migrating south to Africa

one'); the 'hike of the thousand bends' from Sóller through the Biniaraix gorge via the Mirador de Xim Quesada (1,009 m/3,310 ft); and the ascent of the slopes of Puig Major and the Migdia massif to the Comellar de l'Infern ('valley of hell'), all of which are described in Heinrich's guide (see above).

The Sierra de Levante, in the Artà area, is worth visiting and many long walks can be enjoyed from the town itself; for example, taking the northernmost road out of the village, you can follow the narrow country lane up to the Ermita de Betlem. From there a marked trail leads to a viewpoint giving a panoramic view of the bay of Alcúdia.

Climbing: the monastery of Lluc, with its famous image of La Morenita ('the Black Madonna'), is 'the heart of Mallorca' and has been a centre for mountain pilgrimages since the Middle Ages. Modern highways and the commercialization of the

medieval monastery have converted Lluc into more of a tourist attraction, but it remains a starting point for many exciting mountain tours.

The limestone mountains are honeycombed with caves, some of them of great interest to speleologists who have been studying the magnetic orientation of their bottom sediments. Thousands of bats make their home here, and the region's remoteness favours birds of prey — osprey and booted eagle, Eleonora's falcon and Scops owl. Also in the Lluc area are black vultures, and it is one of the few reliable places on the island to see rock thrush.

The mountain hike from Lluc to the Puig Tomir (1,102 m/2,723 ft) by way of Binifaldó is fairly strenuous; another easier walk circles the Puig Roig (1,002 m/3,287 ft). Farther to the north there is the descent from the *finca* (estate) of Mortitx via the Rafal d'Ariant valley to a seaside cave known as the Cova de les Bruixes ('of the witches'); the route is known as the Camí del Ratal and can also be used as an approach to the lunar landscapes of the hidden plateau known as La Malé.

The walk to Castell del Rei, which begins at Pollença, traverses a privately owned *finca*; check with the local tourist office (p169) for information on access. The Castell itself is an ancient fortress-observation post.

Far more demanding is the ascent to the Puig de Massanella (1,348 m/4,423 ft) from the Coll de Sa Batalla ('battle pass') on the road from Inca to Lluc. Since the top of the Puig Major is closed to hikers, the Massanella is the highest accessible mountain on Mallorca. Inexperienced climbers are advised that the going is rough; the excursion is best made with a guide.

Mountain reserves: in addition to S'Albufera, Mallorca has 16 mountain and forest reserves that are publicly owned. They vary considerably in size, but each is a self-contained bird sanctuary and nature reserve. Ask at tourist office (see below) for details.

Caves: the Coves de Campanet, situated 8 km (5 miles) off the C713, about 50 km (30 miles) from Palma, are full of well lit stalagmites and stalactites. The Coves d'Artà are on the PM 404-2 above the Platja de Canyamel; a long stone stairwell takes you up into a vast dark hole in the rock face and the entrance to the caves, which were pirate hide-outs. The Coves del Drach are situated off the PM 404-4, just outside Portocristo.

Gardens: the gardens at Alfàbia have elegant arbours, pavilions and lily ponds; situated on the C711 Palma-Sóller road, 17 km (10 miles) out of Palma.

FURTHER INFORMATION
Tourist office: Aeropuerto de Son San Joán, T/F: 78 95 56; Palma de Mallorca, p169.

Archipiélago de Cabrera

Small islands, whose sparse population makes them a refuge for birds, reptiles and marine life; parque nacional ZEPA 10,021 ha (24,762 acres)

Naturalists are agreed that Cabrera is a great *parque nacional*, despite the fact that the island and its neighbouring islets (notably Conejera) are a military zone, inhabited by a

177

lighthouse keeper and a garrison of about a dozen soldiers who maintain what is essentially an artillery firing range. The island group was made the Parque Nacional Marítimo-Tereste del Archipiélago de Cabrera in 1991, after years of pressure from conservation groups.

Cabrera lies about 18 km (11 miles) from the nearest point on Mallorca — Cap de ses Salines — and 50 km (30 miles) from the Bay of Palma. It measures about 7 by 5 km (4½ by 3 miles) and has a 22-km (13½-mile coastline dominated by two hills, the Puig de Picomosques and the Puig de la Guardia. On the north side a narrow channel guarded by a ruined castle leads into a horseshoe-shaped natural harbour that is completely protected from winds.

The island's vegetation resembles that of southern Mallorca, but its isolation and sparse population have made it a refuge of last resort for several species of plants, birds, reptiles and marine life. The Cabrera sub-species of Lilford's wall lizard are underfoot everywhere, and so fearless they will eat a sandwich out of your hand. Also here are Turkish and Moorish geckoes and Hermann's tortoise. The archipelago harbours important breeding colonies of yellow-legged gulls, shag and Cory's shearwater; also present, though in lesser numbers, are the Balearic shearwater and Eleonora's falcon and two pairs of osprey. There are 450 species of plant on land, while the marine habitat is home to turtles, dolphins and 214 species of fish.

The quality of the sunlight changes the face of Mallorcan landscapes from one minute to the next

Whales, seals and dolphins often visit this coast, for artillery practice takes place so infrequently they have nothing to fear. It is one of the peculiar ironies of the modern world that some of the most undisturbed areas for wildlife are those where military installations keep the rest of the human population at bay.
Before you go *Guide-book:* Ramon Lozano Alvarez, *Itinerarios por La Cabrera* (Lancia, 1996).
Getting there *By sea:* there are organised visits to the island from Colònia de Sant Jordi, in the south of Mallorca; bookings can be made at the Restaurante Miramar, T: (971)

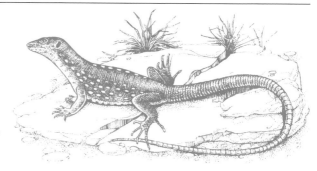

Lilford's wall lizard has died out on the main Balearic Islands, but this dark sub-species survives on Cabrera

64 90 34. It is sometimes possible to 'hitch' a ride with fishermen.

Access and Closures: there are no tourist facilities on Cabrera and visitors are not permitted to stay overnight. *Permits:* to do more than the harbour and ruined castle, you need a special permit, issued in Palma. Enquire at the tourist office.

Menorca

Second largest of the Balearics, at 49 km by 19 km (30 miles by 72 miles); numerous coves and golden beaches; parque natural of S'Albufera des Grao Biosphere Reserve 1,947 ha (4,811 acres)

The windiest and most mysterious of the Balearics, Menorca has managed to preserve something of its ancient splendid isolation. It is the second largest and northernmost of the islands.

It has unique advantages as a summer holiday destination, thanks to the 120 sandy beaches and coves that form the greater part of its coastline: no other Mediterranean island has so many beaches. Most of them have long since capitulated to the tourist invasion, but a few are still deserted and undeveloped — for the simple reason that they can only be approached on foot, along difficult paths. The best of these forgotten beaches lie in the north of the island, between Cala Pregonda (now menaced by urbanization) and Cap (Cabo) Gros, where there are no access roads and where some of the local caves can only be reached by boat.

Apart from the bird sanctuary at S'Albufera des Grao, made a *parque natural* in 1995, Menorca has 19 protected areas, most of which are classified as *Area Natural de Especial Interés*. Much of the interior remains untouched by the fell hand of the 20th century, and no other spot in the world is as thickly strewn with relics of the Bronze Age. In scores of places you come across some of the earliest buildings in Europe, the so-called *talayots*, which resemble stone igloos built by a race of giants. Here and there a side road leads to a miniature Stonehenge: a circle of huge limestone slabs surmounted by a giant T-shaped *taula*, usually interpreted as having been a sacrificial table, although I suspect nothing so sinister, but rather that they were merely meant to be schematic representations of a bull's head.

Although boasting fewer endemic plant species than Mallorca, the island is the only known habitat of the dwarf shrub *Daphne rodriguezii*. This attractive, purple-flowered evergreen grows on the siliceous cliffs of the north-east coast. Another extremely localized species that is restricted to Menorca is the loosestrife, *Lysimachia minoricensis*. The coastal limestone cliffs of the southern shores have an interesting flora: a community comprising species adapted to lime-rich and saline soils.

180

But it is the island's cast of reptiles that really attracts attention. There are only four species of lizard found in the Balearics — and Menorca boasts populations of three. Lilford's wall lizard is a beautiful creature, sometimes green and brown, but also with several melanic populations, black with blue underbellies; it has a distinctive 'turnip-shaped' tail. The Moroccan rock lizard is, as its name suggests, a native of North Africa; it was introduced to this island. It is a small, rather flattened creature, usually with a bronzed, olive skin, and a completely transparent 'window' in the lower eyelid.

The third lacertid is the Italian wall lizard, for which this island is the only Spanish locality. It is vivid olive green with a black dorsal pattern of stripes, and has a long head. It is larger and more robust than the other lizard species of the Balearics, preferring not to climb to hunt its food.

By picking your route carefully, you can back-pack across the island, although asphalt is hard to avoid. The lanes lead past Menorca's spick-and-span dairy farms whose Holstein cattle look strangely out of place in this arch-Mediterranean landscape of rolling hills and whitewashed villages. (Not so long ago Menorcan farmers were in the habit of whitewashing their houses once a week; now, as a concession to the 20th century, they refrain from doing it more than once a month.)

In winter the island is lush and green, and virtually deserted by tourists; in summer the fields turn a predictable beige, brown and ochre. May/June and September/October are ideal times for a visit that might focus on the island's natural beauties rather than its seaside amenities.

BEFORE YOU GO
Maps: IGN 1:25,000 and 1:50,000 Nos. 618, 619, 646, 647 and 673; IGN 1:200,000 Mapa Provincial of Baleares.
Guide-book: Rodney Ansell, *Landscapes of Menorca* (Sunflower, 1996).

GETTING THERE
By air: many companies run frequent international and domestic flights from the mainland and Palma de Mallorca to Maó. Numerous charter flights from northern European destinations also serve Maó airport.
By sea: Trasmediterránea provides frequent car-ferry services from Barcelona and València to Maó, and between Palma de Mallorca and Maó. See p169 for telephone numbers and further details.
ON THE ISLAND
By car: the main route crosses the centre of the island, linking Maó and Ciutadella and branching off to Cala en Porter, Cala Santa Galdana, Fornells and other small coastal towns. There are few coastal roads (and no railway).
To drive to S'Albufera des Grao, follow the road north from Maó towards Fornells; the second fork in the road will take you to Es Grao and the salt marshes of S'Albufera.
By bus: the bus routes are very limited and are mostly confined to the main central road between Maó and the port of Ciutadella. Routes branch off it to the coast.

WHERE TO STAY
Like the neighbouring islands, Menorca has a surfeit of tourist and beach hotels in every price range. Of the numerous hotels in Maó and Ciutadella, try the 4-star Port Mahón, T: (971) 32 26 00, F: 35 10 50, in Maó; and the 3-star Cala Blanca, T: (971) 38 04 50, F: 38 20 00, in Ciutadella. In the country-house style, try the Son Triay Nou, T: (971) 72 15 08, F: 71 73 17, in Ferreries; and the Alcaufar Vell, T: (971) 72 15 08, F: 71 73 17, in Sant Lluís.
Outdoor living: Camping Son Bou, T: (971) 37 26 05, open 4 Apr-12 Dec, with space for 1,000 people, in Alaior; and S'Atalaia, T: (971) 37 30 95, open all year with capacity for 100 people, in Ferreries.

ACTIVITIES
Walking: in the centre of the island, Mercadal is the starting point for the ascent of Monte Toro (358 m/1,175 ft) — the highest point. This is a fairly steep hike of about 4 km (2½ miles) but the view from the top is worth the effort. Some other suggestions: the cliffs around the Platja de Binimel-la offer some good walking routes and there are streams flowing down the beach to the sea; the road from Ferreries to Cala Santa Galdana is lovely, although it does lead, in the end, to the inevitable tourist development; heading south from Ciutadella the rough road leading to Playa son Saura, Cala d'es Talaier and Cala Turqueta makes a good day's outing through green countryside to sunny beaches.
Caves: the Coves d'en Xoroi, near Cala en Porter in the south, have been somewhat commercialized but further round the cliff face you will find more caves. The best way to see these is from the water;

181

Like Mallorca, Menorca (left) has its forgotten pockets of rocky coastline and the remote southwest of Ibiza commands a fine prospect of the islet of Illa Vedrà (above)

---

boat trips are available from the town.

Mopeds: available for hire; ask at the tourist office in Maó for a list of companies. Ensure that your insurance covers theft of the machine. Remember also that petrol stations are few and far between.

Museum: the Ateneo Científico, Literario y Artístico, Maó, is a small museum which has the biggest collection of dried seaweeds in southern Europe.

FURTHER INFORMATION
Tourist office: Maó, p169.

Ibiza

Crowded with pines, and in the summer with tourists; wall lizard and oleander flourish here

In ancient times the whole Balearic archipelago was known as Gymnasiae, as it was believed that the inhabitants ran naked even during the winter; whether this was through ignorance or extreme hardiness is an intriguing mystery. Ibiza (Elvissa or Eivissa) was then the most important of the 'Pityussae' — pine-clad islands — of this group, which comprised Formentera and Espalmador to the south, Tagomago to the east, and Vedrá and Conillera to the west. Sadly, it has become the most over-touristed island of all the Balearics, especially in recent years.

By exercising a great deal of care, it is still possible to get away from the madding crowds

183

who overrun the resorts to search out the island's curiosities. One way to do this is to confine your visits to the autumn and winter.

There are dense forests, with aleppo pine (*Pinus halepensis*) in the higher areas, which make a sharp contrast to the arid environment elsewhere. The dwarf fan palm (*Chamaerops humilis*), the only palm native to Europe, is found in dry sandy areas here and along the Mediterranean coast, and its ½-m (18-in) fronds provide cover for a number of reptile and bird species. Another plant to look out for is the spectacular orchid, *Ophrys bertolonii*, only to be found in peninsular Spain, the Balearics and France; its furry orange-brown flowers are crowned by three slender, pale pink perianth segments.

The most characteristic plant of Ibiza is the oleander, which can be seen overflowing from the dried river beds of the plains in summer. Its grey, leathery leaves are arranged around the stem in whorls of three, and the whole plant is topped with huge pink blooms over 5 cm (2 in) in diameter. It is often found growing with myrtle, and the sight and smell of these beautiful, fragrant plants in full bloom is quite dizzying.

Ibiza's most important animal is the Ibiza wall lizard (*Podarcis pityusensis*). It is endemic to the Pityusae archipelago but has also been introduced to Mallorca and the city of Barcelona. The lizard lives in barren, shrubby areas; it is robust and short-headed, sometimes a vivid green on the back, and may have a spotted throat and belly. Equally interesting is the archetypal hunting dog found on the island, known locally as *ca ervissenc*. Reputedly, this tall,

loose-limbed, fawn-coloured beast was introduced by the Egyptians or Carthaginians, and it is still entirely possible to find animals of almost pure blood line.

Before you go *Maps:* IGN 1:25,000 and 1:50,000 Nos. 772, 773, 798 and 799.

Guide-book: Hans Losse, *Landscapes of Ibiza and Formentera* (Sunflower, 1995).

Getting there *By air:* as well as direct flights from many European cities, there are regular internal flights from the mainland and Palma.

By sea: Trasmediterránea has regular sailings to Eivissa from Barcelona, València and Palma de Mallorca. Flebasa Lines operates services between Denia and Eivissa, and Sant Antoni de Portmany (San Antonio de Portmany), Palma de Mallorca and Eivissa and Eivissa and Formentera. See p169 for telephone numbers and further details.

ON THE ISLAND

By sea: from the main towns, Eivissa, Sant Antoni and Santa Eulària des Riu (Santa Eulalia del Río), there are regular excursion trips and minor ferry routes.

By car: the main route connects Eivissa, Sant Antoni, Portinatx and Santa Eulària des Riu. A good network of minor roads connects the smaller villages, but no coastal route right around the island. Be careful about parking: wheel clamps are used on offending cars.

By bus: the service is fairly comprehensive with regular buses to Sant Antoni, Santa Eulària des Riu, Sant Carles, Es Canar, San Joan de Labritja, Cala Sant Vicent, Portinatx, Salines, Sant Josep, Sant Miquel, Sant Mateu and Santa Agnes.

Where to stay: there is a vast array of accommodation to choose from, especially in

Eivissa, Santa Eulària des Riu and Sant Antoni, although the wise will steer clear of the latter. The 5-star Hotel Hacienda, T: (971) 33 45 00, F: 33 45 14, at Sant Miquel de Balansat, is rather special; the Can Martí, T: (971) 33 35 00, F: 33 31 12, at Sant Joan de Labritja, is also of interest.

Outdoor living: Camping Cala Nova Playa, T: (971) 33 64 31, open 1 Apr-31 Oct, with space for 375 people; and Vacaciones Es Canar, T: (971) 33 21 17, open 20 May-10 Oct with capacity for 249, are both in Santa Eulària des Riu. Camping Cala Bassa, T: (971) 34 45 99, open 1 May-30 Sept, with space for 400 people, is in Sant Agustí des Vedrà.

Activities *Walking:* the road from Eivissa to Sant Miquel takes you through the most attractive parts of the island, where you can readily stop for walks in the hills and through picturesque villages with their groves of almond, carob and olive trees. There is a steepish trail from the port of Sant Miquel which goes over hilly coastal land to Cala Benirras.

Caves: Cova Santa ('the holy cave') lies just off the San Josep-Eivissa road. There is a trail just to the south, from the caves to Cala Yondal.

Museums: the Museu Arte Contemporáneo is situated in Eivissa above the arch of the Portal de las Tablas. The Museu Archaeológica and the Museu Puig des Molins, with finds from the Necropolis, are in the vicinity of the Pl. de España.

Sailing: contact Club Punta Arabí at Es Canar, T: (971) 33 00 85.

Further information *Tourist offices:* Mariano Riquer Wallis, 07840 Santa Eulària des Riu, T: (971) 33 07 28; and Eivissa, see p169.

> 'The landscape was of the purest Mediterranean kind — pines and junipers and fig trees growing out of red earth. Looking down from the hill-top, the plain spread between the sea and the hills was daubed and patched henna, iron rust and stale blood — the fields curried more darkly where newly irrigated, the threshing-floors paler with their encircling beehives of straw, the roads smoking with orange dust where the farm-carts passed...
> The course of Ibiza's only river was marked across this plain by a curling snake of pink-flowered oleanders. Oleanders, too, frothed at most of the well-heads. A firm red line had been drawn enclosing the land at the sea's edge. Here the narrow movements of the Mediterranean tides seemed to submit the earth to a fresh oxidation each day, and after each of the brief, frenzied storms of midsummer, a bloody lake would spread slowly into the blue of the sea, all along the coast.'
> Norman Lewis, *A View of the World*

Formentera

Just south of Ibiza; barren for the most part, but boasting empty, sandy beaches

Of all the islands of the Balearic archipelago, Formentera is closest to the coast of Africa, just 115 kilometres (71 miles) away. The name comes from the island's days as a Roman granary (*frumentaria*). The landscape is quite barren and the highest point (Mola) rises only 192 m (630 ft) above sea level. Like Ibiza, its near neighbour, it has its fair share of pine woods, as well as a healthy population of wall lizard, which is larger than the Ibiza race and often a brighter green. The lizards living on the offshore islets are almost independent of any vegetation cover, and tend to be melanistic, or with brightly coloured flanks of blue or orange.

Before you go *Maps:* IGN 1:25,000 and 1:50,000 Nos. 824 and 825.

Getting there *By sea:* Flebasa Lines operates daily services, either by Linea Jet or regular ferry, the former taking 25 minutes and the latter 60 minutes, between Eivissa and Port de La Savina. See p169 for telephone numbers and further details.

ON THE ISLAND

By car: a car is by far the best means of getting around the island. There are car-hire companies in La Savina and Sant Francesc de Formentera, with four-wheel-drive vehicles being most popular.

By bus: infrequent buses service the towns of Sant Francesc de Formentera, La Savina and El Pinar de la Mola. Bus services are virtually non-existent during weekends, public holidays and winter months.

Where to stay: surprisingly, for such a small, remote island, accommodation is plentiful and varied. Try the 4-star Riu Club la Mola, T/F: (971) 32 80 69, and check the tourist office for a full listing.

Outdoor living: many isolated areas are suitable for camping; for advice, consult the tourist office.

Activities *Bird-watching:* Las Salinas — salt pans in the north of the island between La Savina and Sant Francesc — and the nearby lakes are a haven for bird-watchers, being an important migratory port of call for many birds each year.

Boat trips: in summer there are daily boat trips from La Savina to Espalmador. Check schedules at the Hostal Bahía, T: (971) 32 21 42, in La Savina.

Caves: some small caves, Coves d'en Xeroni, are situated near San Ferran.

Diving: tuition can be arranged at the Riu Club la Mola, T/F: (971) 32 80 69.

Mopeds and bicycles: are available for hire at the Port de La Savina.

Viewpoints: on the Mola plateau, on the eastern edge of the island, is the Mola lighthouse, which is easily reached by car. It provides wide and spectacular views both of the island and of the sea.

Further information *Tourist office:* Formentera, p169.

CHAPTER 8

The Canary Islands

It is a curious legacy of empire that the Canaries are provinces of Spain. Lying 100 kilometres (65 miles) off the coast of Morocco, they are ten times closer to Africa than to the Iberian peninsula. For centuries they were a stopping-off point for explorers, at least as far back as the time of the ancient Greeks: Pliny the Elder described them in some detail. They were claimed for Castile at the dawn of European colonization in the 15th century, when they were found to be inhabited by a native population called Guanches. The islands have never been of any great strategic or economic importance, which is perhaps why they have remained unchallenged in Spanish hands for so long, but they are remarkably rich in flora and geological curiosities.

The origin of the islands has long been the subject of controversy. One ancient theory was that they were the peaks of the legendary lost continent of Atlantis. Now there are two conflicting, but rather more scientific, explanations. One is that the islands rose from the sea bed in independent volcanic eruptions; the other that they were once part of Africa and split off to drift westwards to their present position. It is likely that the truth lies somewhere between the two: the eastern islands — Lanzarote and Fuerteventura — are derived from the same land plate as Africa, while the western islands — Tenerife, La Palma, Hierro, Gomera and Gran Canaria — have volcanic origins.

Of native trees, the one which most successfully exploits the badlands of La Palma is the magnificent Canary Pine

Similarly, there are major climatic differences between the eastern and western islands. A dessicating wind blowing direct from the Sahara scorches the eastern islands for up to a week at a time, while the absence of high ground means that they are unable to intercept the moisture-carrying trade winds from the north. By contrast, the high mountain peaks of the western islands catch these north winds, resulting in one of the western Canaries' most striking features: the ring of cloud that clings to the northern face of each island.

The flora on the islands has clearly been evolving uninterrupted for millions of years, as can be inferred from the large number of species found nowhere else in the world. Fossil evidence has shown that the legendary dragon tree (*Dracaena draco*), the Canary laurels and indigenous fern species may be up to 20 million years old; their nearest living relatives are found today in South America and Africa.

Between them the seven islands, with a total land area of 7,272 square kilometres (2,808 square miles), support an incredible 574 endemic plant taxa, of which 127 are thought to be in danger of extinction. The total flora numbers some two thousand species. Many of these are relics of a sub-tropical vegetation which was previously much more widespread, but has gradually shrunk, due to the desiccation of the area now occupied by the Sahara and the southwards spread of glacial weather during the Ice Ages. The Canaries were protected from these climatic extremes by the moderating influence of the sea and so retained an element of the original flora. In addition, the great height of some of the islands provided a climatic gradient for species sensitive to temperature variation and, as the world climate fluctuated, these species were able

to survive by migrating up and down the mountain slopes.

From the air, the Canaries look like beached shells when the tide has gone out, leaving a white trail. The strong northerly trade winds that blow for most of the year are responsible for the current and the wake of foam that extends southward from the islands.

Yet the initial impression of uniformity is misleading. At sea level the seven main islands are very different from one another, and these differences are exemplified by the four national parks — on Lanzarote, Tenerife, Gomera and La Palma.

Lanzarote, closest to Africa, has the Parque Nacional de Timanfaya that is most interesting geologically, especially to vulcanologists, but by the same token it is virtually devoid of vegetation. The impression that the *parque* makes on its visitors is of a bleak, harsh landscape; windy, dusty and unwelcoming.

Tenerife presents a completely different profile, rising from the rocky shore up through a layer of cloud that clings like a collar around the magnificent peak of El Teide, the Atlantic equivalent of Fujiyama. The vast crater of Las Cañadas del Teide which surrounds this volcanic peak was declared a *parque nacional* in 1954. It is by far the highest of the four national parks, with a remarkable ecosystem famous for its unique alpine flora.

Gomera can be reached only by ferry from Tenerife, less than one and a half hours away. As you sail towards it, a steady stream of clouds pours over the island's peaks like a silent Niagara, shifting continually, but always hiding the heights from view. This crown of moisture-laden clouds gives the Parque Nacional de Garajonay some of Spain's most luxurious vegetation.

A bit farther north-west, La Palma

also has a wholly idiosyncratic landscape. From the sea the island appears less remarkable than the others. Only from the highest points — or from the air — can you gaze down into the vertiginous depths of the deepest crater in the world, La Caldera de Taburiente. This extraordinary phenomenon — an extinct volcano that has streams running within its crater — has been a protected zone and national park for more than 40 years. It is like a milestone set in the sea; from here there is no land westwards until you reach the New World.

GETTING THERE

By air: there are many flights from numerous international and mainland destinations to Tenerife's Reina Sofía airport. There are also flights connecting the main islands, except Gomera, which doesn't have an airport.

By sea: Trasmediterránea, www.trasmediterranea.es, covers the entire Canary Island chain, and operates sailings from Cádiz, on the mainland. Regular crossings take you to all the destinations you require, with the versatility to choose between hydro-foil or jet-foil, or traditional ferries. Contact Cádiz, T: (956) 28 43 11, F: 25 84 33; Santa Cruz de Tenerife, T: (922) 28 78 50, F: 28 61 06; Los Cristianos, (Tenerife), T: (922) 79 61 78, F: 79 61 79; Santa Cruz de la Palma (La Palma), T: (922) 41 11 21, F: 41 39 53; San Sebastián de la Gomera, T/F: (922) 87 13 24; Valverde (Hierro), T/F: (922) 55 01 29; Las Palmas de Gran Canaria, T: (928) 47 41 09, F: 47 41 21; Arrecife (Lanzarote), T: (928) 81 10 19, F: 81 23 63; Puerto del Rosario (Fuerteventura), T: (928) 85 08 77, F: 85 24 08, or Morrojable (Fuerteventura), T/F: (928) 54 02 50.

Fred Olsen Lines, www.fredolsen.es, offers the following four ferry lines: between San Sebastián de la Gomera, T: (922) 87 10 07, F: 87 04 62, and Los Cristianos, T: (922) 79 05 56; Corralejo (Fuerteventura), T: (928) 53 50 90, and Playa Blanca (Lanzarote), T: (928) 51 72 66;

Agaete, Puerto de Las Nieves (Gran Canaria), T: (928) 55 44 62, F: 89 81 99, and Santa Cruz de Tenerife, T: (922) 29 00 11; and Santa Cruz de Tenerife to Los Cristianos to Santa Cruz de la Palma and back to Santa Cruz de Tenerife.

WHEN TO GO

The main tourist season is Jan-Mar; hotels are generally full during these months, and advance booking is strongly recommended.

Spring is the best time for walking in the mountains. The summer months are hot, August's average temperature being 25°C (76°F), but still comfortable enough for hiking. Swimming is possible all year round, though the beaches can get very crowded during the high season.

WHERE TO STAY

All the islands have a very wide choice of accommodation. This can range from 5-star hotels to very simple *pensiones* and *hostales*. Full listings are available from tourist offices.

ACTIVITIES

Mountaineering clubs: Federación Canaria de Montañismo, Heros, 53, sotano, 38008 Santa Cruz de Tenerife, T/F: (922) 22 57 17.

RECOMMENDATIONS

Clothing: tough footwear is a must if you are planning to hike in rocky terrain. In Nov-Apr be prepared for snow at high altitudes.

Drinking water: this can be in short supply, particularly on Lanzarote, and it is advisable to drink bottled water.

FURTHER INFORMATION

Gran Canaria (928): tourist office, Parque de Santa Catalina, 35007, T: 26 46 23, F: 22 98 20. Red Cross, T: 29 00 00, F: 29 64 81.

Fuerteventura (928): tourist office, Avda. Primero de Mayo, 33, 35600 Puerto del Rosario, T: 85 10 24.

Lanzarote (928): tourist office, Parque Municipal, s/n, 35500 Arrecife, T: 81 18 60.

Tenerife (922): tourist office, Pl. de España, s/n, 38003 Santa Cruz de Tenerife, T: 23 95 92, F: 23 98 12. Red Cross, T: 28 29 24, F: 24 67 44.

La Palma (922): tourist office, C/ O'Daly, 22, 38700 Santa Cruz de la Palma, T: 41 21 06.

Gomera (922): tourist office, C/ Del Medio, 20, 38800 San Sebastián de la Gomera, T: 14 01 47.

Hierro (922): tourist office, C/ Licenciado Bueno, 3, 38900 Valverde, T: 55 03 26, F: 55 10 52.

FURTHER READING

Insight Guides, *Tenerife and the Western Canary Islands* (Apa Publications, 1990); David & Zoë Bramwell, *Wild Flowers of the Canary Islands* (Stanley Thornes, 1974); Francisco Javier & Macías Martín, *Parques de Canarias* (Everest, 1997); *Atlas de aves y plantas de la Islas Canarias* (Ministerio de Obras Públicas, Transportes y Medio Ambiente, 1996).

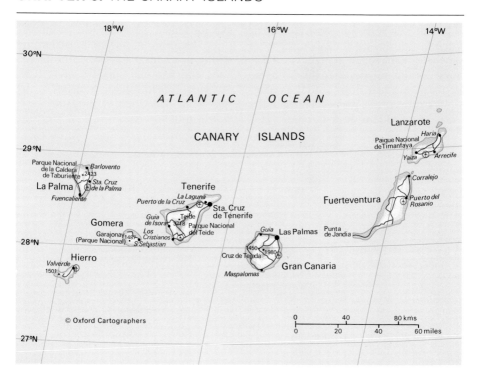

Lanzarote

Largely unspoiled island, with several interesting endemic plant species; home of the Parque Nacional de Timanfaya Biosphere Reserve, ZEPA
5,107 ha (12,620 acres)

No wonder the symbol of Timanfaya is a menacing devil! The feeling, even the smell, of Lanzarote is redolent of sulphur, and the landscape is so hostile it requires an effort of the imagination to conjure up the picture of a fertile agricultural plain, with small streams flowing to the sea, as it was in 1730. Over the next six years a succession of violent eruptions devastated the area, leaving the burned-out husks of volcanoes that dot the plain today.

The entrance to the *parque nacional* is eight kilometres (five miles) from Yaiza, one of the small villages hastily evacuated at the start of the eruptions. The volcanoes rained

down not only rocks and small stones (*lapilli*), but steam and boiling water from the sea. Driving into the park, it is easy to picture the scene from the desolation that remains. An exciting way to travel up to the centre of the park is by camel: half-way along the road from Yaiza caravans wait for visitors to take a leisurely ride. Africa seems very close when the sirocco blows from the Sahara, and the camels plod slowly through the soft, black sand.

The park information centre blends into the landscape, faced with stone from the volcanoes. It is called the Islote de Hilario, after a hermit who lived there with a camel for 50 years; legend says that he planted a fig tree which never bore fruit. Since the earth's crust is still hot here, it is surprising that the fig tree grew at all. Next to the restaurant are tubes in the earth which produce instantaneous geysers, with an impressive whoosh of steam, when water is poured into them. Meals for the tourists are cooked on a geothermal barbecue that uses this

190

The pounding action of Atlantic waves on Lanzarote's lava cliffs (here seen at Los Herrideros) produces the island's famous black-sand beaches

powerful energy source.

If you want to get a good look at the volcanoes you must take a special bus tour. The road runs close to the most awe-inspiring craters, through the immense sea of lava, 'which first advanced as fast as water, forming swirls, and then densely and heavily like honey, destroying villages on the way,' according to the priest of Yaiza who witnessed the eruption. The solidified rivers of lava, called *malpaíses* ('badlands' where nothing will grow), vary in colour and geological formation between black basalt, beige pumice and *amalgras* — burnt red-ochre earth. The commentary on the bus, interspersed with music and bubbling, hissing-sound effects, revealed that there are 36 volcanoes within a triangular area measuring eight kilometres (five miles) along each side. After hanging over an abyss as we negotiated some steep corners on the narrow track,

we believed anything we were told.

One of the volcanoes is yellow, another red; the ground is black, ochre or burnt sienna; the shadows in the deepest craters an intense dark purple. Not a green leaf is visible, just the grey-green of lichen on some northern slopes. The hot, dusty wind of the Sahara blows over this scene, calling to mind the warning from Dante's *Inferno*: 'Abandon hope, all ye who enter here.' An earlier visitor described the volcanoes as 'a scenario by Jules Verne and settings by Noguchi for a film about the moon.'

On our safe return to the haven of the Islote, opinion was divided between those who found the desolate landscape both frightening and disturbing, and those who thought the grandeur elevating — like the Swiss tourist on her twelfth visit to the island who said with eyes shining: 'It's like a cathedral.'

To see a different view of the park, take a turning to the left off the Yaizo-Tinajo road, three kilometres (two miles) beyond the entrance to the park. At present it is marked only by a sign warning 'Camino en mal estado' (road in bad condition), which indeed it is. As you walk or bump over the pot-holes by car, a view slowly unfolds of the wide spaces at the northern limit of the park, with the road winding down to a small beach called Playa de la Madera. From there you look back to see the red volcano and a line of striated cliffs. The silence is absolute, except for the splash of waves on the rocks, the colours shifting as the shadows lengthen. A rabbit appears, the only sign of life; with nothing to eat but lichen, and no water, how can it survive?

For a change from the arid 'badlands' of Timanfaya, I took the road to the north of the island through the vine-growing areas of Uga and La Geria. On sloping ground, every vine is protected from the wind by a semi-circular wall of volcanic rock, with the brilliant green of the vine leaves nestling at the bottom of each hollow. The pattern of the semi-circles on the hills contrasts with the straight lines of the walls in the valleys, covering the countryside in a strange grid.

To get from the vineyards to the ancient capital of Teguise, I drove through the mountains to the Peñas de Chache at 668 metres (2,200 feet): from here the road drops down into the valley of Haría, known as the valley of ten thousand palm trees. Suddenly I noticed that the landscape was looking decidedly Moroccan. The closely shuttered, single-storey houses between the palm trees, an occasional camel to carry heavy loads, the view — all spoke of the proximity of the Sahara.

The highest point on this part of the island is the ridge of Famara, rising to some 700 metres (2,300 feet) above sea level. The sea cliffs at the northern face of the ridge house the majority of the island's rare or endemic species, especially the highly restricted *Echium decaisnei* ssp. *purpuriense* and the composite *Argyranthemum maderense* which, though endemic to Lanzarote, resembles a rather untidy ragwort.

Farther north, you come to a spectacular viewpoint, the Mirador del Río, looking across the straits (El Río) to the two islets of Graciosa and Montaña Clara. The viewing gallery was designed by the local artist César Manrique to blend into the landscape: the dome above the gallery is already acquiring a patina of lichen and the signs are all on wood, so unobtrusive that it is possible to overlook them. Far below at sea level are salt pans, adding a brilliant splash of pink and white to the view.

On my return journey I took a route through Ye to the little fishing hamlet of Orzola, where brightly painted boats bob at anchor in the shelter of a few rocky islets. I can recommend the freshly caught fish — you will never taste better! I drove past the Malpaís de la Corona, where a few tiny beaches have the only white sand on the island, brought in from the Sahara, and forming a dramatic contrast with the black rocks. The caves at Jameos del Agua and the Cueva de los Verdes are worth visiting. The entrances are, like the viewpoint at Mirador del Río, designed by the ubiquitous Manrique; the juxtaposition of large green plants and wooden seats by the pools of water is far more imaginative than cave entrances elsewhere. As at Timanfaya, the recorded commentary in the galleries is accompanied by music, which echoes round the central cavern, 50 metres (164 feet) deep. The level of lighting is low and signposting is poor or non-existent; by refusing to sit and listen to a guide, I took a wrong turning in the gloom and found myself some time later at a dead end. I was glad finally to find the sunlight again. A little further along the east-coast road, around the village of Mala, there are still extensive plantations of prickly pears, grown for their fruit but more particularly for the hemipteran bug (*Dactylopius coccus*) that lives on them, the *cuchinillo* from which the dye cochineal is produced.

The rapid growth of tourism has led to indiscriminate development along the coast and has stretched the Lanzarote's infrastructure to the limit. Fresh water is in short supply: turn on the tap and a malodorous, yellowish liquid comes out. But there are many wild places on the island; the protection of the Parque Nacional de Timanfaya, created in 1974, ensures that the stark beauty of the volcanoes cannot be destroyed.

BEFORE YOU GO
Maps: IGN 1:25,000 and 1:50,000 Nos. 1,079, 1,080, 1,081, 1,082 and 1,084; IGN 1:50,000 No. 1,083, 1,087, 1,088 and 1,089; IGN 1:200,000 Mapa Provincial of Las Palmas.
Guide-book: Noel Rochford, *Landscapes of Lanzarote* (Sunflower, 1998).

GETTING THERE
By air: you can fly to the island directly, or by interchange at Gran Canaria to the airport west of Arrecife.
By sea: Trasmediterránea operates ferries from Cádiz, on the mainland, and from all the other islands to Arrecife.
ON THE ISLAND
By car: cars can be hired at the airport, Arrecife or in other resorts.
By bus: a comprehensive bus system operates on the island. Contact Lanzarote Bus, T: (928) 81 24 58, F: 80 29 45.
  From Arrecife and other resorts there are frequent bus excursions to Timanfaya.

WHERE TO STAY
Arrecife, Puerto del Carmen and Playa Blanca all have a wide variety of accommodation, ranging from the simple to 4-star hotels. For instance, in Arrecife there is the 3-star Lancelot, T: (928) 80 50 99, F: 80 50 39, and in Puerto del Carmen the 4-star Hotel Los Fariones, T: (928) 51 01 75, F: 51 02 02. In Costa Teguise there is the 4-star Hotel Oasis de Lanzarote, T: (928) 59 04 10, F: 59 07 91. Puerto del Carmen and Playa Blanca are both within easy driving distance of the park.

ACTIVITIES
Parque Nacional de Timanfaya: the park entrance is 8 km (5 miles) north of Yaiza. The most spectacular site is the

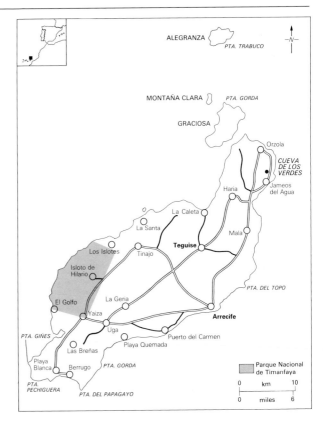

Montañas de Fuego ('Fire Mountains'), at the Islote de Hilario, which are circled by the Ruta de los Volcanes ('route of the volcanoes').
  Bus tours from Islote de Hilario traverse the extensive lava fields and provide panoramic views of this extraordinary landscape; you are not allowed to visit this area independently. The route is 14 km (8½ miles) long and the bus trip takes about 1 hr.
North of Arrecife: you can visit Teguise, with its beautiful Palacio de Spinola, and just to the north, the Castillo de Guanapay, which is situated on the edge of the Guanapay volcano and offers fantastic views across the island. Further on you pass through the highly

cultivated Los Valles and into Haría, one of the most beautiful of the villages, set in a valley filled with hundreds of palm trees. At the northern tip of the island is the tiny village of Orzola, from where you can catch a boat to Isla Graciosa and to a good bathing beach.
South of Arrecife: La Geria is set in an extraordinary black desert-like landscape, which produces the famous Malavisia wines. Here the vines are grown in volcanic ash pits that protect them from the prevailing north-easterly winds.
  From Yaiza, take the road to El Golfo, in which is situated a bright-emerald coloured *laguna* set between the sea and a steep black cliff: a good picnic and bathing spot. Just south is Los

Hervideros, where you can watch the sea 'boil' in caverns formed by lava flow. Down the coast from here are the Janubio salt pans — a spectacular sight with brilliant white pyramidal salt-forms set against the azure water. At the southern tip of the island is Papagayo Point with its splendid walks and relatively deserted beaches.

Mopeds/bicycles: these can be hired from some of the larger hotels or from private companies and are a fun way to explore the island.

Camels: you can ride a camel from Yaiza and do some exploring up Timanfaya, but no solo trips are allowed; an experienced driver leads each caravan of 10 or more camels.

Caves: there are 2 caves famous for being the homes of the *Munidopsis polymorpha*, a 1-cm (½-in) long albino crab, which has not been discovered anywhere else in the world. Los Verdes cave, on the north-east of the island, has about 1½ km (1 mile) of illuminated galleries showing the shaped and coloured rock formations. One of these galleries has been turned into an auditorium, open 11 am-6 pm; guided tours are available.

Just to the east, on the coast, is Jameos del Agua: a sea-water *laguna* in a cave in the lava rock, converted into a concert auditorium by the artist and town planner, Manrique; it also houses a restaurant, swimming pool and night-club.

Diving: the island offers some good diving and there are professionally run diving schools, such as Speedy Diving, in Puerto del Carmen, T/F: (928) 51 14 02, where tuition and equipment can be obtained.

Museums: in Arrecife, the Castillo de San Gabriel (built under Charles III) is now an archeological and

anthropological museum. It stands on the isle of the same name, which is connected to Lanzarote by Puerto de las Bolas. The Castillo de San José, also built during the reign of Charles III, is home to the International Museum of Contemporary Art.

FURTHER INFORMATION

Tourist offices: Avda. Marítima de las Playas, 35510 Puerto del Carmen, T: (928) 81 37 92; and Arrecife, p189.

Fuerteventura

A rich endemic flora thrives on the island, along with many interesting species of bird

In outline, Fuerteventura resembles a northwards-facing tadpole: the 'tail' is the Jandía peninsula, a steeply sloping volcanic ridge that sweeps down to sandy beaches on either side and is joined to the remainder of the island by a narrow sandy isthmus. The northern 'body' of the island is characterized by deeply gullied hills and a central plain, with an extensive sand-dune system along the coast. It is one of the largest of the Canary Islands and the closest to the African coast.

Botanists will find the dune system and the Jandía peninsula particularly exciting. The northern dunes are alive with salt-tolerant species (halophytes), including *Androcymbium psammophilum*, an attractive member of the lily family for which this is the type locality. Other interesting plants, such as the shrubby, yellow-flowered legume *Lotus lancerottensis* and a creeping,

silvery-leaved member of the pink family, *Polycarpaea nivea*, are typical species of the coastal dunes.

However, the island's most diverse flora grows on the Jandía peninsula. The highest point, Pico de la Zarza, is home to many rare plants, some of which can also be found on Lanzarote, at Famara. Of particular interest are the blue-flowered viper's bugloss, *Echium handiense*, which is not found elsewhere in the Canaries and is very rare, and a woody species of hare's-ear, *Bupleurum handiense*, both of which are named after the 'Handia' — or Jandía — locality. There are two extremely rare species growing on the coast in this southern part of Fuerteventura: a fleabane, *Pulicaria burchardii*, to be found only in a few square metres, and a succulent spurge species, *Euphorbia handiensis*, resembling a red-flowered cactus of the spiny variety, which is now in danger of extinction.

Interesting birds also have their home here. Fuerteventura is the stronghold of the endemic Canary Island chat, a sort of 'washed-out' stonechat found nowhere else in the world. With a tiny population, this bird is in great danger of extinction, but may still be seen around the valley, or *barranco*, near the airport. Another Canary Island endemic is Berthelot's pipit, which is relatively common in the same area. The Houbara buzzard has an endemic subspecies (*Fuerteventurae*) on the island, and Fuerteventura is probably the best place to see this magnificent semi-desert bird

The menacing cone of a volcano rises above Timanfaya, on Lanzarote's west coast. Although the last eruption was in 1825, soil temperatures remain high

The viper's buglosses feature prominently in the Canaries' flora

that roams as far east as Pakistan.

Before you go *Maps:* IGN 1:50,000 Nos. 1,092, 1,093, 1,098, 1,099, 1,106, 1,107, 1,114, 1,115 and 1,122. *Guide-books:* John Mercer, *Canary Islands: Fuerteventura* (David & Charles, 1973); Noel Rochford, *Landscapes of Fuerteventura* (Sunflower, 1999).

Getting there *By air:* the island has a small airport, but the ferry is a better option. *By sea:* Trasmediterránea operates ferry services from Las Palmas de Gran Canaria to Puerto del Rosario and Morrojable, on Fuerteventura. *ON THE ISLAND By car:* cars can be hired from several companies in the capital, Puerto del Rosario; driving is the most reliable and convenient form of transport on the island. **Where to stay:** the island's

parador, T: (928) 85 11 50, F: 85 11 58, is situated near the airport at Playa Blanca. Other accommodation can be found at Corralejo, Morrojable and Pájara. Try the 4-star Hotel Riu Palace Tres Islas, T: (928) 53 57 00, F: 53 58 58, in Corralejo.

Activities *Diving:* underwater diving is particularly good off the coast here. For courses or organized dives contact Barakuda Club Corralejo, C/ José Segura Torres 20, Corralejo, T: (928) 88 62 43. *Boats:* can be hired in the small fishing village of Corralejo, for trips to Isla de Lobos where the underwater diving is excellent. *Fishing:* deep-sea fishing for tuna, swordfish, etc. Ask at the tourist office for details.

Further information *Tourist office:* Puerto del Rosario, p189.

Gran Canaria

Island whose mixed climate ensures a great variety of plant life

Gran Canaria is probably the best-known of the Canary Islands. Millions of tourists flock to its capital, Las Palmas, every year. However, once out of the capital the influence of tourism lessens and you will find treasures aplenty waiting to be discovered in these volcanic hills. Like Gomera, the island is almost circular, with a central plateau and large numbers of radial valleys known as *barrancos*. There are also numerous subsidiary cones, which confuse the drainage pattern and create variations in the microclimate that favour certain species of plant.

Gran Canaria occupies a central position in the archipelago and so is subject to the hot, dry climate of the eastern isles and the Sahara, and the oceanic, more humid conditions of the western isles. The rare and endemic plants that grow on the island combine features of the typical flora of both climates.

Unfortunately, the native laurel woods of Gran Canaria have been so severely degraded by timber extraction and visitor pressure that little remains of this primeval vegetation except along the north coast. However, the western side of the island is rich in endemics, in particular the rare and endangered *Dendriopoterium menendezii*, a tall, palm-like burnet and one of the few members of the rose family to be found in the archipelago. It is confined to this area of Gran Canaria, growing with a tree-like knapweed, *Cheirolophus arbutifolius*.

The Barranco de Guayedra supports three rare composite species — *Tanacetum ferulaceum*, *Sonchus brachylobus* and *Argyranthemum frutescens* — but it is higher up on these cliff faces that one of the rarest plants in the whole of the Canary Islands is to be found. Although it is a member of the daisy family, the foliage of *Sventenia bupleuroides* resembles that of spurge-laurel, with leaves arranged in whorls; the yellowish flowers, however, indicate its true status, being similar to those of the closely related sow-thistles.

Other plants of interest on Gran Canaria are: the very rare St John's wort, *Hypericum coadunatum*, which grows on wet cliffs in the area around one of the highest points to the east of the island, Cruz de Tejeda (1,980 m/6,500 ft);

Orchis canariensis, a pink-purple species, and one of only five orchid species that occur in the Canaries; and two of the multiple species of *Aeonium* that abound on the islands, both of them fleshy, yellow flowered shrubs endemic to Gran Canaria: *A. undulatum* and *A. manriqueorum*, of which the second is also found on El Hierro. The rare composite *Tanacetum ptarmiciflorum* grows in the south of the island, around Paso de la Plata, and nearby you might see the equally scarce member of the potato family, *Solanum lidii*.
Before you go *Maps:* IGN 1:50,000 Nos. 1,112, 1,113, 1,120, 1,121, 1,125, 1,126, 1,128 and 1,129.
Guide-book: Noel Rochford, *Landscapes of Gran Canaria* (Sunflower, 1994).
Getting there *By air:* a wide choice of flights, both international and domestic (from the mainland and the other islands), arrive at Gran Canaria.
By sea: Trasmediterránea operates ferry services from Santa Cruz de Tenerife, Puerto Rosario and Morrojable, Arrecife and Cádiz to Las Palmas de Gran Canarias.
ON THE ISLAND
By car: cars can be hired at the airport and in Las Palmas; it is wise to book in peak season.
By bus: a good local bus service covers the whole island; tourist offices have up-to-date schedules.
Where to stay: certainly no shortage of accommodation on this island. Most communities offer a choice of places, with a surprising number being 5-star or 4-star hotels. Also some interesting country hotels: try the Casa de los Suárez, T: (928) 12 41 83, in Agüimes; La Cuevita (yes, really a small cave), T: (928) 66 16 68, F: 66 15 60, in Artenara; El Ingenio,

T: (928) 66 16 68, in Santa Lucía; and El Pinar, T: (928) 66 16 68, in Valsequillo.
Outdoor living: Camping Temisas, T: (928) 79 81 49, open all year, in Agüimes, and the Guantánamo, T: (928) 56 02 07, open all year, in Mogán.
Activities *Walking/climbing:* in the north of the island, at Arucas, you can follow a road up past the church and on to Montaña de Arucas, where there is a superb view of the town and the hinterland. The cliffs around Gáldar are honeycombed with caves. The well-known Cueva Pintada with its decorative wall paintings is here. Just north of the town is the Guanche Necropolis, and south, on the way to Agaete – a small, attractive village, not spoilt by tourism and worth a visit in itself – are the Cuevas de las Cruces.
La Caldera de Bandama can be thoroughly explored from Bandama, as can the Pico de Bandama. It takes about ¼ hr to climb the peak of the volcano, and a further 1 hr to make the strenuous descent into the crater. The walk round the perimeter of the crater takes less than an hour.
Also in the north but inland is the town of Teror ('town of balconies'). There are wonderful views from the road and it is an excellent starting point both for walking and for exploring parts of the interior. From here the road continues to twist its way to Artenara, the island's highest village. It is another extremely convenient base for good hikes.
The centre of the island: heading south from Tejeda on the C811, turn right on to the 17-3 to reach the small village of Cueva Grande. From here you can walk up the massive Cueva de Rey – a steep 10-15 min ascent which begins

alongside the first house in the village. Another fine crater is the Caldera de los Marteles situated off the 18-3. Both this and the luxuriant *barranco* right next to it are favourite hiking areas for locals and visitors. For the more ambitious, the strenuous hike to the top of the Pico de las Nieves (1,947 m/6,388 ft) should not be missed. This peak can be approached from Cruz Grande on the 815 and takes about 1½ hrs to reach.
The Ojeda, Inagua and Pajonales nature reserves can be explored from the small town of El Juncal on the 17-2; take the road opposite the church which leads you right down to the floor of the valley.
In the south, Los Palmitos makes a good base for interesting walks in this area, including a 3-hr hike to the Guanche Necropolis, just south of Arteara.
The Barranco de Arguineguín between Cercado Espina and Soria provides a memorable setting for walks among palm trees.
Mopeds/bicycles: these are a popular way of exploring the island, and can be hired.
Gardens: Aruca's municipal park has an interesting collection of native plants, and its Gothic church stands amid a variety of fruit trees. Tafira Alta also has an excellent botanical garden.
Museums: the Canarian Museum, on C/ Dr. Verneau, Las Palmas, has an extensive collection of Guanche and other pre-Hispanic art as well as artefacts from the island.
Sailing/diving: the Sporting Centre of the Hotel Don Gregory, San Agustín, T: (928) 76 26 62, hires out equipment and arranges tuition.
Further information *Tourist office:* Las Palmas de Gran Canaria, p189.

Tenerife

Largest of the Canary Islands, with a diverse endemic flora; home of the Parque Nacional de las Cañadas del Teide
European Diploma
13,571 ha (33,535 acres)

Teide, at 3,718 metres (12,198 feet), is the highest mountain not only in the Canary Islands but in the whole of Spain. Its volcanic peak dominates the island, floating serenely in sunlight above a constant sea of clouds; when the weather is fine it is clearly visible from the other islands of the group. This peak and the sandy areas to the south are enclosed within the steep, almost sheer, encircling walls of a vast crater, which forms the boundary of the *parque nacional*.

The view from Teide's peak is breath-taking, with the islands of Gran Canaria, Gomera, El Hierro and La Palma spread across the sea, and the jagged peaks of the *caldera* rim all round below you. The varied colours of the many different types of volcanic rocks are seen most clearly from here: ochre and rust, black and beige. Bushy clumps of the Teide daisy shine on the highest slopes.

Tenerife is a large, triangular island traversed from the centre to the northern end by a deeply serrated ridge. The northern coast is bordered by steep cliffs, but the southern part of the island slopes down to one of the few regions of level coastal plain in the volcanic islands of the archipelago.

Arriving by air, the first you see of Tenerife is the peak of El Teide, surrounded by its collar of cloud. As you descend through the cloud layer the mountain is suddenly lost to view, until you emerge into the sunlight again, over the harsh arid south side of the island. Driving from the airport to the park of Cañadas del Teide takes more than an hour. You wind slowly upwards through the small villages of Granadilla and Vilaflor, where vines are cultivated on terraces; then upwards again through chestnuts and scattered pines until the pine forest becomes dense, the trees' spreading branches meeting overhead as the cloud layer closes in. The light is soft and diffused within the clouds and when you climb out into the sunlight, the burst of colour is momentarily blinding. The pines thin out, the rocky rim of the crater encircles the sky, a narrow defile at the Boca de Tauce leads into the stony plains of the high plateau and the great summit of Teide soars high above everything in all its shimmering majesty.

The last time I visited, children were collecting pine-needles in the forest, piling them into bundles; a woman was walking gracefully towards a little truck with an immense bundle balanced on her straw hat, looking in the misty light like a hallucinatory moving mushroom. Later, further down the mountain in the vineyard area in Valle San Lorenzo, I saw the practical reason for this mirage-like activity: the needles were being spread on the vine terraces to supply a slow-acting mulch on top of the thin layer of soil, then covered with pumice to retain the moisture.

The flora of Tenerife is almost as diverse and restricted in its distribution as that of Gran Canaria. Some outstanding botanical spots include El Fraile, on the northern cliffs, which harbours such rarities as *Lavatera phoenicea* and *Marcetella moquiniana*, members of the mallow and rose families respectively. This area also boasts some 300 species of flowering plant in only a few hectares, one of the richest botanical assemblages in the islands.

Some interesting endemics grow elsewhere on the island: for instance, the white-flowered trailing vetch *Vicia scandens*, which grows on the *caldera* cliffs, and the xerophilic species on El Medano at the southern tip of the island, where plants have adapted to the almost Saharan conditions that prevail there. The cliffs of the Ladera de Güimar, on the eastern coast of Tenerife, harbour such rare endemics as *Monanthes adenoscepes* and *Micromeria teneriffae* (a succulent of the stonecrop family and a labiate, respectively), as well as being the only known Tenerife locality for *Pterocephalus dumetorum*, a pink-flowered scabious (it also grows round Roque Nublo in Gran Ca-

The explosive history of Tenerife is recorded in multi-coloured layers of lava deposits near El Teide

naria and on La Palma).

Within the park there is very little indigenous fauna but both the endemic Canary and the blue chaffinch are found here, the latter feeding around picnic sites just like their more widespread relations elsewhere. In May and June the spectacular red spikes of the Teide viper's bugloss (*Echium wildpretii*) bloom; the flowers grow to two metres (six feet) and the spikes remain standing long after the flowers have died.

For centuries the most notable botanical feature of Tenerife was the legendary 6,000-year-old dragon tree (*Dracaena draco*) at Orotava on the north coast, which unfortunately perished in the hurricane of 1867, but was reputed to have been more ancient than the Pyramids. This giant among trees measured some 24 metres (78 feet) in circumference and more than 23 metres (75 feet) in height. The dragon tree yields a red gum, known in some circles as dragon's blood, which was believed by the alchemists of the Middle Ages to carry mystical and healing powers. Wild specimens of dragon tree today are very rare, although it is extensively cultivated in botanical gardens; it is one of the few woody members of the lily family in Europe. A less ancient but hardly less venerable dragon tree survived the hurricane and can still be seen in the north-western village of Icod.

The islanders have become concerned about preserving the delicate equilibrium between people and nature. In peak season, the hordes of tourists and foreigners already heavily outweigh the local population and there is a long-term strategy now in place to re-evaluate and reduce planning permission for hotels and tourist developments in order to curtail the growth of tourism and safeguard the island's unique natural heritage.

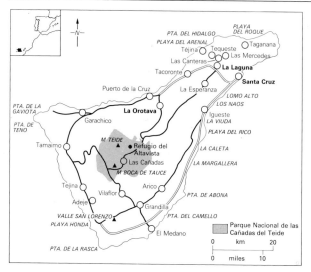

BEFORE YOU GO
Maps: IGN 1:25,000 Nos. 1,088, 1,089, 1,091, 1,092, 1,096, 1,097 and 1,102; IGN 1:50,000 Nos. 1,096, 1,097, 1,102, 1,103, 1,104, 1,105, 1,109, 1,110, 1,111, 1,118, 1,119 and 1,124.
Guide-books: Myrtle & Philip Ashmole, *Natural History Excursions in Tenerife* (Kidston Mill Press, 1989); Enric Balasch & Yolanda Ruiz, *El Parque Nacional de Teide* (Planeta, 1998); Noel Rochford, *Landscapes of Southern Tenerife and La Gomera* (Sunflower, 1995); Noel Rochford, *Landscapes of Tenerife* (Sunflower, 1999).

GETTING THERE
By air: Tenerife has two airports. The newer one at the south-east corner of the island, Reina Sofía, T: (922) 75 92 00, is used for international flights; the old one in the mountains of the north, Los Rodeos, is vulnerable to poor weather conditions and is now used only for domestic and pleasure flights.
By sea: Trasmediterránea runs ferry services between Santa Cruz de Tenerife and Cádiz, Las Palmas de Gran Canaria and Santa Cruz de la Palma; and between Los Cristianos, in the south of the island, and San Sebastián de la Gomera and Valle Gran Rey (Gomera) and Valverde on Hierro.

ON THE ISLAND
By bus: TITSA, T: (922) 53 13 00, F: 21 72 63, operates an extensive network of bus routes covering the whole of the island, including the Parque Nacional de las Cañadas del Teide. Services operate daily and on a regular basis.

A good local bus service runs regularly from both Santa Cruz and Puerto de la Cruz through the park, with stops at the cable car and the *parador*, both in easy walking distance of Monte Teide.

WHERE TO STAY
The Parador Cañadas del Teide, T: (922) 38 64 15, F: 38 23 52, is situated within the park, with a magnificent view of the volcanic peak. Throughout the island there is a wide array of accommodation, with many 4- and 5-star hotels. Try the 2-star

Pensión Silene, T: (922) 33 01 99, in La Orotava, or the 3-star Los Príncipes, T: (922) 38 33 53, F: 37 00 01, in Puerto de la Cruz.
Outdoor living: there is one official site, Camping-Caravaning Nauta, T: (922) 78 51 18, F: 79 50 16, in Cañada Blanca-Las Galletas (Arona). Elsewhere, you must apply for a permit to be able to camp.

ACTIVITIES
Parque Nacional de las Cañadas del Teide: located in the centre of the island, the park can be approached from the north via the Orotava road; from the south via the Vilaflor road; from the east via the lateral road starting at La Laguna; and the west via the Chío-Boca de Tauce road.

There is a cable car less than 2 km (1¼ miles) beyond the Parador de las Cañadas del Teide; it can carry you more than 1,000 m (3,300 ft) upward in about 15 min to just below the summit. When walking here you will find the wind chilly, even on a sunny day.

Within the park there are 2 forest access roads: the route of the Cañadas skirts the edge of the crater in parts; from the Orotava-Vilaflor road there is a route up the side of Montaña Rajada leading as far as

The giant red-flowered spikes of *Echium wildpretii* provide welcome splashes of colour on Tenerife

Montaña Blanca.

The park contains an extensive network of footpaths, and you are advised to pick up a local map of these from the information centre. Not all areas of the park are open to the public; you must follow the marked paths. Walking on solidified lava can be extremely difficult and somewhat treacherous — wear flat, comfortable shoes; the volcanic rock is very sharp, and small stones will get into sandals.

North: the Anaga region's rough landscape includes the famous *laurisilva* forest around Pico del Inglés. The town of La Laguna is situated on the southern edge of the mountains in the north, on the fringe of the Laurisilva de las Mercedes. Here are found 2 of the Canary Islands' 7 endemic species of birds — Boll's laurel pigeon and the white-tailed laurel pigeon. These dark forest birds have only recently been separated by ornithologists and are difficult

to locate. Their future depends entirely on the survival of these forests. The trade winds blowing down from the north-west produce clouds over the islands which are then prevented from rising and dispersing by the trade winds from the north-east; the condensation is trapped by the foliage of the laurel forest and the pine woods, and serves as a vital source of fresh water, as the rainfall is very low.

Near the town of Tacoronte is a steep road leading down to the Playa de Las Gaviotas, a black sandy beach where nude bathing is permitted.

South: even the tourist zone has some rugged features, notably the Barranco del Infierno ('hell's gorge'), near the town of Adeje, renowned for its botanical and zoological variety. Its vertical walls are perforated with burial caves and are largely overgrown; young dragon trees cling to the cliffs above the head of the

barranco.

Fishing: contact Golden Marlin, T: (922) 71 49 67, F: 76 54 71, in Puerto Colón or Marítimos Acantilados, T: (922) 86 19 18.

Museum: the archaeological museum, T: (922) 60 55 74, is at C/ Fuentes Morales, s/n, Santa Cruz.

Sailing: for details contact Real Club Náutico, Carretera de San Andrés, Santa Cruz, T: (922) 27 78 50, or Escuela de Vela de Puerto Colón, T: (922) 79 50 73.

Underwater diving: for details contact the Park Club Europe Tenerife, Playa de las Américas, T: (922) 75 27 08; or Coral Sur-Ten Bel, Hotel Park Ten Bel, Las Galletas-Arona, T: (922) 78 52 31.

FURTHER INFORMATION
Tourist office: Santa Cruz de Tenerife, p189.
Park information: Ecological Centre of La Laguna, T: (922) 25 99 03.

Gomera

Tiny volcanic cone, tranquil and densely forested; home of the Garojonay National Park
World Heritage Site, ZEPA
3,984 ha (9,845 acres)

The islanders of Gomera are justly proud of their history and traditions. Christopher Columbus set sail from here hoping to find either the westward passage to Asia or the Tierra Incognita; the islands he discovered became known as the West Indies. On my last trip I found Gomera to be still remarkably unspoilt, its people welcoming of strangers. When a passing peasant woman stopped to talk to me, and I said 'how beau-

tiful your island is,' she replied with a little smile: '*Disfrutamos de la tranquilidad*' ('we enjoy the tranquillity').

This tiny circular volcanic island rises to a central peak of almost 1,490 metres (4,890 feet), the cone scoured by radiating *barrancos* or valleys that terminate suddenly some way above sea level. The more barren parts of the island, often composed of raw basaltic rock, have their own characteristic flora, as do the steep-sided *barrancos* which shelter more sensitive species from the extremes of climate which are often experienced here. Particularly interesting species include the legume *Lotus emeroides*, which is endemic to the island, as are the blue-flowered *Echium acanthocarpum*, the shrubby crucifer *Crambe gomerae*, a yellow-flowered composite *Argyranthemum callichrysum*, and two species of sow-thistle which occur on Gomera only in the area around Agulo in the north-east of the island: *Sonchus gomerensis* and *Taeckholmia regis-jubae*, which is also present on Gran Canaria, Tenerife and La Palma.

I drove down the luxuriantly cultivated slopes of Vallehermoso ('beautiful valley') to the town of the same name. At siesta time on a hot day it was as deserted as the *Marie Celeste*, though brilliant with geraniums and bougainvillea. Suddenly, rounding a corner, I caught sight of three huge figures seated round a table; two more figures were placed at either end of a bench, in what seemed to be a children's playground. The figures were more than three metres (ten feet) high, seated. I searched in vain for the name of the sculptor, or for an explanation. One had a stylized helmet, in Henry Moore mode, which made me wonder if they represented the Guanche ancestors in conference — then I found at each end of the bench the letters PAPA and MAMA. It would have been interesting to see the children at play among them, but the siesta hour was sacrosanct and my curiosity was left unsatisfied.

It was a totally unexpected touch of fantasy in a practical agricultural community, busy producing tomatoes, maize and bananas — everywhere bananas. On the eastern side of the island I drove to the port of San Sebastián around the lower slopes of the mountain, through prickly pears, palm trees and an infinite variety of tree spurges. With El Teide a silent presence across the sea, like a Pillar of Hercules, the islands are truly the gardens of the Hesperides.

How easy it is to get lost in the wilder parts of the island! Driving towards the Parque Nacional de Garajonay, I stopped to ask the way. Do not place too much confidence in the islanders' ability to give directions; asking for the nearest road to the park, I was told to carry straight on. The narrow road turned into an unpaved track that clung to a steep mountain slope, then, rounding a sharp corner, it disappeared into the waters of a new reservoir. Thankful that it was daylight, I retraced my route with difficulty and started again.

Walking over the jagged volcanic rocks of Las Cañadas del Teide can be painful, and is never to be undertaken lightly

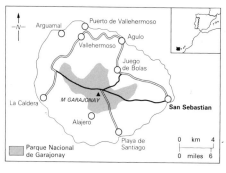

When I finally arrived in the park, worse was in store. As I drove through the forest, the cloud cover became thicker, the road more winding, until I became disorientated: no sun, no sound, no view further than six metres (20 feet) ahead, above or below. The cloud layer that rests almost permanently on the shoulders of Gomera streams down through the trees, catching and blowing free like fleece on bushes. Again I was completely lost, this time for more than an hour, and was eventually relieved to see an ordinary black chicken cross the rutted track.

Relating the story later to one of the park guardians, he said severely that no one should ever go into the forest alone or without a good map of all the tracks. He told me of two tourists who disappeared from their hotel, failed to return in the evening, and were eventually found 36 hours after they had set out, suffering from exposure and dehydration, after all the police and park wardens had been mobilized in the search.

Here, in this forest, Canary willow and holly (*Salix canariensis* and *Ilex canariensis*) grow together with *Laurus azorica* and the aromatic evergreen myrtle, *Myrica faya*, which also grows in sandy localities of

southern Portugal. The woodland is of particular interest for its lush vegetation, nurtured by the abundance of moisture. Several ferns flourish here, including *Asplenium onopteris*, *Diplazium caudatum* and *Woodwardia radicans*.

The north-western tip of the park includes some rocky open terrain, close to the attractive hamlet of Arguamal. The rocks by the road are studded with rosettes of succulents: *Aeonium nobile*, green with pink-tipped leaves and pink flowers; and many varieties of golden-flowering broom.

The contrast between the vegetation of La Gomera and nearby Tenerife is striking: the greenness of Garajonay has no rival on the larger island of Tenerife except for the relatively small area of semi-tropical *laurisilva* on its north-facing flanks.

The varied trees of the Gomera forest, so densely packed and often clinging to precipitous slopes, provide the green lung for the whole island. The cistus and heather of the lower slopes, becoming denser and taller towards the heights, mixed with the shiny foliage of the laurels, the bright yellow of Canary broom and trailing lengths of lichen, create a living tapestry of plants that must be seen in order to imagine how the islands must have looked in the days of the Guanches, the aboriginal population.

From their early folklore comes the name of the park: Gara was a beautiful Gomeran girl who fell in love with a boy named Jonay from Tenerife, who would swim to visit her. Her relations were bitterly opposed to her union with an outsider, so the couple fled up into the heights of the mountain, where they died in each other's arms, pierced through by the thorn of a tree — hence Gara-jonay, to commemorate the union.

BEFORE YOU GO
Maps: IGN 1:25,000 Nos. 1,095 and 1,101; IGN 1:50,000 Nos. 1,108, 1,109, 1,116 and 1,117; IGN 1:50,000 Isla de la Gomera.
Guide-books: Noel Rochford, *Landscapes of Southern Tenerife and La Gomera*

(Sunflower, 1995); P. Romero, *Parque Nacional de Garajonay, Itinerarios Autoguiados* (Icona, 1987).

GETTING THERE
By air: this is not an option.
By sea: Trasmediterránea operates ferry services between

San Sebastián de la Gomera, Valle Gran Rey, Los Cristianos and Valverde (El Hierro). Fred Olsen Lines operates a ferry service between San Sebastián de la Gomera and Los Cristianos.

ON THE ISLAND
By bus: for information about

buses and taxis contact the tourist office (p189).
By car: cars are available for hire by the ferry port at San Sebastián but not elsewhere. Many petrol stations on the island close on Sundays and public holidays.

WHERE TO STAY
The Parador de San Sebastián de la Gomera, T: (922) 87 11 00, F: 87 11 16, is one of the most beautiful *paradores* in Spain. It is ideally situated above the port of San Sebastián to command a good view and benefit from a sea breeze. Most of the other accommodation is also in San Sebastián or Playa de Santiago.
Outdoor living: camping is forbidden within the limits of the park. There is a camping area around the Caserío de Cedro.

ACTIVITIES
Parque Nacional de Garajonay: it takes nearly 1 hr to get to the park from San Sebastián. Although the park is open to visitors the information centre is closed on Sundays and Mondays. Refreshment amenities are limited, so be sure to take some supplies with you — especially water and fruit — if you intend to walk in the forest for any length of time. It is advisable to carry waterproofs and a thick jumper with you since it is often cold and wet in the cloud. The tourist office can arrange visits to the park.
Valle Gran Rey makes a good day excursion. From San Sebastián, take the Playa de Santiago road, but instead of turning in to the town go straight ahead towards the Valle Gran Rey. At Guadá you get fantastic views over the whole valley. Further north at Arure, in the Cueva de María, fine pieces of Gomera pottery

are for sale and there is a magnificent view down to the little village of Taguluche, nestling by the coast.
Los Organos is a 100 m (330 ft) cliff facing the Atlantic Ocean, with the appearance of massive organ-pipes. There are many gorges worth exploring in the area, but they can only be seen by boat.
Museum: the San Sebastián museum has a fascinating collection of historical items found on the island.
Sailing: contact Club Nautique, C/ del Conde, T: (922) 87 10 53, in San Sebastián de la Gomera.

FURTHER INFORMATION
Tourist office: San Sebastián de la Gomera, p189.
Park information: Information Centre, Las Rosas, T: (922) 80 09 03.

Hierro

Smallest island of the Canaries group, with pine and laurel forests clinging to the near-vertical slopes of a high central ridge

This roughly triangular island has the distinction of being both the southernmost and westernmost of the Canaries archipelago, and is reputed to have been formed from the fragment of an ancient volcano; the evidence is a central semi-circular ridge oriented to the north-west. Although Hierro is the smallest of the seven islands, its highest point exceeds 1,500 m (4,900 ft); the slopes down to sea level are thus almost vertical in places.
The crater area is known as El Golfo, and it is this semi-

circular cliff and bay area that holds the most botanical interest. The steep backdrop to the bay supports dense pine and laurel forest, which seems to cling precariously to the cliffs. Parts of the forest have a canopy dominated by the huge spurge *Euphorbia regis-jubae*, known locally as *tabaiba*, and often growing with the mocan tree (*Visnea mocanera*). Rarities of the El Golfo area include the pink-flowered *Echium hierrense*, the endemic sow-thistle *Sonchus gandogeri*, the knapweed *Cheirolophus durannii*, which is rare in the lower cliffs of this bay and found nowhere else, and the pink-flowered campion species *Silene sabinosae*.
El Hierro is also home to the giant lizard *Gallotia simonyi*, which can reach up to two metres (over six feet) in length. The population of between one and two hundred is found mainly on Risco de Tibataje, an inaccessible area of steep slopes and precipices to the south-east of El Golfo.
Before you go *Maps:* IGN 1:25,000 Nos. 1,105 and 1,108; IGN 1:50,000 Nos. 1,123, 1,127 and 1,130; and IGN 1:50,000 Isla del Hierro.
Guide-book: Noel Rochford, *Landscapes of La Palma and El Hierro* (Sunflower, 1993).
Getting there *By air:* there is a small airport at Tamaduste.
By sea: Trasmediterránea operates ferries between Valverde and San Sebastián de la Gomera.
Where to stay: the 3-star Parador del Hierro, T: (922) 55 80 36, F: 55 80 86, is about 10 km (6 miles) from Valverde. Other accommodation can be found in Valverde and Frontera.
Activities *Walking:* along the rim of El Golfo from the Roques de Salmor to Sabinosa there are fine walks through

laurels, giant briars and banana trees. In Sabinosa itself is a spa renowned for the medicinal qualities of its water. La Dehesa, too, offers some interesting walks. A large pine wood at El Pinar on the eastern side of the island is a beautiful place in which to stroll.

It takes about 15-20 min to walk from Guarazoca up to the belvedere of El Hierro from where the whole crater can be viewed; west of San Andrés runs a track to the Mirador de Jinama; El Rincón is approached by a track across La Dehesa.

Diving: the island offers superb underwater diving off its rocky coast. La Restinga, to the south of the island, is probably the best region for diving and snorkeling.

FURTHER INFORMATION
Tourist office: Valverde, p189.

La Palma

Exceptional among the Canaries for the fertility of its cultivated areas; includes the Parque Nacional de la Caldera de Taburiente
ZEPA
4,690 ha (11,589 acres)

From sea level the island of La Palma rises steeply to wooded, rocky heights; only from the highest points can you see into the deepest crater in the world, La Caldera de Taburiente. The slopes of the *caldera* are forested with pine trees, in some places of massive girth (the most famous has a circumference of eight metres/26 feet). Beneath the trees grow thick bushes of broom with bright yellow flowers.

Because of the numerous springs on the island, the cultivated areas are very fertile. A great variety of tropical fruit is grown: papayas, pomegranates, pineapples and avocado pears, oranges, loquats and small sweet mirabelle plums.

Banana plantations cover the lower slopes of the mountains, protected from the winds by perforated walls. Above these are narrower terraces for tomatoes and cabbages, then vines where the slopes become so steep that only the most determined *campesinos* would plant anything. Nevertheless, the ground is good enough to grow good grapes from which a delicious white wine is produced. The other Canary speciality, a banana liqueur, is an acquired taste which I have not yet acquired.

Gomera flourishes in the humidity of its almost permanent cloud-cover, which has produced this dramatic rainbow (left)

Above the last terraces the chestnut trees start, then the bracken and broom between scattered pines, until at last you reach the top of the *barranco* in full sunlight, looking down at the thin layer of clouds below.

Woods of lime and laurel grow on the heights of Los Sauces, as well as an astonishing variety of wild flowers. Plant species which are endemic to La Palma include the forest-dwelling *Echium pininana*, which produces huge spikes, up to four metres (13 feet) of pale blue flowers, and of which only a few specimens remain; the bright yellow-flowered composite *Gonospermum canariense*, from the north-eastern forests, known locally as *faro* ('lighthouse') because its flowers shine like beacons; another composite, *Argyranthemum webbii*; and the viper's bugloss named after the same botanist, *Echium webbii*. *Taeckholmia heterophylla*, found on Gran Canaria and Gomera, was recently rediscovered on the coast of La Palma, near Barlovento, after

Species such as the introduced prickly pear cactus compete with the native shrubs of La Palma

an absence of more than a century.

The southern tip of the island is worth visiting to see the black landscape produced by the eruption, in 1971, of the Volcán de Teneguía. In this most recent occurrence of volcanic activity on the islands, Teneguía spouted fire, rocks and lava in a short-lived but violent eruption, and showers of volcanic pebbles (*lapilli*) rained down on the surrounding countryside. Taking the road south from Santa Cruz through the little white villages of the lower slopes, such as Breña Baja, you come to a pottery in a windmill selling attractive black 'pinch' pots; they are made by hand, not thrown on a wheel, exactly as the Guanche ancestors used to make them. Other island crafts are still thriving: lace-making, embroidery and weaving of beautiful baskets made of palm fronds, wicker and even long, pliant brambles. Understandably, the last is now a dying art, since the young no longer have the patience to learn such a prickly *métier*.

Near the town of Fuencaliente ('hot spring'), the earth turns black, and looking south you can see two volcanic cones, those of San Antonio and Teneguía. Vines have been planted since the 1971 eruption, appearing brilliantly green against the black background, and the first wild plants have gained a tentative roothold. In fact, the Roque de Teneguía is the only known locality of the shrubby, mauve-flowered knapweed *Cheirolophus junonianus*; many typical Canarian species also favour this area but grow in stunted dwarf varieties, such as the composite *Phagnalon umbelliforme*.

Returning northwards to Santa Cruz on the coast road, I walked along the sea front enjoying the evening breeze blowing in from the Atlantic. Glancing up a side turning, I chanced upon a wooden ship riding a concrete wave, bow pointed out to sea; a monument to the courage and imagination of Christopher Columbus in setting off on an Atlantic crossing in such a cockle-shell of a craft. To the east lies Africa and the other Canary Islands, including Gomera, from where he embarked on his first voyage of discovery; to the west, the open sea, the islands of the Caribbean and the continent

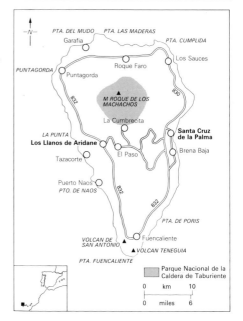

which Columbus finally stumbled upon in his search for the Indies. For Columbus, the Canaries provided a last landfall before the rigours of the ocean crossing. The islanders are naturally proud of their connection with these historic expeditions.

La Palma's Parque Nacional de la Caldera de Taburiente is a fascinating place. Unlike the bleak, apocalyptic landscape of Lanzarote, the Taburiente crater is lined with pine woods, and near the base there are deciduous woods with streams flowing along the floor of the crater. The 770-metre (2,525-foot) walls are vertiginous from above and impressive from below; the sunlight filtering through the branches of the huge Canary pines makes it seem almost as if the vegetation had tamed and softened the harsh volcanic rocks.

The trees are the volcano's first line of defence against the crumbling effects of wind, rain and sun. Their roots stabilize the steep slopes of the volcano, slowing the natural processes of erosion which cause long screes to form. I became aware of this precarious balance on a walk in the *caldera* one summer. A track from the entry point at La

Cumbrecita to the Lomo de las Chozas was blocked to cars after a rock fall, but some people were walking across the fall on foot. As I started across, the heap of loose rock and small pebbles began to bounce down; I beat a hasty retreat. In a flash, the pebbles became bigger stones, like an avalanche of dust, sliding down the mountain. The brave walkers who had already managed to cross it found their return journey considerably more difficult.

Because of the tendency for the rocks to crack in hot and dry conditions, rock falls are a dangerous possibility in the summer, and few guided walks are arranged at this time of year. There is also a great risk of forest fires, and a well organized corps of fire-watchers maintains a constant vigil from vantage points in the pine woods. Although the differential between summer and winter temperatures is not great — only 6°C (12°F) — the greater humidity of winter makes walking in the *caldera* much safer then.

On the northern tip of the crater is the Roque de los Muchachos, the best viewpoint on the island at 2,423 metres (7,950 feet), from which you can look south into the abyss, or north to the sea. You will also find a well developed sub-alpine flora, containing a number of extremely rare species.

BEFORE YOU GO
Maps: IGN 1:25,000 Nos. 1,083, 1,085 and 1,087; IGN 1:50,000 Nos. 1,085, 1,090 and 1,094; and IGN 1:50,000 Isla de la Palma.
Guide-book: Noel Rochford, *Landscapes of La Palma and El Hierro* (Sunflower, 1993).

GETTING THERE
By air: there is an airport at Santa Cruz de la Palma.
By sea: Trasmediterránea and Fred Olsen Lines operate ferries between Santa Cruz de la Palma and Santa Cruz de Tenerife, Las Palmas de Gran Canaria, San Sebastián de Gomera and Valverde (El Hierro).
ON THE ISLAND
The only means of transport to the Parque Nacional de Taburiente are tourist bus, taxi or hired car; there is no regular bus service.

WHERE TO STAY
The 3-star Parador de Santa Cruz de la Palma, T: (922) 41 23 40, F: 41 18 56, on the sea front at Santa Cruz, is an attractive old balconied building. Try also the 4-star Hotel Taburiente Playa, T: (922) 18 12 77, F: 18 12 85, at Breña Baja o San José. Other accommodation can be found around the island in such places as Barlovento, Los Llanos de Aridane and San Miguel.

ACTIVITIES
Water flows in abundance through this volcanic landscape; as you walk in the crater you will see 'fountains', springs and waterfalls. At the falls of Desfondada a small stream drops 150 m (490 ft); the cascade is a 1-hr walk from Taburiente. The cave at Tanausú, situated half-way between Tenerra and the few houses of Taburiente, is also worth a visit.

From El Paso, there is a 9-km (5½-mile) route up to the Mirador of La Cumbrecita where from the look-outs of Las Chozas and Roques you will get splendid views of the park from the very edge of the crater. From Los Llanos de Aridane, take the rough road to Lomo de los Caballos, then to the 'cliff of anguish' and up to La Farola; the bridle path begins from here, taking you into the *caldera*. From Mirca, continue to Los Andenes (33 km/20 miles) and on to Roque de los Muchachos (36 km/22 miles) where you can walk to the highest *mirador* (viewpoint) on the island.

Other interesting places: the Teneguía volcano is still active (it last erupted in 1971). It is near Fuencaliente, the most southern town of the island. When heading north to the *parque nacional*, driving from Santa Cruz to Los Sauces, you pass many caves — most of which are abandoned and overgrown — and an abundance of terraced banana plantations.
Beaches: Las Cançajos, near Santa Cruz at Breña Baja; Tazacorte and Puerto Naos are the main bathing beaches.
Caves: the Guanche caves of Hoya Grande and Fuente de la Zanza have prehistoric inscriptions decorating their walls, as does the cave of Belmaco in Mazo. Cueva Bonita is notable for its dramatic, completely natural, light show.

FURTHER INFORMATION
Tourist office: Valverde, p189.
Park information: Parque Nacional de la Caldera de Taburiente, Visitor Centre, T: (922) 41 31 41, F: 41 34 48.

A sub-tropical sunset (overleaf) may be brief, but over cloud-capped La Palma it is an unforgettable sight

GLOSSARY

Albergue, modern building in the Spanish style which can be found on the roadsides; similar to a motel. The maximum stay is 48 hours and reservations are not accepted. Also sometimes used to describe accommodation, often in dormitories, for groups, especially children; popular with mountaineers.

Biosphere Reserve, a site included in the UNESCO Man and the Biosphere (MAB) programme, which aims to develop reserves of sustainable biodiversity and promote interdisciplinary research and training. This conservation project began in 1971 and by April 1996 covered 337 sites in 85 countries.

Casa de Huespedes, a guest-house, similar to a *fonda* (see below).

DGCN, Dirección General de Conservación de la Naturaleza (Directorate General for Nature Conservation), which has superseded ICONA (see below).

EC, European Council. A summit of Heads of State, meeting at least twice a year as part of the Council of the European Union.

European Diploma, EC Diploma for Conservation. A prestigious, if little-known, award given for good management of protected areas.

Fonda, equivalent to, but cheaper than a one-star *hostal.*

Hostal, similar to a *pensión* (see below).

Hotel Residencia, similar to a hotel, but without a restaurant and serving breakfast only.

ICONA, Instituto Nacional de la Conservación de la Naturaleza (National Institute for Nature Conservation), replaced by the DGCN (see above).

IGN, Instituto Geográfico Nacional (National Geographical Institute). Produces a variety of map series. The most frequently cited in this book are the large-scale (1:25,000 and 1:50,000) and provincial (1:200,000) maps (*Mapas Provinciales*).

Michelin, publishers of a small-scale (1:400,000) series which covers Spain in eight maps.

Parador, state-run luxury hotel, usually superbly located in a converted castle or historic building. Some are in the four- and five-star classes. The amenities are usually excellent.

Paraje Natural (natural place), small natural park.

Parque Nacional, national park, of which Spain has ten.

Parque Natural, natural park managed by one of Spain's 17 autonomous regional governments (*autonomías*).

Pensión, modest place rated with one to three stars, usually one floor in an apartment block. You are often required to take half-board (breakfast plus either lunch or dinner).

Ramsar, wildlife designation providing protection under international law for wetlands, particularly those used by wintering wildfowl and wading birds. Sites around the world provide a network of areas for migrating birds. The name Ramsar is taken from the Iranian town where this convention was adopted in 1971.

Reserva Integral (integral reserve), an inner sanctum within a national or natural park.

Refugio (refuge), alpine hut that caters for climbers and walkers. They are usually rough-and-ready and operate on a first-come, first-served basis. Some are open all year round, unstaffed and unlocked. Others can only be used if you pick up the key from a local village before you set off.

World Heritage Site, listed under the UNESCO Convention Concerning the Protection of the World Cultural and Natural Heritage. This international agreement, signed by more than 150 countries, was adopted by the General Conference of UNESCO in 1972.

ZEPA, a site covered by the 1979 EC Directive for the Conservation of Wild Birds, the Spanish equivalent of a UK Special Protection Area. The declaration of ZEPA sites was started in Spain in 1987, and today more than 130 areas merit this distinction.

FURTHER READING

A. Allee, *Andalusia — Two Steps from Paradise* (Nelson, 1974).

A. Bonner, *Plants of the Balearic Islands* (Editorial Moll, 1985).

A. Chapman and W. J. Buck, *Wild Spain* (London, 1893).

A. Chapman and W. J. Buck, *Unexplored Spain* (London, 1910).

J. Crozier, *A Birdwatching Guide to the Pyrenees* (Arlequin Press, 1998).

C. Finlayson, *The Birdwatchers Guide to Southern Spain and Gibraltar* (Prior Huntingdon, 1993).

C. Finlayson, *Birds of Iberia* (Mirador, 1993).

C. Grey-Wilson and M. Blamey, *The Alpine Flowers of Britain & Europe* (Harper Collins, 1995).

P. Lucia, *Through the Spanish Pyrenees* (Cicerone Press,1996).

R. Macaulay, *Fabled Shore* (Oxford University Press, 1986).

G. Mountfort, *Portrait of a Wilderness: the story of the Coto Doñana* (Expeditiona, 1968).

A. Paterson, *Birdwatching in Southern Spain* (Golf-Area S.A., Costa del Sol, 1987).

A. W. Taylor, *Wild Flowers of Spain and Portugal* (Chatto & Windus, 1972).

A. W. Taylor, *Wild Flowers of the Pyrenees* (Chatto & Windus, 1972).

K. Whinnom, *A Glossary of Spanish Bird Names* (Tamesis Books, 1966).

USEFUL ADDRESSES

GOVERNMENT ENVIRONMENTAL DEPARTMENTS

NATIONAL

Dirección General de Conservación de la Naturaleza: Ilmo Sr D. Enrique Alonso García, Director General de la Conservación Naturaleza, Ministerio de Medio Ambiente, Gran Vía de San Francisco, 4, 28005 MADRID
T: (91) 597 54 00
F: (91) 597 55 64

REGIONAL

Junta de Andalucía: Director General de Gestión del Medio Natural, Avda Acacias, s/n La Cartuja, 41071 SEVILLA
T: (95) 448 02 07
F: (95) 448 02 20

Diputación General de Aragón: Director General del Medio Natural, Pº Mª Agustín, 36, Edif. Pignatelli, 50071 ZARAGOZA
T: (976) 71 48 10
F: (976) 71 48 17

Principado de Asturias: Director Regional de Montes y Medio Natural, C/ Coronel Aranda, 2, 3ª, 33005 OVIEDO
T: (98) 510 56 85
F: (98) 510 56 55

Gobierno de Islas Baleares: Director General de Estructuras Agrarias y Medio Natural, C/ Foners, 10, 07006 PALMA DE MALLORCA
T: (971) 17 61 03
F: (971) 17 61 58

Gobierno de Canarias: Viceconsejero de Medio Ambiente, Avda de Anaga, 35, 7ª planta, 38001 SANTA CRUZ DE TENERIFE
T: (922) 29 11 23
F: (922) 28 71 15

Gobierno de Cantabria: Director Regional de Montes, Caza y Conservación de la Naturaleza, C/ Rodríguez, 5, 1º, 39002 SANTANDER
T: (942) 20 75 93
F: (942) 20 75 97

Junta de Castilla y León: Director General de Medio Natural, C/ Muro, 9, 47071 VALLADOLID
T: (983) 41 19 41
F: (983) 41 19 78

Junta de Comunidades de Castilla-La Mancha: Director General de Medio Ambiente Natural, C/ Pintor Matías Moreno, 4, 45002 TOLEDO
T: (925) 26 67 09
F: (925) 26 67 16

Generalidad de Cataluña: Director General del Medio Natural, C/ Gran Vía, 612-614, 08007 BARCELONA
T: (93) 304 67 26
F: (93) 304 67 60

C. A. Extremadura: Director General de Medio Ambiente, C/ Juan Pablo Forner, 9, 06800 MERIDA (Badajoz)
T: (924) 38 13 68
F: (924) 38 13 60

Xunta de Galicia: Director General de Montes y Medio Ambiente Natural, C/ San Lázaro, s/n, Edif. San Cayetano, 15771 SANTIAGO DE COMPOSTELA (La Coruña)
T: (981) 54 61 09
F: (981) 54 61 01

Comunidad de Madrid: Director General del Medio Natural, C/ Princesa, 3, 8ª planta, 28008 MADRID
T: (91) 580 54 25
F: (91) 580 38 68

Región de Murcia: Director General de Medio Natural, C/ Luis Fontes Pagán, s/n, 30071 MURCIA
T: (968) 36 26 28
F: (968) 36 28 94

Gobierno de Navarra: Director General de Medio Ambiente, C/ Alhóndiga, 1, 31002 PAMPLONA
T: (948) 42 14 97
F: (948) 42 75 73

País Vasco: Director General de Ordenación e Investigación del Medio Natural, C/ Duque de Wellington, 2, 01010 VITORIA
T: (945) 18 96 52
F: (945) 18 96 02

Gobierno de la Rioja: Ilmo Sr D. Miguel Urbiola Antón, Director General de Medio Natural, C/ Prado Viejo, 62 bis, 26071 LOGROÑO
T: (941) 29 13 60
F: (945) 29 13 56

Generalidad Valenciana: Director General de Desarrollo Sostenible, C/ Arquitecto Alfaro, 39, 46011 VALENCIA
T: (96) 386 76 86
F: (96) 386 50 91

NON-GOVERNMENTAL BODIES

Jardin Botanico de Cordoba: D. Esteban Hernández Bermejo, Avda Linneo, s/n, 14004 CORDOBA
T: (957) 20 00 77
F: (957) 29 53 33

Parque Zoologico de Barcelona: D. Esteve Tomás, Parque de la Ciudadela, 08003 BARCELONA

T: (93) 221 25 06
F: (93) 221 38 53

Andalus: D. Enrique Alés
Gómez, C/ Marqués de
Paradas, 18, 1°, puerta 7, 41080
SEVILLA
T: (95) 421 42 51
F: (95) 421 42 51

Amigos de la Tierra: Dª
Carmen Espina, Avda de
Ajalvir a Vicálvaro, 82,
MADRID
T: (91) 306 99 00
F: (91) 313 48 93

Asociacion Amigos de Doñana:
D. Manuel Español González,
C/ Panamá, 6, 41012 SEVILLA
T: (95) 423 65 51
F: (95) 423 07 99

ADENA/WWF: D. Juan Carlos
del Olmo, C/ Santa Engracia, 6,
28010 MADRID
T: (91) 308 23 09
F: (91) 308 32 93

Aedenat: D. José Luis García
Cano, C/ Campomanes, 13,
28013 MADRID
T/F: (91) 541 10 71

Adenex: D. Jan-Erik Petersen,
C/ Cuba, 10, 06800 MERIDA
(Badajoz)
T: (924) 37 12 02
F: (924) 37 31 18

CODA: D. José Santamarta,
Pza Santa Mª Soledad Torres
Acosta, 1, 3° A, 28004
MADRID
T: (91) 531 27 39
F: (91) 531 26 11

FEPMA: D. Julio Martín
Casas, Pº de la Castellana, 8,
5° I, 28046 MADRID
T: (91) 575 41 68
F: (91) 577 09 53

Fundacion Bios: D. Carlos
Segovia Espiau, Avda Manuel
Siurot, 3, San Leandro, 41013
SEVILLA

T: (95) 461 56 79
F: (95) 421 42 51

Greenpeace: D. Xavier
Rodríguez Pastor, C/ Rodríguez
San Pedro, 58, 28015
MADRID
T: (91) 543 47 04
F: (91) 543 97 79

GOB (Ornithological society):
C/ Verí, 1-3R, 07001 PALMA
DE MALLORCA
T: (971) 72 11 05
F: (971) 71 13 75

DEPANA: Dª Purificación
Canals, C/ San Salvador, 97,
Bajo, 08024 BARCELONA
T: (93) 210 46 79
F: (93) 285 04 26

Silvema: D. Saturnino Moreno
Borrel, Apartado de Correos
4046, 29080 MALAGA
T: (95) 222 95 95
F: (95) 260 16 91

AMPAR: D. Pedro J. Romero
Manrique, Urb. Radazul Alta,
El Paraíso, 5ª fase, n° 23, 38109
EL ROSARIO (Sta Cruz de
Tenerife)
T/F: (922) 62 14 32

**Instituto de Investigaciones
Ecolgicas:** D. Mario Robles del
Moral, Apartado de Correos
15521, 28080 MALAGA
T: (95) 260 35 40
F: (95) 260 06 67

**Asociacion Española de
Entomologia:** D. Eduardo
Galante Patiño, Departamento
de Ciencias Ambientales y
Recursos Naturales,
Universidad de Alicante, 03080
ALICANTE
T: (96) 590 35 56
F: (96) 590 38 12

Sociedad Biosfera: D. Jesús
Vozmediano Gómez-Feu, C/
Pedro del Toro, 2, 41001
SEVILLA
F: (95) 421 76 55

Ecomediterranea: D. Rafael
Madueño Sedano, Gran Vía de
les Corts Catalanes, 643, 3°,
08010 BARCELONA
T: (93) 412 55 99
F: (93) 412 46 22

**Fundacion Naturaleza y
Hombre:** D. Carlos Sánchez, C/
18 de Julio, 25, entresuelo,
39619 EL ASTILLERO
(Cantabria)

**Consejo Iberico para la Defensa
de la Naturaleza:** D. Francisco
Blanco Coronado, C/ Cuba, 27,
06800 MERIDA (Badajoz)
T: (924) 37 12 02
F: (924) 37 31 18
C/ Cava Alta, 10, Ofic. 6-7,
28005 MADRID
T/F: (91) 365 20 24

**Fondo Iberico para la
Conservacion de la Naturaleza:**
Dª Angeles de Andrés
Camarés, C/ Marcenado, 2,
28002 MADRID
T/F: (91) 416 17 20

**Fondo Patrimonio Natural
Europeo:** D. Juan Serra Martin,
C/ Hapitán Haya, 23, Escalera
2, planta 9, puerta 2, 28020
MADRID
T: (91) 556 93 90
F: (91) 556 98 95

**SEO (Sociedad Española de
Ornitologia):** D. Alejandro
Sánchez Pérez, Ctra de
Húmera, 63, 1°, 28224
POZUELO DE ALARCON
(Madrid)
T: (91) 351 10 45
F: (91) 351 13 86

**Coordinadora de las ongs para
el Desarrollo:** D. Miguel
Romero Baeza, C/ Reina 17, 3°,
28004 MADRID
T: (91) 521 09 55
F: (91) 521 38 43

Michelin Maps:
C/ Doctor Esquerda, 157,
28007 MADRID

T: (91) 409 09 40
Web-site: www.michelin-travel.com

PRINCIPAL IGN MAP OUTLETS

E-mail: webmaster@cnig.ign.es
or consulta@cnig.ign.es
Web-site: www.cnig.ign.es

MADRID (Servicios centrales)
C/ General Ibáñez de Ibero, 3,
28003 MADRID
Información General:
T: (91) 597 94 53
F: (91) 553 29 13
Venta de Publicaciones (Sales):
T: (91) 597 95 14
F: (91) 535 25 91

ANDALUCIA OCCIDENTAL
Avda San Francisco Javier, 9,
Edif. Sevilla, 2, 8° (módulo 7),
41018 SEVILLA
T: (95) 464 42 56
F: (95) 466 13 77

ANDALUCIA ORIENTAL
C/ Divina Pastora, 7 & 9, 18012
GRANADA
T: (958) 29 04 11/29 04 50
F: (958) 27 10 14

ARAGON
C/ Coso, 55, 5°, 50001
ZARAGOZA
T: (976) 39 59 10
F: (976) 29 57 93

ASTURIAS
Plaza de España, 3, 1°, 33071
OVIEDO
T: (98) 524 49 00/523 62 00
F: (98) 523 94 62

CANARIAS
Centro Geofísico de Canarias,
La Marina, 20, 2°, 38001
SANTA CRUZ DE TENERIFE
T: (922) 28 70 54/28 70 66
F: (922) 24 30 17

CANTABRIA-PAIS VASCO
C/ Vargas, 53 Edif. anexo, 8ª
planta, 39010 SANTANDER

T: (942) 23 55 99
F: (942) 23 56 36

CASTILLA-LA MANCHA
C/ Disputación, 2, 2°, 45004
TOLEDO
T/F: (925) 22 43 17

CASTILLA Y LEON
C/ Jesús Rivero Meneses, 2, 7°
dcha, Edif. de Servicios
Múltiples, 47014
VALLADOLID
T: (983) 33 10 66
F: (983) 37 32 26

CATALUNYA
Carrer de la Marquesa, 12,
08003 BARCELONA
T: (93) 304 79 36/37/38
F: (93) 304 79 44

EXTREMADURA
Avda de Europa, 1, 6ª planta,
Edif. de Servicios Múltiples,
06004 BADAJOZ
T: (924) 25 93 61 ext. 150
F: (924) 22 36 09

GALICIA
C/ Salvador de Madariaga, s/n
9° (ala norte), Edif. de Servicios
Múltiples, 15008 A CORUÑA
T: (981) 29 23 46
F: (981) 29 36 67

MURCIA
C/ Pinares, 1, 30001 MURCIA
T: (968) 21 34 25/21 41 00
F: (968) 21 58 19

LA RIOJA
C/ Miguel Villanueva, 7, 7°,
26001 LOGROÑO
T: (941) 25 22 07/24 43 44
F: (941) 23 47 67

COMUNIDAD VALENCIA
C/ Joaquín Ballester, 39, 5ª
planta, Edif. de Servicios
Múltiples, 46009 VALENCIA
T: (96) 388 11 85
F: (96) 388 11 84

ADDITIONAL IGN MAP OUTLETS

BALEARES
Casa del Mapa de **Palma** , C/
Juan Maragall, 3 bajo, 07006
T: (971) 46 60 61
F: (971) 77 16 16

CANARIAS
Casa del Mapa de **Las Palmas de Gran Canaria**, Paseo Tomás
Morales, 56, 35003
T/F: (928) 37 08 47

GALICIA
Casa del Mapa de **A Coruña**,
C/ Salvador de Madariaga, s/n
9° (ala norte), Edif. de Servicios
Múltiples, 15008
T: (981) 29 23 46
F: (981) 29 36 67

MURCIA
Casa del Mapa de **Murcia**, C/
Pinares, 1, 30001
T/F: (968) 21 41 00

OVIEDO
Casa del Mapa de **Oviedo**,
Plaza de España, 3, bajo, 33071
T: (98) 523 62 00 ext. 183/523
23 50
F: (98) 524 49 00

SANTANDER
Casa del Mapa de **Santander**,
C/ José Ramón López Toriga,
6, 39003
T: (942) 22 14 32
F: (942) 23 56 36

INDEX

Species are indexed only where information is provided in addition to general description and location. and where they are illustrated; page references in *italics* refer to illustrations.

WILD SPAIN

PICTURE CREDITS

Jacket Front Cover — Fred
Grunfeld. 10/11, 14 — Richard
Kemp/Remote Source. 19 —
A.G.E. FotoStock. 22 — David
Simson. 23 — Tony Stone
Worldwide. 26/27 — Fred
Grunfeld. 30 — David Simson.
31 — Fred Grunfeld. 34/35 —
Teresa Farino. 43 — M.
Chinery/Natural Science
Photos. 46, 47, 51 — Teresa
Farino. 54/55 — Firo-Foto.
58/59 — Paul Sterry/Nature
Photographers Ltd. 62 — Fred
Grunfeld. 66 — A.G.E.
FotoStock. 67 — Natural
Science Photos. 70/71 — Paul
Sterry/Nature Photographers
Ltd. 75, 78, 79 — A.G.E.
FotoStock. 82/83 — Kevin
Carlson. 87, 90, 91, 94, 95 —
Fred Grunfeld. 98 — J.L.G.
Grande/Bruce Coleman Ltd.
102 — Kevin Carlson. 103,
106/107 — Teresa Farino.
114/115 — David Simson. 118,
119, 123, 126 — A.G.E.
FotoStock. 127 — Kevin
Carlson. 130/131 Robert
Harding Picture Library Ltd.
135 — Christopher Grey-
Wilson/Nature Photographers
Ltd. 138, 143, 147, 151 —
A.G.E. FotoStock. 155 — Brian
Hawkes. 158 — Fred Grunfeld.
159 — R & J Kemp/Remote
Source. 163 — Charles
Henneghien/Bruce Coleman
Ltd. 166/167 — Archie Miles.
170, 174 — Prisma/Planet Earth
Pictures. 175, 178/179 — Fred
Grunfeld. 182 — Robert
Harding Picture Library Ltd.
183 — Agencia Zardoya.
186/187 — George Wright. 191
— David George/Planet Earth
Pictures. 195 — Firo-Foto. 199
— Ernest Newal/Planet Earth
Pictures. 202/203 — Alex
Williams/Planet Earth Pictures.
206 — Prisma/Planet Earth
Pictures. 207, 210/211 — George
Wright.

ACKNOWLEDGEMENTS

The editors owe a major debt
of gratitude to the Directorate
General for Nature
Conservation (Dirección
General de Conservación de la
Naturaleza) in the Spanish
Ministry of Environment
(Ministerio de Medio
Ambiente), in particular to
Ilmo Sr Don Enrique Alonso
García, Director General
Conservación Naturaleza, for
his invaluable guidance and for
his kindness in making
available the services of his
department and staff, including
Sr Don Borja Heredia, who
knowledgeably answered many
questions on natural history
and protected wild places, and
Sra María Jesús Gonzalez for
her bibliographical assistance.

Special thanks are also due to
Dr Iain Bishop, Martin
Gardiner, Sr Don Felix
Gonzalez, Tony Hare and Cdr
and Mrs J. L. Rigge for their
assistance; and to Anthony
Bonner, Valerie Chandler,
Franky Eynon, Antonio
Lardiez, Irene Martin, Timothy
Osborne, Maria Teresa Palau,
Mike Rosenberg, Charlie
Spring-Rice, Mercedes Sus,
Teresa Tinsley and Brigitte
Vienneaux.